D1136002

JAPAN'S COMMERCIAL EMPIRE

by Jon Woronoff

LOTUS PRESS
Tokyo, Japan

Published in Japanese by Toyo Keizai Shinposha
under the title of *Keizai Teikoku-Nihon no Sugao*

First Edition

Published by Lotus Press Ltd.
Chofu P.O. Box 15, Chofu-shi, Tokyo, 182–91 Japan
© 1984 by Jon Woronoff
ISBN: 4-89788-022-X
Cover design by Akira Tsuchiya

Printed in Japan by Komiyama Printing Co.

Contents

Foreword

The shadow play is very popular in Asia. Rough figures are cut out of leather or molded into papier maché and a light is focused on them so that a huge shadow appears on the screen. The further away from the screen the figure is, the larger it becomes. On occasion, it can be absolutely monstrous. To make things perfectly obvious, there is a broad characterization of the personalities and behavior. This way the audience immediately knows who is who. It can readily distinguish the good guys from the bad guys and respond accordingly.

Unfortunately, all these efforts make the characters more visible... and less real. By doing away with details and ignoring nuances, it is possible to obtain simple and sharp outlines. But this creates not clarity so much as confusion and bias. And the crude personification, along with invariable and predictable story lines, result in a cast of caricatures rather than recognizable persons and scenes.

One of the most striking shadow plays nowadays is the explosive resurgence of the Japanese economy and, as a particular attraction, the invasion launched by its aggressive investors. The shows that are presented will vary tremendously depending on whether they are directed by Japanese or foreigners. But there is always the same gross exaggeration and simplistic plot and action.

In its own road show, Japan depicts itself as good and helpful. Its investors come to tap natural resources, sell essential products and upgrade domestic industry. The employers treat their staff well and look after their interests. In the end, they are rewarded for their kindness and generosity. Meanwhile, in local theaters, the complete opposite is portrayed. Here, the Japanese are reviled as exploiters and neocolonialists, greedy people who take everything they want and give precious little in return.

Such portrayals, alas, are not restricted to street players and untutored troupes. The descriptions of Japanese investment, like those of American imperialism, and European colonialism before it, are amazingly onesided and unreliable. This applies to those for *and* against. They try to convince by appealing more to emotions than reason, by playing on fears and prejudices rather than proving their point with facts and figures. They evoke applause, but very rarely understanding. Yet, the authors are noted academics and journalists, businessmen and politicians.

In this book, an attempt is made to deflate the exaggerations by contrasting the opposing views. Biases on both sides are used to disprove one another. This is not as difficult as it may seem. The instant one starts collecting information objectively, without a predetermined plot or an urge to show which side is right, the result is a much more variegated picture. Piecing the parts together, it quickly becomes manifest that neither side is systematically the hero or the villain, the victor or the victim.

While this presentation may be somewhat less dramatic, and does not conclude with a simple and easy-to-remember moral, it does have its advantages. It is certainly closer to reality. It shows how the various actors behave in different situations and what their deeper motivations may be. It provides a broader variety of scenarios, some with a happy ending, others banal or tragic. And, it reduces the antagonisms and confrontations to their true proportions rather than blowing them up to impress the public.

JON WORONOFF

1
Reviving The Empire

The Japanese Return

"We never thought they would come back," grumbled an elderly Filipino worker who had once helped construct a bridge for the Japanese and was now part of a crew building a factory just outside of Manila. When he was working on that bridge, some forty years ago, it was not because he applied for the job. All the people in his village had been rounded up at gunpoint and told to work. Now he was drawing a salary. He would build a factory for the Japanese as willingly as one for the Americans or local capitalists . . . or almost. The difference is that he was not really pleased to have the Japanese back.

The surprise is universal. No one expected the Japanese to recover from their defeat for decades. The battle was hard won and the victors wished to see the foe restricted to its crowded islands and perhaps reduced to a more primitive and pastoral life. It was only when new opponents arose that the United States decided Japan should not be stripped of its machinery and have its companies disbanded. But even the Americans never expected Japan to reconstruct as quickly as it did and then expand its economic power around the world.

This is not the first time the Japanese have astonished their neighbors. The erstwhile Japanese empire, which reached its maximum extension in the Greater East Asia

Co-Prosperity Sphere, was built in the twinkling of an eye if compared to most other empires, from the Roman to the British. It was not until 1879 that Japan, just "opened" to commerce in 1854, made its initial move abroad by incorporating Okinawa. In 1895, it took over Formosa (now Taiwan). In 1910, it annexed Korea. Then it carved out more spheres of influence in China. The progression became lightning swift once the Japanese decided to risk everything. In about a decade, from the Manchurian Incident in 1931 to the time it reached the peak of its expansion, the imperial army conquered or controlled most of China, Indochina, Thailand, Burma, Singapore, Malaysia, the Philippines, Indonesia and the Pacific islands.

The only historical event that could beat that for speed was the rapid disintegration of the Japanese empire. Driven out of New Guinea in 1944, the Japanese were chased from island to island by the American navy. Meanwhile, they lost Burma and the Philippines. Then came the raids on Tokyo and atomic bombings of Hiroshima and Nagasaki. When the emperor surrendered in August 1945, the rest of the empire collapsed like a house of cards.

The Japanese hurried back to the motherland. Even those who had been in Taiwan or Manchuria for years, some for a whole lifetime, found it wiser to retreat promptly. There were over six million of them between soldiers and settlers who were added to the islands' already huge population of over seventy million. If forced to live as humble peasants and restricted to some rudimentary industries at best, they might have vegetated and disappeared as an active and vital part of humanity. When allowed to restore the economy completely, they were reinvigorated and the energy generated by that unprecedented effort carried them abroad once again.

This could hardly be avoided and should not really have surprised anyone. Few contries are as bereft of natural resources as Japan. Simply to survive, it must import vast quantities of food from abroad. Once its industries were revived, it naturally needed raw materials. The list of those sought is almost endless: coal, iron ore, bauxite, tin, zinc, lead, timber, pulp, cotton, and many more.

Then, as the economy soared, it was no longer a question of modest amounts of coal or iron but huge quantities to feed the biggest, most efficient and most voracious steel mills in the world. The same applied to everything else. From 1960 to 1980, Japan increased the value of imports of raw cotton and wool three times over. During the same period, the import value of metal ores and scrap was multiplied by 13, of foodstuffs by 27, of solid mineral fuels by 62, and of crude oil by 113. No matter how impressive any of these figures may seem, they are nothing compared to what they should be in another ten, twenty or thirty years.

Japan also needed markets to sell the prodigious amounts of goods it produced. It is hard to tell whether it produces so much to buy the raw materials it wants or it needs so much raw materials because it has gotten into the habit of producing so much. Some of the finished products have to be exported to the countries which supply the raw materials. They also had to be exported to many others to get the wherewithal to purchase capital goods, especially in the early days, and increasingly foodstuffs.

Gradually, as its economic machine got back into gear, Japan found that even its huge population, the many millions of people it thought could never find a job, was not quite big enough. Or, even if there were enough Japanese, they had become too costly compared to people living in relatively backward countries. Industrialists needed more hands to run the factories and, since they could not be brought to Japan any more, the factories were moved to them.

This is exactly the same combination of causes that led to the effect of a growing colonial empire before the Pacific War. Then, too, it needed raw materials and cheaper labor. It needed markets. And the needs were seen as so pressing and overwhelming that Japan resorted even to aggression to obtain or preserve them.

Obviously, this process could no longer be repeated. But there are more ways than one to reach the same end. A far more peaceful means is through international trade and overseas investment. Lest it be forgotten, that was also the alternative before Manchuria was invaded and it had been preferred by many businessmen. But the businessmen were overruled by the military. Now there is no real military and the businessmen reign supreme. Thus, what would perhaps always have been their first preference is being applied not only because Japan has no choice but because this is a good alternative and so far has proven extremely effective.

So, the Japanese have returned. And this return, no matter how sensational (and, for some, troubling) is still at its beginnings. Overseas investment is comparatively new and has grown most rapidly since the 1970s. If not for the oil crisis, which slowed it down temporarily, the Japanese would have expanded far more than they did. But, whatever was not accomplished in the 1970s will most assuredly be done during the 1980s and 1990s if the world is not turned upside down again.

Pushing Outward

Nothing was left of Japan's old empire after the war. Defeated militarily, forced to accept unconditional surrender, it was quickly shorn of its colonies. The factories and mines it had developed were lost. It was not even able to hold on to any property or assets that had been come by legitimately. To the contrary, not only did it lose all its wealth abroad, it was condemned to pay reparations to the subject countries.

Nevertheless, in 1951, only six years after the war ended, Japan began launching its first overseas projects. For a long time this remained at a very low level. Obviously, a devastated nation had little money to invest abroad. Its own companies were desperately borrowing funds to resume operations and the government imposed very tight restrictions on overseas investment. Moreover, once the economy did get moving again, the greatest opportunities existed at home.

Still, by 1969, the government was willing to relax the regulations somewhat and the flow of investment began to swell. Then, during the 1970s, it introduced five rounds of liberalization and thereafter funds could flow quite freely. But there were other factors which encouraged investment yet more. As Japanese companies gradually exhausted the possibilities of expansion at home, they had to think more in terms of expansion abroad. What was more, increasingly they had the money for this. Investment grew rapidly, only dipping after the oil crisis, and then showing a renewed upsurge.

The peaks of investment, however, were not only related to the general economic situation and the state of company finances. Two incidental factors played a crucial role. One was the fluctuations in the trade and payments balance, whose massive surpluses on occasion led the government to incite more investment. The other was the resulting appreciation of the yen. The more the yen was worth, the more it could buy in foreign currencies. The exchange rate also played tricks with the statistics, which were usually in dollars, since the same amount of yen converted to more dollars than ever. This happened just before the oil crisis, periodically in the late 1970s, and would probably continue more moderately throughout the 1980s.

These factors help explain the extraordinary progression of direct overseas investment during the past decades. This might be traced first in terms of number of projects. During the 1950s, there were only about a hundred cases of investment a year. Over the 1960s, this built up to an average of several hundred a year. During the 1970s, the average ranged around 2,000 cases a year, with a peak of 3,093 cases in 1973. This was a quantum leap. At the same time, the amount of money invested in each case was also growing. The average case involved about $1 million right through the 1960s. However, by the early 1980s, the average case rose above $2 million, a figure evidencing considerable advance despite the effects of inflation and currency appreciation.

These two elements, more cases of investment and larger amounts per case, combined to bring about an explosive growth. Thus, the total amount of investment per year kept on rising throughout the 1960s, when it never exceeded $1,000 million, and then into the 1970s, when it was almost always above $2,000 million. It reached a first peak in 1973, at somewhat under $3,500 million and climbed again to nearly $9,000 million in 1981. By the end of fiscal 1982, the total cumulative investment was some $53,131 million.[1]

While the new commercial empire has been increasing in value, it has also been expanding in geographical extension. By now, Japan has investments in just about every country in the world, no matter how remote and no matter how different. Sometimes, but not always, the strongest bases are the very same countries that once were englobed in its co-prosperity sphere. But this conceals the essential fact that the empire was put together almost in reverse order after the wartime defeat.

Despite seemingly compelling economic reasons, it was extremely hard to enter the nearby countries, those which were its natural trading partners and catchment area for investment. The first experience of relations with Japan, and the crude exploitation involved, left behind tremendous resentment which took many years to subside. Instead, it turned to countries that were relatively neutral and even some that had been enemies.

In an amazingly short time, as tension grew between the East and West blocs, the United States turned into Japan's leading friend and ally. It was also rapidly becoming its largest, and certainly most affluent, market. As early as the 1950s, the Japanese were making investments there and this has never ceased. Some of them, especially at the outset, were to obtain vital raw materials, others were to establish the necessary sales and distribution facilities, and more recently to produce locally.

Another early field for investment was Latin America. Entry was eased by a lack of antagonism and also because of Japanese migration, in smallish numbers to Peru and some other countries, but resulting in a reasonably large and influential community in Brazil. When Brazil stabilized politically under a series of military regimes, and launched a major drive for development, the involvement grew. Brazil clearly obtained the lion's share of the investment and the rest was distributed more sparsely.

It was not really until the early 1960s that the walls of hatred began crumbling in certain parts of East and Southeast Asia. A first, modest breach, was made in Hong Kong, a British colony applying a free trade policy, which was always willing to accept investment from anywhere. Japan joined in the circle as a junior, then a senior, member of the club. Singapore showed a somewhat similar attitude.

It followed a very open policy under Lee Kuan Yew and, when the economy began developing, the Japanese were attracted quite naturally.

No sooner were relations restored in 1952 than Taiwan became a favorite site for investment which grew rapidly with the booming economy. Given the extended period of Japanese colonization, many Taiwanese spoke Japanese, had been educated in Japanese ways, and could deal with them suitably. Of course, they had their own reasons for cooperation. It was necessary to obtain substantial investment, and higher technologies, to upgrade industry. It was also desirable to make Japan a stronger ally by tying it down economically. This worked, and investment flowed swiftly and smoothly even into the 1970s when the other China became an alternate pole.

Korea remained closed for a much longer time. Under the rule of Syngman Rhee, policy was very nationalistic, autarchic and anti-Japanese. Not until Park Chung Hee came to power could the situation be turned around. One aspect was to open the economy and try to develop rationally, accepting whatever cooperation was available. The other was to end the legacy of the war by restoring diplomatic relations, something that was not accomplished until 1965. Then it was possible to build on the base of familiarity and cultural similarities between Japanese and Koreans as well as a common interest in building the economy, despite the very different goals of each partner.

Meanwhile, the movement continued further into Southeast Asia. Thailand became rather popular after the government adopted a favorable investment law in 1962 and launched various programs of industrialization. The Philippines also rose to prominence when Marcos introduced his "new society," putting an end to the political chaos that kept investors away. Malaysia, with considerable natural resources, soon attracted investment. But the most interesting spot was Indonesia, a source of vital raw materials and especially oil as well as one of the biggest potential markets in the region. Nothing much could be done as long as Sukarno ruled, stirring up a nationalism that worried foreign investors and meanwhile dilapidating the economy. When the Suharto regime came to power, stabilized the political situation, and then adopted a foreign investment law in 1967, the time had come.[2]

While the Japanese economy gathered speed in the 1960s, the lack of raw materials became its major bottleneck and vigorous efforts were made to expand the range of suppliers. Australia, which resisted Japanese incursions due to bad wartime experiences or for domestic reasons, opened up periodically. Yet, not until the mid-1970s did it become a major source. Meanwhile, investments spread to more remote places like Zaire, Niger, or South Africa, for a broad range of raw materials. Since oil was rapidly becoming the crucial resource, Japan also found itself investing heavily in the Middle East and later Mexico.

Europe had never been a major concern since it had no raw materials to offer and its labor costs were high compared to Asia. But it did have a large market dispersed among its many countries. When EFTA and the early Common Market, followed by the expanded European Community, turned these fragmented markets into larger, more compact ones, and then started surrounding them with common tariff walls, it made much more sense to penetrate from within. The easiest point of entry was Great Britain. A waning economy and labor unrest discouraged too much investment so it was spread more broadly, including places like Ireland, Belgium and Spain. Yet, only Germany really appealed to the Japanese, who concentrated their commercial operations there, creating a "little Tokyo" in Frankfurt. In due time, even East European states and the Soviet Union were covered by smaller offices while the possibilities in Siberia were mulled.

Finally, late in the 1970s, the People's Republic of China began lowering the "bamboo curtain." It had been hard to maintain proper relations after the war due to accumulated hatred which turned yet more intense as Japan drew closer to Taiwan and Korea. The differing political regimes and economic policies did not help either. Even when economics imposed on politics to the extent of a gradual increase in trade, communism and especially the policies followed by Mao Zedong and his supporters clearly excluded any closer involvement. However, as the whole system was transformed under Deng Xiaoping and his team, some things suddenly became possible.

By then, the circle was pretty much complete. There were likely to be few additions to what amounted to most of the countries in the world. And the additions would be cancelled out pretty much by those withdrawing one way or another. In some countries, Japanese investments were nationalized, in others they did so poorly there was no sense in keeping them. Uncertainty about the financial, and sometimes political, situation in Eastern Europe inhibited relations there. In Iran, it became hard, if not impossible, to operate. And continuing unrest in Indochina kept Japanese investors out of what had once been a prime target.

At present, the pattern of investment has more or less stabilized and the relative share of each component makes much better sense than in the early days. In fiscal 1982, the United States still had the highest cumulative total and a share of about 26%. Latin America had slipped back to 17%, and Brazil had nearly half of that. Meanwhile, Asia had clearly risen to the top, with 27% for the region, and 14% for Indonesia alone. Europe's share was 12%, that of Oceania (mainly Australia) 6%, the Middle East another 5%, and Africa also 5%.[3] But this does not exclude further shifts in the relative composition as raw materials or manufacturing become more or less important or one country or another provides a better investment climate or becomes decidely inhospitable.

Japan's old co-prosperity sphere was nothing compared to the present commercial empire in extension or value of the investments. This time it stretches clear around the world and not only to places within reach of the Japanese army and fleet. It is found not only in friendly countries but also some whose relations are barely correct or even a bit tense. Investment has also moved into sectors that would have been unthinkable before, not only raw material processing but marketing and local manufacturing. Once upon a time, the sun never set on the British empire. Now it has not ceased rising on Japan's empire.

Rekindled Fears

If the Japanese were delighted with their progress, that delight was hardly shared by many of the countries they entered. It is perfectly natural that the sudden and un-expected resurgence of Japan as an economic power that is not only selling its products all over the world but also investing in many countries should arouse some concern. The sheer elements of size, speed, and scope of its invest-ment are surprising and thus alarming. The fact that Japan is such a formidable, and manifestly expansive, economic power means that any anxiety must grow among those who cooperate or compete with it.

No matter what benefits this appearance may offer for other countries, they are often so worried about the side effects and possible negative consequences that they cannot deal with it as rationally as the investment or presence of smaller countries or less ruthlessly efficient companies. The same sort of fear that Latin Americans have about any action of their big brother to the north, or the former colonies about a British or French presence, is felt just as profoundly about the Japanese. And it is tinged with anger and bitterness since the Japanese, unlike the other imperial powers, lost the war and had hopefully been relegated to a lesser role.

Obviously, the fears are much keener in areas formerly ruled over by the Japanese. Repeated surveys of people living in the ASEAN countries, four of which were occupied and the fifth dominated by Japan during the Pacific War, show that they have not entirely forgotten the past, nor really forgiven it either. Most are willing to deal with the Japanese but they cannot fully trust them. Obviously, this affects the older generations most. But younger people, sometimes more nationalistic and emotional, often have just as strong feelings.[4]

The situation has gradually been evolving over the years and as the Japanese presence becomes more familiar. It can improve as the advantages of dealing with the Japanese emerge for the government, which may receive aid or loans, and local business circles, some of which are partners or clients. Yet, even as regards a very nebulous concept like the Pacific Basin Community, which could be in the interest of all concerned (and surely would have to offer benefits to the smaller states or they would not join), it is not that easy to let bygones be bygones. Even a conservative and highly reputable newspaper, like the *Business Times*, in a relatively moderate and no-nonsense country like Malaysia, finds it hard not to reminisce:

"The enthusiasm with which Japan is currently engaged in promoting the Pacific Basin concept. . . may give rise to unwholesome speculation as to the motives behind Japan's eagerness. To ASEAN countries, in particular, the concept may freshen memories of the somewhat similar idea Japan had of co-prosperity in the 1930s. Although circumstances have changed, and there is no evidence suggesting any intention to revive the ill-fated scheme, there is still the niggling fear at the back of the collective ASEAN mind, that the Pacific Basin concept is a device to ensure a steady supply of raw materials for the industrial Pacific countries, particularly at this juncture, when the industrial countries have become aware of the growing scarcity of natural resources and the need for some form of guarantee of supplies."[5]

This sort of comment is still closer to one end of the spectrum, the view of those who are willing to examine any project rationally and decide which of the two sides will benefit most and then try to move the balance in their favor. There are others who see no good whatsoever in the Japanese presence. They include activist groups like radical students, left-wing political organizations and tougher trade union bodies. Although they frequently represent a minority, and a small minority at that, they can exploit the vast reserves of fear and resentment that Japan's reappearance has laid bare in much broader segments of the population.

Thus, while Japan's investment in Asia mounted during the 1970s, it sparked a campaign aimed against the growing presence of its businessmen. This involved strikes and boycotts but is best remembered for the rather nasty reception Prime Minister Tanaka found when he arrived in Thailand and Indonesia early in 1974. He was met by angry demonstrators carrying banners condemning "Japanese economic imperialism," "neocolonialism" and "neocapitalism." Since then, things have remained relatively calm on the surface, but anti-Japanese tracts and newsletters continue to circulate. When Prime Minister Suzuki visited the Philippines in January 1981, one of them warned that he had come to "facilitate the smoother and more aggressive entry of Japanese capital into practically all fields of local industry."[6]

Indonesian Students Rally Against
Japanese "Economic Imperialism"

Credit: AP Radiophoto

This incipient hatred and quiescent anxiety exist in other parts of the erstwhile empire, perhaps nowhere quite as strongly as in Manchuria, which was once Japan's main source of raw materials and seems destined to open up its riches once again. Even further afield, the Japanese can count on a less than positive mind-set. There are many in Australia who are suspicious about Japan's ability to cooperate frankly and fairly. America still has its traditions of a "yellow peril," this time regarding trade offensives and market penetration, and Europe deems itself a greater victim. Although France is one of the countries least affected by the Japanese onslaught, either for exports or investment, it has been reacting nervously and in some cases almost neurotically, as this quote from the superficial but popular *Paris Match* will show:

"It's war and the Japanese army, the strongest and most disciplined in the world, counts 54 million magnificently equipped combattants under the flag. It's war and it serves no purpose to say, in an understatement, that it's economic. Quite to the contrary, while the Japanese run no risk of seeing their factories turned into ashes by atomic bombs, they can in return engage with impunity in economic Pearl Harbors throughout the world without any fear of annihilation. For this is the industrial war...."[7]

In such an atmosphere, it is not surprising that otherwise rational problems are sometimes dealt with irrationally. Nor are the fears all imaginary. If Japanese investment is not received properly and used to the best advantage, if the Japanese do not behave correctly and those in the host country behave unwisely, the result can be painfully negative. Such an outcome has been evident in any number of countries which have fallen prey to more economically advanced powers.

This is argued by various groups. Among the most cogent are those who go by the name of "concerned scholars," for whom concern occasionally becomes more important than scholarship and who repeatedly make the mistake of assuming that only by worrying about the supposed underdog or the exploited masses can one truly show concern. They have built up a rather solid case to show that *certain* investments, by *certain* companies, in *certain* countries have brought more bad than good. Many of their examples nowadays involve Japan (a close runner-up to the American imperialists).

They point out, among other things, that some intrusions by multinationals have resulted in exploitation of the workers, or in destruction of the existing small-scale industries or local entrepreneurs, or a rise in the price of goods, or serious outbreaks of pollution. They have even demonstrated, quite adequately, that some countries ended up worse off after receiving massive investments than they were to begin with and certainly did not reap the harvest of economic development they had hoped for and that had been promised to them. The weakest point in their argument is that they then generalize these bad examples to smear all others and fail to seriously consider the advantages.

The "concerned scholars" also provide ammunition for any number of others who are intensely concerned but boast no scholarship whatsoever. There are the hordes of prating politicians, ranging from village bosses to parliamentarians and prime ministers, who have spun fact and fiction into a dense web of ideology. There are also untold masses of angry students, aggrieved workers, dispossessed peasants, and other alienated groups which trace many of their misfortunes to foreign influences or regard the foreign presence as a prop for their own intensely distrusted and stridently denounced government. These diverse sectors can readily turn against the investors.

Although the factual bases are very shaky, the broad and excessively vague foundation for the concept of "neo-colonialism" has become terribly rigid and almost unshakable. This theory, espoused shortly after many colonies became free and when they wanted complete and untrammeled independence, is now over thirty years old. It has thus developed its own traditions and vocabulary. A ritualistic incantation of the evils that can be sworn up by allowing in foreign capital is one of its standard practices. This pseudo-scientific worldview mixed with nationalism does much to keep investment out or undermine its value even when accepted.[8]

But it is not only academics, politicians, students or trade unionists who are wary of investment. Those at the opposite end of the ideological scale are also worried when they learn that "the Japanese are coming." Local businessmen know what investment is, they engage in it themselves, and they are no strangers to competition. But they obviously do not like it when newcomers appear and especially when they arrive with more advanced techniques, larger sources of capital, and backup from huge companies at home. Some of the businessmen will make their separate peace and become agents or partners. The vast majority are left outside and fearful for their position.[9]

Frequently, the strongest lobbying against Japanese incursions comes not from the unions or opposition politicians but local businessmen, including some of the most successful and influential. This does not occur in every country. Some are more open, others more closed and protective. Yet, one need merely read the newspapers or hear the speeches in chambers of commerce to realize that this is regarded as a very serious matter. It is not just a question of making an investment. No, the Japanese are getting a foothold in the American semiconductor industry. Sony can penetrate the European Community by opening a factory in Wales. Japanese traders are cornering Australia's coal resources. And so on.

Such views are already quite prevalent although not a majority opinion in most places. They are, however, gaining ground and are more likely to advance than recede. The first few decades after the Pacific War were a time of unprecedented growth and prosperity for many countries when trade expanded and living standards rose. During much of this period, other nations were basically pleased to buy Japanese exports and receive Japanese investment. Since the oil crisis, things have changed dramatically. Competiton will be much fiercer and the chances of everyone winning will be much smaller. The future will be a period when successes are no longer admired but envied and when a presence of the successful is both coveted and despised.

Updated Responses

Faced with such arguments, and noticing their increasingly unfavorable image, the Japanese are not so much annoyed or angered as puzzled and uncomprehending. They do not refute the charges of neocolonialism, they don't seem to grasp what is meant. They do not explain away the drawbacks of some of their investments, they have trouble understanding what can be wrong with investment as such. When people in host countries complain that investors are self-centered or greedy, they do not deny this. They simply cannot conceive of it. The Japanese claim, and many perceive it thus, that their presence arises out of the finest and purest motives.

First, the Japanese point out that they have changed completely and that Japan is not, and never again will become, a militaristic power such as it once was. In fact, there is hardly a country in the world that spends a smaller share of its wealth on defense or has more groups committed to world peace. The Japanese have not forgotten the experience of the atomic bomb, something no other country has suffered, and this has tamed any desire to play at being a major power. Instead, all of the nation's energy has been channelled into other activities, mainly economic.

It does not occur to the Japanese that this unbounded preoccupation with economic development, one which has long since spilled over the nation's borders and invaded much of the world, is striking fear in the hearts of others. The Japanese think it is perfectly right to produce, and produce, and produce, and then to export their products far and wide even if they stunt the growth of industry in other countries. They heartily believe in the virtues of affluence and prosperity and assume that a profusion of material goods will lead to peace and happiness. That their presence can also create friction and anxiety escapes them.

If questioned as to why their influence has spread so rapidly in the world and their presence dominates certain sectors in countries thousands of miles from home, they don't seem to get the point. Aren't they helping the countries they are in? Aren't they buying raw materials from people who depend on such earnings to survive? Aren't they introducing new technologies to more backward countries that could not develop otherwise? Aren't they putting up productive facilities so that goods formerly imported can be manufactured locally? What is wrong with all these things?

Just like the British who once bore the burden of empire as an (at least verbal) sacrifice, the Japanese have developed their own ideology of international cooperation. They are providing grants to poor countries and loans to those somewhat better off. But, they point out—and with reason—that neither grants nor loans, especially if devoted mainly to creating infrastructure or social installations, will generate much development. Development only comes from mines, and factories, and shops. The Japanese know that. That's how their own country developed. And they are now making investments such as they made at home with the sole difference that these are made abroad.

This makes the Japanese approach range from neutral to highly positive. They do not think in terms of exploitation. Indeed, they hardly even think in terms of business as usual. Most of their pronouncements speak rather of contributions to peace and prosperity. This sort of thing quite naturally comes strongly from the government. The Ministry of International Trade and Industry includes direct overseas investment under the heading of economic cooperation, since such investments "have the effect of not only increasing funds, but also facilitate the creation of employment, technology transfer, and regional development."[10] Moreover, what could possibly be wrong with investment when it is part of the new wave of international cooperation?

"Moral significance is what serves as the foremost premise in thinking about the significance of economic cooperation. When the significance of economic cooperation is considered on this premise, the purpose of economic cooperation lies, first of all, in speeding up economic development and promoting welfare in developing countries. If the well-being of developing countries is improved as a result of the progress achieved in economic development, their livelihood will be settled and their political and social stability will be secured. Thus, they will contribute ultimately to world peace and stability. In addition, the formation through economic cooperation of relationships of mutual prosperity will build the foundation for the security and stability of our access to natural resources and energy necessary for the development of the Japanese economy. Moreover, economic cooperation is conducive to the stable expansion of the trade relationships between Japan and developing countries."[11]

While the overall policy is defined and packaged by the government, the more particular aspects of investment policy are developed by private business circles. They also have their own ideology of economic cooperation and it is no less high-sounding and well-intentioned. Everyone likes to put a good face on things. But this is rarely done with the flare or thoroughness of the Japanese. The following proposal for a new dimension in Japan's approach comes from Keizai Doyukai, a group of enlightened business leaders who often introduce new trends.

"The basic idea of the new dimension of internationalization may be put thus: Japan's people and industry have an active role to play and a contribution to make in maintaining humanity in a flourishing condition in a limited world. Stated differently, this means that Japan secures its own life in a new world order by playing an active role in shaping that new world order in which all peoples alike enjoy well-being. Heretofore Japan has thought only of its own development and profit as it sought to catch up with and overtake the advanced nations. But now the country needs to awaken to the social responsibility appropriate for its present position of political and economic power. Action in the new dimension demands an about-face in thinking to considerations of what Japan should be and what it should do about the well-being of the world. With a clear perception that the country's own way lies in accelerating the achievement of well-being in the developing countries, there must be close thought on what major role Japan may play in world development. It is of the utmost importance that we change our idea of internationalization, recognizing clearly that only in contributing to world well-being may we maintain our own well-being and survive."[12]

Even on a more practical level, such as specific commercial investments, Japan's business leaders like to speak of a contribution to world prosperity, the need to help others, or the greater well-being of humanity. Some insist that the investment was made more at the request of the host country than out of their own wishes. One of many such comments comes from Masaharu Matsushita, chairman of various companies in the Matsushita group (makers of National and Panasonic brand products).

"In our second half-century as a corporation, we want to contribute to world development to the fullest extent possible. This has always been the ideal of our management philosophy; now we have reached the business scale where the ideal can be put into practice. When we establish local factories, we do so in such a way as to benefit local industry as a whole. We want to be looked upon as a useful member of the community, and not as an intruder out to grab all he can get."[13]

While such sentiments may sound strange to people living in host countries which have ample experience of Japanese investment, they are no more strange than the seemingly wild charges that Japanese investors are crudely dominating countries which are sometimes heard. Such a possibility hardly occurs to the average Japanese. Ever since they were children, they have been brought up with a completely different image, namely that of a poor and dependent country. Japan is small, it has little arable land, it has inadequate raw materials, it must export its products to live. In this struggle for survival it turns to much wealthier countries to buy them and it relies on much luckier countries to provide raw materials. If any country is to be pitied, is it not Japan?

This view has as good a basis as the opposing concept. A look at Japan's raw material imports, for example, will show that it is sorely dependent on them for nearly everything. Food is also in great shortage. Japan could not get by a month if all shipments were cut off. The other side, that countries would be severely hurt if Japan stopped buying their goods, or switched sources, or used the fact that it is a massive purchaser to rig or depress prices, is ignored. That excessive investment could give it undue control over crucial aspects of the economy is forgotten. Even those who engage in such practices regard them as defensive, to keep the good ship Japan afloat.

This self-image is extremely powerful. And it has not been possible to convince the Japanese that others are weaker than they intrinsically and that even the more powerful are in some ways dependent. There is not much hope that the Japanese will change this view in the future either, not only because it has its own foundation in reality (while carefully evading the other side of the story), but also because it has extremely deep roots. The idea of a poor, weak, dependent Japan that must fight to survive is an old one. It was born under the Meiji state when Japan was first opened to the world and has flourished even while Japan subjected other peoples and eventually conquered half of Asia so that it could not be deprived of food, raw materials, or markets.

This may explain some of the gap between the high ideals of official policy and the coarser practices applied in implementing them. More than others, more than the Americans, British or French, the Japanese feel compelled to succeed and are less concerned by what may happen to anyone else. The second explanation is much simpler. The various generous principles and kindly virtues of Japan's international policy and the more practical implementation of its economic cooperation are handled by quite different people. The noble pose is struck by politicians and senior businessmen back home. The dirty work is left to local employees who have little time or inclination to listen to charitable advice and are overwhelmed by the daily routine of running an overseas venture.

This may lead some to feel that there is a good deal of duplicity in Japanese policy. Perhaps there is. Perhaps it only seems that way. However, while we are trying to determine whether it is intentional or accidental, we might just as well consider the fact that the main reason many of the foreign investors are so frustrated and angry is that they, too, perceive a tremendous gap between the official pronouncements of the host governments or the local businessmen, including their own partners, who warmly welcome them in touching speeches and flashy gestures . . . only to make their lives miserable when it comes to making the project work.

Reciprocal Self-Interest

These very divergent views of one another (and of themselves) by the investors and host countries certainly do not create the ideal climate for foreign investment. Some may be tempted to claim that since so much "cooperation" and/or "neocolonialism" does exist, the problems have been exaggerated. They most definitely have not. The fact that investments run into billions of dollars annually does not in any way exclude the possibility that they could run into much more if a better atmosphere were created. It is a moot point whether this would be two times more or ten times more.

There is no doubt that some countries have preferred an inward-looking policy of self-sufficiency or autarchy which keeps them out of the economic and technological mainstream. Others merely make it hard to invest. And some leaders have pushed the fear of entanglement so far that their countries were cut off from international intercourse nearly as much in the midst of the twentieth century as Japan in Tokugawa days. Burma and Sri Lanka, ideal sites for investment but long closed to such activities, are obvious examples. Meanwhile, other countries have lost out because of exceptional instability or hostility, Vietnam and Iran being cases in point.

Moreover, most of the investment that is actually generated, and supposedly bears witness to how countries can compose their differences when necessary, could be much more effective if seen in the right light. Although the projects do exist, the likelihood of their bearing the promised fruit is certainly reduced when many of the local politicians regard them as a form of contamination, because they are capitalist, because they are modern, or simply because they were created by foreigners. Excessively suspicious bureaucrats, immigration officials who harass the foreign experts, customs inspectors who block essential imports, or fiscal examiners who cannot imagine that they are not being cheated (but will forget this for a bribe) only complicate the situation. Not feeling overly wanted, the foreigners may live up to their reputation and become cruder and more aggressive than if well received. And the crucial goal—which is not merely the installation of some facility but the ability to run it efficiently in the new environment—can be missed.

It is therefore obvious that something must be done to shape relations so that, as a minimum, the crucial contacts and essential transfers can be accomplished smoothly. Otherwise, this eternal distrust can turn honest mistakes into assumed incompetence or supposed sabotage and justify attempts at outmaneuvering or simply ripping off the opposite party, seen as an opponent and not a partner. Unless both sides understand one another better (and also admit their own true intention) they can scarcely start building a solid basis for cooperation. Even then, it will be hard to work out the exact details of agreements that can bring this about.

Thus, attempts have been made at finding a middle ground. Often this is done on an equally ideological level by trying to infuse both parties with a feeling of "one world solidarity" or of being together "in the same boat." Appeals are made to their finer sentiments, their hopes for a better future, and so on. These PR efforts are certainly laudible. But many of them are so patently fake or grossly overdone that they only contribute to greater suspicion.

One high sounding justification of foreign investment is interdependence. It is particularly apt when one considers that Japan has been able to cooperate with so many

GM's Smith and Toyota's Toyoda
Celebrate Another "Historic Occasion"

Credit: Foreign Press Center/Kyodo

countries of different types and categories. Politicial differences have not prevented this since Japan has been able to invest in the Soviet Union, the East bloc, and China. Indeed, sometimes relations there were calmer than with its partners in the "free world." Social differences did not keep it from working in such disparate places as the Christian West, the Muslim Middle East or Hinduistic India. Differences in the level of development, rather than hindering, often provided one more reason to cooperate. The troubles have not been systematic with any type of country but sporadic, and sometimes temporary, when some regime did not feel that cooperation was to its advantage.

Mutual benefit is another nice way of presenting the case. It is obvious that there would never have been relations if both parties did not need one another. If Japan did not need raw materials, it would not have bought them, and they would never have been sold if the owner did not need the money. Japan would not have used local labor in most cases if it were not cheaper, and the workers involved would not have come unless they got more than otherwise. If Japan did not sell what others wished to buy, there would never have been trade. And, if it did not want the added income from local production, the investments would not have been made. In all these cases both the foreigners and locals benefit.

But this is not truly the same thing as mutual benefit. For each party derives completely different advantages in fundamentally different ways. It is much more a case of each party getting what it wants than both of them benefiting from the same thing. This makes the exchange somewhat more complicated. But it also provides room for all sorts of trade-offs and compensation when one finds a particular aspect of the deal distasteful, but will go along with it for other gains. By satisfying the self-interest of the various parties it is possible to bring about a venture which was not sought in that specific form by any but helps them all.

Thus, reciprocal self-interest is far better an explanation of what actually happens than the more idealistic promises or demonic ulterior motives. Japan did not invest to contribute or to control but to obtain what it wanted, labor, sales, profits. The host countries only accepted this to get what they wanted, wages, earnings, tax revenues. There was pitifully little altruism on either side. If the Japanese thought an investment had poor prospects, they would not make it. The host country did not throw open its doors in the name of some vague partnership in progress but because that was the only way it could develop.

Reciprocal self-interest is an even more accurate description of the process on the level at which it usually takes place, namely that of commercial dealings. No matter how great the government's interest, most investments are made by private companies and most of those in the host country directly affected by them are other companies (private or state), the labor force, and the public (as consumers, taxpayers, etc.). All of them react as a function of their own interests and with very slight concern as to the interests of anyone else. A company will only open a factory if it expects to make a decent profit, a worker will only accept a job if the pay is good, a purchaser will only buy a product if the price is right.

In this context, most of the people actually involved would regard appeals to mutual benefit or interdependence as so much hot air. This is not because they are without feelings. Nor is it that do not have higher aspirations. It is simply because that is the way they usually function. A worker cannot get by without a salary, a consumer cannot meet his needs without suitable products, and a company cannot last very long without profits. Asking them to behave otherwise is absurd. It is tantamount to asking them to ignore the primary motives and decisive signals that in ordinary circumstances determine their success or failure or, more accurately, their survival or disappearance.

So, in many ways, an investment is successful only when the reciprocal self-interests of those concerned converge and mesh and it only remains viable as long as that is the case. When trouble arises, appeals to higher principles or complaints of base motives, like generosity or exploitation, only confuse the situation. What is needed is more likely to be higher wages, cheaper prices for goods, perhaps more local equity, easier repatriation of capital, and the like, very specific points that make any business deal a success or failure and should be negotiated in a businesslike manner.

When approaching the phenomenon on the basis of reciprocal self-interest, other extremely useful judgements can be made which do not even appear in the context of "cooperation" or "neocolonialism." Not only can one deal more rationally with the flaws of any arrangement and see how they can be overcome by minor modifications rather than blanket approval or rejection, one can examine the posture of both sides far more objectively. It is ridiculous to regard either the investors or the hosts, the outsiders or the locals, the Japanese or the others as always being the winners and the losers, the exploiters and the exploited, the donors and the beneficiaries. Depending on the circumstances, these terms can apply equally well to any party.

Rather than waste time by pinning labels on the countries and companies and deciding who is the good guy and who the bad guy, one might try to determine which side was aware of what its self-interest really was, which followed it more intelligently and effectively, and which succeeded in attaining its goals. That could be either Japan or the host, neither in some cases, and both in others.

Therefore, if a country did lose in its relations with Japan, it would be absurd to place the blame solely on

Japan. Why did the country allow Japanese investment in? Why didn't it work out more valid counterproposals? Why did it only discover that it was being taken so late in the day? And why was it not gaining anything when other countries clearly were? Instead of shifting all the blame to Japan for any difficulties, one might let the other party share the blame for its own mistakes and for letting Japan misbehave!

Moreover, although rarely considered by the rival theories (both cooperation and neocolonialism), there is no reason to believe that the investing country always comes out on top. Sometimes it loses, and badly. Many Japanese investments turned sour and some ventures should never have been launched in the first place. Japanese companies have repeatedly failed to get as much out of projects as they planned, although they rarely admit it. And, in some cases, they were tricked or mistreated by the host country. How could this happen? Why did the Japanese allow it to happen?

NOTES

1. Ministry of Finance, *Japan's Direct Overseas Investment*, 1983.
2. For more on Japanese investment in the region, see Kunio Yoshihara, *Japanese Investment in Southeast Asia*, pp. 13–90.
3. Ministry of Finance, *op. cit.*
4. Ministry of Foreign Affairs, *Public Opinion Survey Concerning the Attitudes of Five ASEAN Countries Towards Japan*, September 1979.
5. *Business Times*, March 11, 1980.
6. *Solidaridad II*, January 1981, p. 6.
7. *Paris Match,* September 29, 1980.
8. See Jon Halliday and Gavin McCormack, *Japanese Imperialism Today.*
9. See Yoshi Tsurumi, *The Japanese Are Coming.*
10. MITI, *Economic Cooperation of Japan*, 1980, p. 45.
11. *Ibid*, p. 28.
12. Keizai Doyukai, *Toward A New Dimension of Internationalization*, February 1976, p. 7.
13. Rowland Gould, *The Matsushita Phenomenon*, Tokyo, Diamond Sha, 1970, p. 200.

2
The Colonizers

Grounds For Investing

Overseas investment is nothing new. It was not invented by
the Japanese *zaibatsu*, nor by the European imperialists,
nor by the classical school of economics, nor even by the
Romans and Phoenicians. It is a normal and purposeful
commercial exercise in the right circumstances and has
repeatedly been applied by those who praise it as well as
some who decry it, at least when undertaken by others,
including a number of developing countries and also
socialist states.

According to economic theory, investment can increase
the benefits a country derives by making better use of its
capital, knowhow or entrepreneurial skill. When trade has
reached a given level, overseas operations may become
viable and more profitable. Or, if for some reason trade is
impeded, investment may be the only alternative. Very
learned economists have worked this out nicely on paper,
refining their theories and plotting their graphs to determine the best possible conditions. Few businessmen
have ever seen them, and fewer could comprehend their
meaning, but they have all had a gut feeling somewhere
along the line that investment was the best approach to a
given project.

Although each Japanese company has its own specific
grounds for launching an investment abroad, the types

of reasons are relatively limited and can be grouped into three rough categories. Two of them concern basic inputs which are needed for production, namely raw materials and labor. The third has to do with the market for products. The same motives apply to all countries even if each will have different priorities and preferences.

Japan, as has been said often enough, is short of just about all raw materials and has to import them. Even to that end, it is advisable to establish a minimal infrastructure for the firms that handle imports so that they may check on the sources better, get to know their suppliers, and see to it that the goods are delivered on time and in proper condition. They may eventually go a step further if they find that not enough raw materials are available by joining in the search. And then they may take a second step by processing some raw materials on the spot.

Normally, labor is not the sort of thing one buys or sells on the international market. If a country is short of labor, it would tend to replace it with machinery. But not all tasks can be mechanized and sometimes large amounts of labor remain necessary. One approach has been to accept migrants or seasonal workers. In Japan, where this solution would cause more problems than it solves, the alternative has been for industries that need labor to go abroad where it can be found.

Japanese goods must find a market. And some investments can be made to set up offices that will prospect the local market, get to know the buyers, find out what the regulations and fashions are, develop a feel for prices, and feed this information back home. If enough goods are exported, a further step might be to open actual sales outlets or set up a network of dealers and agents. Other institutions like banks, insurance companies, and so on, might also advance to broaden their clientele.

The big step forward comes when manufacturing companies which had previously only exported go over to local production. There can be any number of reasons for that. They may find that some of the essential raw materials are readily available. Land, water, energy may be cheaper. Even the local labor costs may be lower or, at any rate, not high enough to negate the other advantages. Once they reach a sufficient size to obtain economies of scale it would make little difference where they manufacture and they could also save on transport.

There is one further explanation for such investment. It may happen that the local government adopts trade restrictions or imposes regulations that make former exporters produce locally or risk losing the market. Thus, there is a much greater ambivalence about this kind of investment. It may not always correspond precisely to economic logic and it may not be entered into as spontaneously. Especially for a country like Japan, it has the big drawback of inhibiting trade flows.

It is not all that easy to know just why a given project was launched. Sometimes there is one predominant reason. More often, there is a combination of reasons, with many factors entering into the calculation: availability of raw materials, cost and efficiency of labor, utility rates, size and accessibility of market, etc. Indeed, a more cautious investor would want everything to be in his favor before taking the move. On the other hand, if certain incentives are adopted in the host country or sufficient pressure exerted, earlier doubts might vanish.

Investment is classified in various manners, depending pretty much on who does the research. Each one is logical in its own context and irrelevant in the others. Thus, it is worthwhile considering how the information is presented to avoid confusion when applying it.

The statisticians of the Ministry of Finance, who keep close watch over the amounts of money invested abroad, have a rather simple classification by purpose. Those in the Ministry of International Trade and Industry find it no less useful. For, it basically follows the various sectors of economic activity which are familiar to all. Mining, agriculture, forestry and fishing make up the primary sector. Manufacturing is the secondary sector, with its various branches such as textiles, chemicals, machinery, and so on. And the tertiary sector includes things like commerce, finance and insurance.

On the basis of this breakdown, which is the only one that provides actual figures, we can see just how much money is devoted to investment in each sector or branch. From a look at the statistics, it clearly appears that manufacturing is the largest category with almost a third of the total. Next come the various activities in the tertiary sector, with commerce getting the bulk of that, some 16%. Agricultural investment is very slight, while mining attracts substantial amounts, nearly 20%. This is a fluctuating pattern, however, and relative shares tend to rise or fall.[1]

These figures are very interesting since they show where investment is directed. But they do not tell us very much about why. Projects in the very same sector can be made for a variety of reasons and those wishing to understand the workings of investment will doubtlessly want that additional bit of information. Thus, many economists and academics have developed a different categorization based largely on motivation. This also results in a three-way division consisting of natural resource-oriented, labor-oriented and market-oriented investment. The principal concern here is not the sector but the economic advantage.[2]

This classification coincides partly, but only partly, with the first. Obviously, the natural resource-related projects involve those in agriculture and mining. But they also include timber, which is listed under manufacturing in the standard statistics. Labor-oriented investment is almost

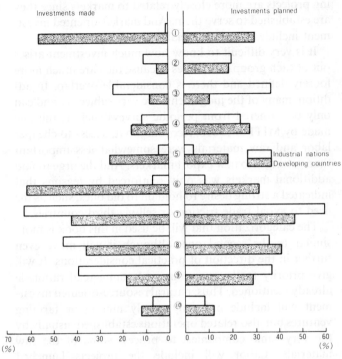

Why Japanese Firms Invest Abroad

Investments made | Investments planned

① Advantages in wage costs
② Advantages in production costs other than wage costs
③ Effects of defusing trade friction
④ Stable access to raw materials resources
⑤ Advantages for the export to third countries (preferential duties, etc.)
⑥ Advantages of preferential treatment given by local government
⑦ Diversification and internationalization of operations
⑧ Diversification of export markets
⑨ Expansion of the service sector
⑩ Others

Industrial nations
Developing countries

Source: *White Paper on International Trade*, 1981, MITI.

entirely in manufacturing. However, as we shall see, it is limited to certain branches in practice. Other manufacturing projects are more closely related to markets since they are established to serve them. And market-oriented investment includes many financial and service operations.

It is very difficult to know how much investment arises out of each group of motives because they are much more loosely defined and there is considerable overlap. In addition, many of the judgements are very subjective and can only be gathered from periodic surveys such as the one made by MITI in 1981. According to it, access to cheaper labor and raw materials were somewhat less important than getting into new export markets. And the urge to find additional markets was only reinforced by reasons that indicated a strong desire to hold on to old ones, such as the need to avoid trade friction or sell via third countries. [3]

The categorization that will be used in this book is more similar to the second one, although it will move even further in the direction of practical considerations. It will give priority to the economic and commercial rationale already mentioned. Thus, natural resource-oriented investment will include not only purely mining or farming ventures but also related operations established, usually by the very same companies, to process some of the raw materials. Labor will include the projects launched specifically to use cheaper labor in developing countries as well as those which use more expensive labor in the West. For, similar labor problems arise for every venture, whatever the place or sector. Finally, in market-oriented investment, commercial operations are only a first step. Whether the investors know it or not, this can lead to many more and bring them into full-fledged manufacturing.

Again, there is some difficulty in comparing this division with the standard statistics since the sectors and branches merge or overlap. The natural resource group this time will clearly eat into manufacturing investment, for metals, petrochemicals and pulp in particular. Manufacturing will be listed largely under market-oriented investment although some projects are really made more to save on labor. And much of the material relating to labor-oriented projects will refer to the whole context of Japanese labor practices and management.

Whatever may be lost by breaking the tight bonds of customary statistics or academic schema will be more than compensated for by creating a much more realistic approach to investment. This is the approach taken not by statisticians in their musty offices, or academics in their ivory towers, but by businessmen and entrepreneurs who are actually making investments. By the way, it also ties up nicely with the concerns of those in the host country who must approve of or participate in projects or direct the general economic policy.

Keeping Up With The Mitsuis

In addition to the various economic grounds for making investments abroad, there are a number of less rational and sometimes downright extraneous or foolish reasons for doing so. Not even in the toughest, most tightly-run multinational anywhere are business decisions entirely sheltered from passions like the lust for adventure, dreams of glory, or empire building. And, the bigger and looser a company, the more Parkinson's laws seem to apply. In Japan, there are a few business practices and mind-sets that also influence decisions which might better have been protected from them.

The first arises from an almost unbroken period of growth that was only slowed down, without being brought to a complete halt, by the oil crisis. Ever since the postwar reconstruction began, Japanese companies have been springing up and expanding in many ways. The number of personnel has grown, turnover has increased, the range of products has broadened. For a long time, it was assumed that any company worth its salt would be growing at a rate of about 15% to 20% a year, which meant that it was keeping ahead of the overall expansion of the economy. In fact, it was felt that not to expand was a sign of weakness or incompetence and thus there was a constant urge to find new outlets.

Meanwhile, the individual companies were becoming increasingly complex. They had ever more sections and divisions internally, each with its managers. They were also spawning new branches and subsidiaries and opening new factories. In certain subtle ways, they almost had to given the customary employment system in which those at the bottom work patiently and diligently for many years on the assumption that when they reach a certain age there will be a managerial post waiting for them. The habit of expansion plus the need to satisfy the staff, which has a great say on how things are done, has led to forced growth. Once a company had pretty much stabilized at home, it became natural to look for possibilities of expansion abroad.

The drive for expansion was further whipped up by Japan's great stress on ranking. Rather than follow its profits to judge a company's success, most observers kept an eye on size. Factors such as market share, number of employees, or number of subsidiaries both domestic and foreign, were crucial in rating them. This was not purely a matter of prestige but had practical implications as well. With a larger market share, one could produce at economies of scale and block the competition. A larger staff attracted the best recruits and offered the greatest opportunities of promotion to ambitious employees. Banks loaned money more readily to solid firms. Customers felt reassured in dealing with them. And the government could be counted on to help big companies while tending to neglect the small ones.

With this sort of mentality, it did not take long for the major companies to start rivalling one another on an international basis as well. The first to set up foreign offices were the trading companies. If Mitsui set up an office in a major capital, so did Mitsubishi, and Marubeni. Once the top traders were there, the smaller ones refused to be outdone and joined them. Then the large trading companies began setting up offices in lesser known countries. Whether they had any business there or not, other trading companies soon also opened offices. The same thing happened with the leading manufacturers and even department stores.

During these movements, it would seem as if they lacked confidence in their own judgement since quite often the decision taken by one automatically triggered parallel action by the others. But the syndrome went even deeper than mere copying. In Japan, businessmen had learned to their regret the risks inherent in letting their competitors get a head start on any market. For, they then staked it out and blocked entry. Forgetting that foreign markets were ruled more by price and quality than control of distribution channels and government support, they feared that letting a competitor act alone would lead to irretrievable losses. This resulted in a very noticeable "bandwagon" effect.

Although the directors of many companies were quite amenable to plans of overseas expansion to fill in gaps in their ardently desired growth strategy, there were times when any constraints on action hardly existed. Since profits were not an overriding concern and dividends were often just regular and token payment, periods when the company did well could lead to surplus cash flow . . . at least in the eyes of the responsible executives. These large sums might only be a temporary phenomenon while any investment implied a long-term commitment, yet they tended to launch projects with great abandon at such times. This was even more striking in the various years when the yen appreciated substantially and more foreign currency could be acquired for the same money.

Close relations with the banks further smoothed this path. In some cases, the banks were even too bullish on investment. As the domestic economy expanded less rapidly, they found there was not as much demand for loans. They could have finally developed lines for smaller companies or individuals but preferred working on large operations, even at smaller interest rates, and further encouraged their best customers to look abroad. By now, the banks also have branches or subsidiaries in many parts of the world and could thus service companies at both ends. When the amounts were too large, they would band together in a consortium. And this backing became even more solid with support from the Ministry of Finance or loans from the Export-Import Bank.

As if it were not enough for businessmen to have conditioned reflexes that pushed them toward expansion, and friendly bankers who would facilitate credit, they were also periodically prodded by the government to make greater efforts. Some of Japan's general policies implied making more investments in certain countries than would normally have arisen in the course of business. It is not that the businessmen were unhappy to make investments. But, by letting politics get mixed up in the process, they were induced to make investments they did not want that badly or to make them earlier, larger and sometimes granting more advantageous terms than desired.

One series of investments has arisen out of Japan's overall policy of keeping up steady supplies of raw materials. Companies were urged to scour the world to find new sources and were given exceptionally generous backing when they entered into such projects. Since most of these projects were rather large, this implied considerable burdens on all concerned. However, given Japan's complex about the need to have enough raw materials when it wanted them, projects could be launched that were unnecessarily large or involved costs and risks that ordinary investors would shun.

Another series of investments arose because of trade friction. Whenever Japan exported too many goods abroad, such as television sets or automobiles, it come under pressure to cut back. When the overall trade balance became too lopsided, there were broader threats of protectionism. To avoid this, Japan was offered the alternative of making investments in the countries concerned. This would affect the payments balance rather swiftly as funds were transferred abroad and would gradually improve the trade balance as Japanese companies produced more abroad and less was imported. This proved a more acceptable (politically, not economically) manner of allowing Japanese companies to expand.

A final series of projects derived from various attempts to patch up or improve relations with certain crucial countries. One of the most important efforts was made to get on better terms with the oil producers, whether in the Middle East, Indonesia, or Mexico. Another was to resume good relations with some areas exposed to its earlier imperialism, and ASEAN became the main focus here. There were also general efforts to establish links with China. In such cases, the Japanese representatives usually made promises of substantial aid and loans and this tended to attract further business involvement, sometimes in the form of investment.

All of these are rather dubious reasons for making investments. Empire building within the company, need to promote aspiring young salarymen, excess liquidity, are elements that push one to take decisions or facilitate them when in fact a decision on overseas investment should mature naturally and be part of a broad and clear international strategy. No matter what the competitors do, it may be just as well to refrain or at least check on the circumstances more thoroughly. Pressure from the bank or government doubtlessly expresses their interest without in any way proving that the project concerned is likely to succeed. Nor can government guarantees entirely compensate a company for eventual losses.

Moreover, an overseas investment is always an alternative to something else. It is true that growth opportunities are drying up at home and more and more one has to look abroad for expansion. But it is not as if the Japanese companies did not have other uses for their money. They could buy newer machinery, pay higher wages, or distribute larger dividends. They could diversify into other fields. Finally, they could pay back more of the tremendous debts they had incurred with the banks because of their earlier expansion. Instead, they often borrowed yet more and then tied the money up in overseas investments that would take years to bear fruit.

Just as it is not easy to separate out the various grounds for making investments, whether to obtain raw materials, labor or market share, it is not easy to distinguish the deeper motives for launching any specific project. They are always presented as if the rational arguments were uppermost and indeed opportunism or emotion played no role. But it is clear that even when they were not predominant, they could be decisive by tipping the balance one way or the other. There is no sense in trying to estimate just how often this happened. The best that can be said, as we shall later see, is that it was more often than was wise.

Spawning Multinationals

Probably the best known agents of Japanese penetration are the general trading companies or *sogo shosha*. They deal in just about everything and can be found just about everywhere. Originally, they only engaged in import-export but they have since expanded their activities in many ways that bring them into marketing and even manufacturing abroad. This has led them to make substantial investments not only for themselves but also on behalf of many of their clients, some of whom would probably never have strayed abroad otherwise.[4]

What is strangest about these powerful companies is that they first arose as an admission of weakness and ignorance by Japan's business community. When Japan was first opened to commerce with the world, not much more than a century ago, its businessmen were anything but accustomed to trading with foreign countries. After nearly three centuries of seclusion, there were not many people who spoke any foreign language or had any experience in dealing with foreigners. Even fewer knew where to obtain raw materials or how to enter foreign markets. Moreover, since industrialization was proceeding apace, many businessmen were too occupied with their own specific concerns to develop these skills. Thus, trading activities were spun off to a growing number of companies, large and small, highly specialized or more comprehensive.

Some of these companies became highly proficient in the essential skills and they contributed greatly to prewar economic development. Unfortunately, they also got mixed up in politics. Mitsubishi was particularly noticeable in many of the Meiji governments' ventures. Some of the trading houses were also members of the *zaibatsu* which became active in the move to colonize China and played a role in the Pacific War. In retribution for this, they were dissolved by the occupation forces into a welter of smaller components. Yet, since the war, the general trading companies have reappeared as smaller firms grew and pieces of the older ones came together again. They proved no less aggressive than their predecessors and showed some abiding taste for grandiose projects and a willingness to serve the state.

At present, there is a multitude of trading companies, perhaps 8,000 of them, ranging from minute to monumental. But it is usually the ten (and then nine) top ones which attract most of the attention given their vast size and turnover. The two largest are Mitsubishi and Mitsui. Then comes a second batch with C. Itoh, Marubeni, Sumitomo and Nissho Iwai. And finally a group of somewhat smaller ones like Toyo Menka, Kanematsu-Gosho, Nichimen, and formerly Ataka. The rivalry among them is fierce, so much so that Ataka collapsed in an attempt to rise a notch higher. Between them they have some 65,000 employees and showed a turnover of about $334 billion in 1980. Among them, they control approximately half of Japan's total imports and exports.

Why the *sogo shosha*, and the other trading firms to a lesser extent, are so important for investment immediately becomes clear upon examining their primary activities. To this must be added the fact that, after the war as well, they were allowed considerable leeway by and took major initiatives for their clients.

The trading companies have traditionally supplied Japan with most of its food and industrual raw materials. This was obtained through normal commercial channels in most cases. However, over the years, the needs became so great that it was increasingly necessary to do a bit more. Thus, they began seeking new sources of food and raw materials and entering joint ventures to produce the goods they eventually brought back to Japan. This could involve

Trading Room In A *Sogo Shosha*
Credit: Mitsubishi Corp.

merely buying into an existing company on their own or in cooperation with the clients which would ultimately purchase the materials. From this more passive role, they went over to actively organizing projects, including numerous partners, on an unprecedented scale.

Traditionally, the trading companies have sold most of Japan's goods abroad on behalf of the manufacturers, a practice less commonly applied by other countries. This side of the operation they could only hold onto through their clever use of commercial channels and by keeping their margins extremely low. However, as the cost of some Japanese goods rose or when developing countries or industrialized ones put up tariff barriers, the trading companies realized that they (and their clients) might soon be losing the business. To overcome the cost problem or get around protectionism, they sometimes persuaded their clients to go over to production on such markets. And sometimes they did this themselves.

The trading companies were crucial in such ventures due to their knowledge of the market and conditions in foreign countries, something many mining or manufacturing companies lacked. They could locate suitable partners, negotiate proper arrangements with the local authorities, and help in setting things up. In such operations, they often invested along with the mining or manufacturing companies to keep their foot in the door and be assured of continued patronage. They were also useful as project organizers because they knew where to obtain the necessary plant, equipment and knowhow at reasonable prices. They could more readily field an effective team for even the most complex ventures since they maintained so many links with other Japanese companies, some of them a part of the same group.

To fulfill the more usual import-export functions efficiently, the trading companies had to provide certain auxiliary services which also grew and became more sophisticated with time. One of them was to pay close attention to matters that concerned any of their clients and supply vast amounts of information that was gathered through an increasingly dense network of offices scattered around the globe. In this way, the trading companies helped keep Japan provided with new technologies at cheap rates. They also notified their clients about the possibilities of sales or the need to shift to manufacturing. All this induced investments, by the trading companies or their clients, individually or jointly.

Finally, since they were constantly handling tremendous sums of money and enjoyed exceptional creditworthiness as well as special relations with the banks, they could get funds at particularly favorable rates. These funds they were then able to relend to their own clients at a better rate than some of them could get directly from the bank. In the case of smaller companies, the traders were often a major source of borrowing. This money could be used for current business or, if so desired, to float a new project. When it came to financing major investments, the top traders could more readily raise the funds and obtain any necessary bank support.

With all these assets, it is not surprising to find that the *sogo shosha* adopted an aggressive approach to overseas investment. "We must become true coordinators of the world's industry," urged Marubeni President Matsujiro Ikeda. "We must positively engage in natural resource development programs. We must make heavy investments in international projects for dividend revenues." He was echoed by C. Itoh's Executive Director Isao Yonekura. "*Sogo shosha* will work as expeditionary forces of the government in its overseas assistance programs."[5]

But the other companies were increasingly important. This was partly because they, too, entered a phase of internationalization and were at the same time becoming less dependent on the trading houses. This could be seen for the steelmakers and metal refiners which made greater efforts to cover their own needs of basic inputs and did not hesitate to invest in overseas projects. It was even more noticeable for some of the leading manufacturers which preferred establishing their own offices abroad and occasionally went over to local production. This did not occur in all sectors, but it was striking for textiles, electronics, motor vehicles and some others. Given the size of the Japanese companies, their solidity and efficiency, even a timid step toward investment could make waves. But some were anything but timid, launching literally dozens of ventures of one sort or another.

There were a number of other Japanese companies that eventually appeared on the scene. Prominent among them were the banks and securities companies. Given the intimate relations with their clients, they were easily convinced to establish branches abroad and this, in turn, encouraged other Japanese companies to come. To handle the growing trade, there were also shipping, forwarding and insurance firms. Tourism brought the airlines, hotels and travel agencies. Even some of the leading retail chains set up shop.

However, it was hardly expected that smaller manufacturers would also enter upon the course of foreign investment. Most multinationals are, almost by definition, large, well-endowed companies with very distinctive products or highly advanced technologies. Small Japanese companies offered none of this and, to boot, they had almost no experience of operating abroad. Most of them did not even handle their own exports and left it to trading companies or at most to periodic trips abroad by their salesmen.

In addition, the smaller companies occupy a rather subordinate position in Japan's dual economy. Whereas the larger companies, which represent less than 1% of the total number, employ about 30% of the labor force and produce about 50% of the value of shipments, hordes of lesser ones fight over the rest. In addition to being smaller, and weaker, they usually show lower productivity and pay their workers somewhat less. In fact, they increasingly find it hard to obtain workers at any price for their aging factories and hard or dirty manual labor. Defined as companies that have a paid-in capital of ¥100 million or less, they hardly look like candidates for multinationals. And this becomes more pointed when it is considered that they are concentrated largely in more labor-intensive and declining industries.

These firms would find it almost impossible to move abroad on their own. However, they have been assisted by the trading companies which distributed their products. As soon as it became obvious that a Japanese exporter was in trouble or that the importing countries were liable to put up trade barriers, the trading company warned it. If the only way to survive was by seeking cheaper labor abroad, the trading company knew how this could be done. It then helped find a local partner for a joint venture, since a small Japanese firm might not know how to operate alone in another country. It advanced some of the funds needed. And frequently the trading company took a small share of the equity since it hoped to act as agent for the purchase of raw materials or machinery and then later for the export of finished goods.

There was another basic pattern to this "migration" by smaller Japanese manufacturers, this time with the large assemblers playing the crucial role. In Japan, most of the leading companies surround themselves with a vast number of suppliers and subcontractors and the relations can be very close, based not merely on commercial ties but also partial ownership of the smaller firms. It is therefore not surprising that, when such a company decided to go into production in another country, it was followed by some of its associates. They knew that this step might bring a loss of production in Japan while setting up their own operation abroad could boost sales. Moreover, if they moved at about the same time as their primary buyer, they could count on considerable business fron the outset plus a good deal of support.

Thus, small and medium-scale enterprises have come to hold a sizeable portion of Japan's overseas investments. Over 40% of the total number of manufacturing projects were launched by them, although their position is much less impressive in value terms, under 10%. And they are barely represented in the primary and tertiary sectors. While relatively few of them moved to advanced countries, in Asia where most of their ventures are concentrated they are a major factor.

Nor could one really forget the banks. Their role is far greater than the investments they made directly by setting up branches abroad. In fact, they were the biggest financiers of Japan's outward movement. This includes both the commercial banks and the state-run banks and financial agencies. Sometimes they cooperated by taking equity in major projects. More often, they offered credit. Just as most Japanese companies are built on debt and not equity, their overseas ventures are also solidly embedded in loans. Actually, over the years, the share of debt acquisition has been catching up with securities acquisition and now represents nearly half the total value of direct foreign investment. Without this backup from the banks, it would never have been possible to expand the empire so rapidly.

Japanese investment may have been slow in starting, but it quickly snowballed into a mutually-reinforcing process in which one partner encouraged the other. Given the close relations that exist between Japanese companies and their proclivity for dealing with one another, as well as often crossownership and other links, this was not at all unusual. Trading companies paved the way for their clients, the banks followed, and then yet more hesitant investors felt it was safe to advance. Major manufacturers would set up a factory and soon be joined by their habitual suppliers and subcontractors. Meanwhile, the preference for living among Japanese or difficulties in getting over the hurdle of entering the indigenous society attracted even smaller operations including shops, restaurants and professionals to serve the growing community.

The Empire Builders

The Japanese have always entrusted their young men with the task of invading enemy territory, storming a castle, or launching new economic ventures. Young men are more daring, more energetic, and can take more deprivation. They are usually under very broad direction from above but left with a fair amount of discretion on the ground. They draw up their own plans and proceed to implement them, reporting back once things have started moving smartly. By then, it may be too late for counterorders, were any to come. But the only concern is really success no matter how it is achieved.

When the Japanese multinationals, especially the large and conspicuous ones, the *sogo shosha* and the banks, the huge manufacturing monoliths and dynamic young companies, began opening their offices abroad, almost as a matter of course they were staffed with younger salarymen and managers. These were employees recruited directly from school, trained in the ways of the company and who showed some promise in their first years there. They were not just strays picked up locally or a manager brought in from outside to handle affairs. Thus, they had the company's interest very much at heart.

Equally important, they had their own personal success at heart. One can say what one wants about loyalty to the company and group spirit, each individual Japanese also hopes that among all the others he will be singled out for somewhat faster promotion and some dream of rising to the top. An overseas assignment is a particularly good way of testing the metal of these young men and seeing which of them can be brought onto the special track that leads to top management. If they succeed, the path lies open; if they fail, they will languish among the multitudes of salarymen who never quite made it and perhaps be pensioned off earlier.

It is this sort of people who arrived in countries they had never seen before and whose language they often did not speak. They were unfamiliar with the customs and wary about the inhabitants. Often, they shut themselves off from the rest of this strange environment and devoted themselves entirely to building up the local office or getting the local manufacturing plant going. They would not hesitate to put in long hours each day or to spend evenings and weekends at work as well. The first batches even came without their wife and children and could more readily lead such a dedicated life. Even now, when things are much easier and the family is allowed to come, sometimes a few months later, they are not known for knocking off at five o'clock and rushing home.

Naturally, one person could not hold out alone and the Japanese like to work in groups anyway. Thus, the staff members coming from the head office quickly form close relations with one another and adopt many of the same methods used back home. This includes group meetings and the numerous *nemawashi* contacts that lead to reaching a consensus, a technique so intricate no foreigner could really apply it. The whole team leads a relatively Spartan life and shares the hardships and misfortunes together. Obviously, for the Japanese employees, this relationship is helpful and supportive. But it cuts them off even more from those around them and the host country in general.

All this while, they maintain very close contact with the head office and owe their allegience primarily to the parent company and not the subsidiary. This arises already out of the kind of relations that exist among Japanese, where formal relations can be much less significant than informal links and frequently the personal ties between employees and their superiors are decisive. A man is usually seconded not only by the company but comes from a given division, to which he may return. He is representing this division, and the company, in the subsidiary, and he will write copious notes home to inform people of how things are going. There is also a steady stream of higher-ups from the head office visiting the local office, whose staff will be forced to spend an exorbitant amount of time with them, not only on business matters but social and entertainment.

Although these close relations are essential for smooth and efficient operations, they can also create some impediments. The local personnel, and the local society more generally, may not share all of the corporate goals conceived in the inner circle of management or an even more remote head office. Trying to impose them only causes friction between the expatriates and their colleagues. The fact that, following the standard routine, the Japanese are rotated every two or three years and will rarely spend more than one or two stints in the same subsidiary already makes the relationship quite tenuous. Linguistic barriers and an undeniable clannishness broaden the gap yet further.

The eager young men, however, are not the only ones who carry the flag of empire. Oddly enough, the other contingent comes from the opposite end, namely older businessmen, sometimes entrepreneurs and company executives in their own right, but who run some of Japan's smaller firms. As the cost of labor went up, as competition became more intense, they often had to move the bulk of their manufacturing operations abroad to benefit from cheaper labor. Gradually, more and more of the production came from these overseas ventures and thus the primary concern was to keep them running well while the parent company in Japan became little more than an assembly plant or distribution channel.

Those who came were frequently the older managers since the stagnant office and factory in Japan hardly recruited young people any more. Yet, since the quality had to be as good as in Japan, a fair-sized general staff might arrive to keep a good watch over things. Actually, the older men of Pacific War vintage occasionally had more experience of living abroad than the younger ones and, despite any animosity that remained, they tended to chose some of the places they had once been stationed in or where the people spoke some Japanese, like Korea or Taiwan. Working in much smaller operations, in closer contact with the locals, they could be a bit friendlier and more relaxed. In addition, they were likely to stay for many years and not just a brief stint.

Yet, there was one thing they shared with the young men sent by the big multinationals, they had to succeed. They did not have to succeed for their future career; they had to succeed or there would be no future career. The companies they left behind, where they had worked and which some had founded, were in no position to survive if the flow of cheaper components and articles ceased. Nor could they just let the home company collapse and go somewhere else. In Japan, only young workers are sought after, older ones have trouble finding a job, and what they get is usually none too good. There are also terribly few old age benefits for that generation. Success in the overseas venture was clearly the only real hope.

So, both of these rather disparate groups of empire builders were driven by the same urge: the need to succeed come what may. This means succeed in the sense of doing the company's bidding or achieving concrete targets such as a given level of sales or flow of products. Under such conditions, they have little time to think of broader and fuzzier corporate aims such as winning the favor of the local population or government or even improving the image of their own company and Japan in general. They are periodically given such directives, and doubtlessly the company president will make philosophical statements about forgetting their everyday cares and working for the future or realizing that the company's true ambition is a happier world and the like. But, in the hustle and bustle of their assignment abroad, they have few incentives to do much about this.[6]

Japan, Inc.

Japan's emergence as a major overseas investor, like its economic rise, owes much to close cooperation between the three partners running the country's economy, namely the business community, the bureaucracy, and the ruling politicians. Although not really a coordinated policy, the fact that businessmen can count on a degree of government support has made it far easier for them to launch, and especially finance, overseas ventures.

As we shall see, the Japanese government provides an expanding program of development aid. As we shall also see, much of this assistance is directed toward countries with which Japan already has close relations or with which it wishes to improve relations, in most cases for economic reasons. Reparations, and then normal aid, have served to smooth over difficulties or relax friction and also helped open doors. This results not just from a generally improved atmosphere but because business interests know how to use the aid machinery to their advantage.

No matter what economic theory may state, most projects are not the result of an objective and disinterested examination of a country's development needs and potential. Nor is the prime mover always the local government or population. What happens with startling frequency is nearly the complete opposite. Japanese businessmen may find a project that appeals to them and which they then bring to the notice of local interests which get it accepted by the host government. The government thereupon makes a formal request to the Japanese aid-related agencies which are quite likely to approve it, after all the Japanese promoters are busily working behind the scenes to that end. Such schemes usually do have some merit, and there are justifiable grounds for including them in a development plan. Yet, there are equally important gains for the Japanese companies, this often being to build the project or supply plant and equipment. In some cases, it may be an otherwise comercial venture which they wished to invest in anyway.

Selecting projects, whether endorsed by the local and/or Japanese government or restricted to private parties, is only a first step. Financing is no less crucial, especially for companies that have as little internal capital as the Japanese do. Much of the funds come from the commercial banks which are only willing to advance as much as they do for overseas investment because they know that the government takes a positive view of such activities. If they feel sufficiently reassured, the banks may subsequently lend liberally to the overseas venture itself and even the foreign partners.

In addition, the government has established several institutions that provide supplementary funding. The Export-Import Bank can extend substantial loans to Japanese investors to finance their purchase of equity in overseas ventures. It can also make loans to the venture itself for the purchase of plant and equipment from Japan. For projects which are too large for the private sector to handle, and which may be established under government auspices, the Overseas Economic Cooperation Fund (OECF) intervenes. It makes loans or buys equity in a consortium formed by Japanese firms. Whereas the Exim Bank's loans are offered at modest interest rates, revolving around 8%, the OECF grants even more generous terms, in the region of 3% and with longer grace and repayment periods. Meanwhile, the Japanese International Cooperation Agency (JICA) can provide loans or technical assistance for promising economic development projects.[7]

Smaller companies attempting to invest abroad are even more sorely in need of support and special efforts have been made for them. During the 1970s, the Japan Overseas Development Corporation (JODC) made feasibility studies of projects being considered in developing countries and, if they were approved, granted rather extended interest-free loans for part of the necessary capital. Financial assistance is still provided by various institutions set up specifically to aid small-scale enterprises such as the Small Business Finance Corporation, the People's Finance Corporation, and the Central Cooperative Bank for Commerce and Industry.

For natural resource development, the Japanese government has created a number of specialized bodies which try to organize and channel national efforts and can contribute financial or other support as well as participating directly in certain projects. One of the earliest was the Metal Ore Exploration Promotion Agency. Then came the Japan Petroleum Development Corporation (JPDC) and the Japan National Oil Corporation (JNOC). More recently, the Power Reactor and Nuclear Fuel Development Corporation (PRN) was added. In the private sector, there is also a Light Metal Development Company for bauxite and a broader, mixed organization, the Overseas Mineral Resources Development Company.

Some more general measures have also encouraged investment. One is a tax incentive whereby companies could set aside reserves of 30% for most investments in developing countries and as much as 100% for resource projects. They were even more pleased to be covered against unforeseeable risks such as expropriation and nationalization by a special overseas investment insurance system. This fund will reimburse as much as 90% of the contracted amount and is fed by a premium of less than 1% of the contract value, income from the use of internal reserves, and whatever assets can be recovered from the other country. By 1980, the special account was generating an annual income of some ¥40 billion. Hopefully this would be enough to meet any contingency.

But nothing was more desirable than having a venture singled out as a "national project." Just what this means is far from clear and the term national does not imply that it is in any way a government project. At most, it is a very large-scale operation, often too large for anything but a group of private companies, and which is felt to be in the national interest. The reason may be that it consolidates relations with a crucial country or, as often as not, facilitates Japan's access to resources. For such reasons, the government agrees to promote it politically and financially (usually through the OECF), although the exact extent of this backing has never been defined.

While most of this is rather straightforward and not very different from what happens elsewhere, more informal yet apparently persuasive tactics are also used. Investors occasionally get a helping hand from prominent politicians, some of whom seem to have a knack for unlocking doors. Links between major companies and leading Liberal Democratic Party politicians are very close while the LDP has established good relations with many politicians abroad. They were influential in creating an atmosphere in which Japanese investment would be welcome in Taiwan under the Kuomintang and in Korea after Park come to power. They were also credited with opening up Indonesia after the fall of Sukarno and Brazil under General Geisel. A flurry of visits to the Middle East just after the oil embargo resulted in Japan's being placed on the list of "friendly" countries and being eminently eligible for many projects since then. Major state visits also paved the way to

interesting contacts with ASEAN, Mexico and the People's Republic of China.

Of course, it was not so easy as just shaking a couple of hands and whispering a few words in someone's ear. On occasion, very specific projects were discussed by people who had a vested interest in their coming about. More generally, Japan's leaders have had to spread largesse on a grand scale to overcome certain inhibitions or show just how fine a partner it could be. Some of the gifts they brought were truly magnificent. During a whirlwind tour of the Middle East in 1974, Iraq was apparently offered $1 billion in loans while Iran, out of sheer self-respect, settled for twice that. The Brazilian President was promised $3 billion when he visited Tokyo. Prime Minister Fukuda pledged $1 billion in loans to finance a project for each of the five ASEAN countries in 1977 and, soon after, Prime Minister Ohira offered $1.5 billion to China. By the time Mexico was granted a $1 billion loan, this was no longer exceptional. And it was easily topped by Prime Minister Nakasone's offer of $4 billion to Korea in 1983.

While these pump-priming endeavors certainly helped the Japanese businessmen increase their sales and investment, the outcome was not always positive. One scenario that was repeated more often than desirable went as follows. The leader of some strategic nation had set upon a major, highly visible and spectacular project which he proclaimed was in the national interest. A visiting Japanese politician, poorly briefed and hard put to refuse, then blindly promised support of the project and lavishly offered loans to finance it. He eventually had to lean heavily on business interests, while making some key concessions to them, so that the project could be carried out and he would not lose face. Some of these projects looked pretty risky from the outset and the Japanese companies only accepted because of promises of government support.

But it was not always the businessmen who had to honor the face of the politicians. Japanese companies periodically got involved in projects whose original rationale was shattered by subsequent events. The cost of investment might have risen, the market for the finished product shrunk, or the political situation soured. If the project had not progressed very far, the company might try to extricate itself. But that was not so easy, especially not for "national" projects. It could also happen that a new, more nationalistic or leftist regime would decide to expropriate a foreign venture or financial constraints would make it impossible to repatriate capital. In such cases, the businessmen did not hesitate to call on the government, both bureaucrats and politicians, to obtain redress or compensation.

These forms of cooperation within Japan, Inc. leave a rather mixed impression. Because of the close links between business and government it is possible to carry out major projects that could not be launched normally and to spread Japanese influence abroad faster than otherwise. At the same time, the cooperation sometimes makes it too easy to go ahead and political meddling in essentially commercial affairs can get businessmen involved in the wrong projects. The massive use of credit in general allows Japanese firms to expand more readily but leaves them prey to serious repercussions if anything goes wrong.

One final drawback is hardly ever noticed because not much attention is paid to the interests of the general public. The individual Japanese citizen, as a consumer, taxpayer, bank depositor, or in any other capacity that makes it possible for the system to continue, is rarely consulted. If foolish investments are made or if compensation is found for unlucky companies, then someone must lose somewhere. This is obviously not going to be the politicians and bureaucrats but rather the public.

Aid Or Charity?

In the bad old days of unrepentant imperialism, foreign investment was usually imposed by strong and aggressive nations on their weaker subject or client states. The stick was wielded with a heavy hand and such projects were rarely rejected, although there may have been a degree of passive resistance. Nowadays, the carrot is much more noticeable. Not only are the fine points of specific projects vaunted, the investor's home country will often toss in some bonus like cheaper loans or the gift of a school or hospital.

It is not really certain why that has become the fashion since, if a project will not bring sufficient reward to those concerned, it should never be launched. And, to the Japanese at least, the inherent advantages of overseas investment are quite adequate to include it among the various forms of "international cooperation." They are, as outlined in *Economic Cooperation of Japan 1980*, "not only increasing funds within the country, but also facilitating the creation of employment, technology transfer, and regional development."[8] Still, if granting a bit of assistance will make countries more amenable to accepting the benefits of investment, why not?

Anyway, as a rising economic power and a proud member of the so-called "advanced nations club," Japan has had little choice but to follow the fashion and increase its foreign aid as well. Its first step in this direction was hardly a happy one, since it was forced to grant reparations to many of the countries its troops had occupied and devastated during the war. They included the Philippines, Korea, Burma and Indonesia, but ultimately not the biggest victim, China, which renounced the right. The amounts were substantial both in cash and kind, start-

ing in the 1950s and building up to something over ¥600 billion.

Meanwhile, Japan became a member of the United Nations and, like the other developed countries, came under relentless pressure from the developing countries to expand its aid. When it joined the Organisation for Economic Cooperation and Development, the only Asian country to do so, it was urged to make ever larger contributions by the rest of the Development Assistance Committee (DAC).

Some of Japan's contributions could qualify as "aid" in the sense of a transfer of funds not resulting from normal commercial interests or, in looser terms, "charity." This applies to the two basic categories included by the DAC in official development assistance (ODA). One is grants, either in money or goods, given free of charge. The other, namely concessional loans, is already somewhat less disinterested since they must eventually be paid back. The main advantage is that the terms are exceptionally lenient with very low interest rates and long repayment periods. By 1981, the government had granted nearly ¥3,940 billion.

When it comes to ODA, Japan's performance has been both impressive and disappointing, depending on how you look at it. By now, it has risen to fourth position as regards the total absolute amount. For the 1981-85 period alone, Japan intends to provide nearly $21 billion worth. But the ODA/GNP ratio is relatively low, showing how little the Japanese contribute per capita. As late as 1982, it was 0.29%, well below the average of 0.33% and even more so the target of 0.70%. Japan's grant element was also somewhat beneath the average. Thus, it has come under continuing pressure to increase its official development assistance and especially the amount of grants. This resulted in two ODA-doubling campaigns which led to a substantial, if not wholly satisfactory, improvement.[9]

Prime Minister Ohira Visits China
Credit: Foreign Press Center/Kyodo

The other problem with Japan's aid effort, as opposed to the actual size, was that in earlier days many of the contributions were "tied." Reparations consisted basically of products that were made in Japan and shipped to the beneficiaries. Later on, when Japan offered assistance, the sums were usually linked to purchases of its goods. This meant that the recipient country was formally bound to procure any goods and services from Japanese companies whether they were the best and cheapest suppliers or not. It also annoyed other advanced countries whose companies wished to bid for the projects. Japan eventually fell into line and promised to "untie" the bulk of its aid. It actually has done so. But most of the money it offers still ends up with its national companies somehow.

This is only partly due to the definite bias in Japan's distribution of grants and loans, one that runs very much

parallel to its underlying economic interests. Basically, it channels the bulk of its assistance to Asia, especially East and Southeast Asia. The Middle East, despite its small size and population, also receives a disproportionately large share. Africa and Latin America (aside from Brazil), on the other hand, have to get by with much less. This means that the countries which do the most business with Japan, either as raw materials suppliers (like Indonesia) or purchasers of capital goods (like Korea) do particularly well. It helps complete the circuit in the flow of resources from Japan to the developing countries and back.

Aside from what can properly be regarded as aid, Japan adds many other items to its "total" economic cooperation. One of these elements is export credits and other loans. They are considerably less disinterested since Japan is repaid, this time at the going bank rates or slightly lower. In addition, most of these loans and credits are used specifically to purchase Japanese goods, frequently including plant and equipment, which might never have been sold if such financing were not provided. Even private loans to the same end are included under economic cooperation.

Finally, direct overseas investment itself is added. Although this does involve a transfer of capital and technology from one country to another, it is quite difficult to imagine the Japanese doing this out of anything but self-interest. These are purely commercial transactions in which the companies involved not only expect to get back their initial outlay but also earn a profit which is at least equal to what could have been made domestically. They may be wrong. But they were hardly acting out of higher motives. The same applies to imports from developing countries, another element Japan is trying to slip into the very elastic concept of cooperation.

Admittedly, there is one peculiarity of Japanese investment that makes it somewhat more akin to aid if seen in a

certain light. More than other investors, the Japanese tend to build their ventures on debt, taking out loans from commercial and state banks. While it is only natural for them to raise their share of the capital, they often go much further. They extend or arrange loans to their overseas venture as well, even when it is not wholly owned. And, on occasion, they obtain loans for their foreign partners. In so doing, they must act as guarantor and accept the responsibility for massive amounts of loans that are not even contracted directly by them. Of course, this is done to keep the venture going. But it is a very big risk.

While most of this is business as usual, it is absurd to go as far as some critics and claim that these efforts cost Japan nothing and only brought it gains. It is pointed out that reparations started the flow of trade and aid has often resulted in much more sales and investment than before. They may well be a counterpart, and also an entry point, but they are not free of cost as far as Japan is concerned. Whether it provided goods or the money to purchase goods, there was a real transfer of assets that would not have occurred otherwise. And it was most definitely a one-way flow, from Japan to the other countries. The return of some of that money might just as well have taken place anyway as long as Japan provided the goods that were needed.

Also, although trade and investment are clearly self-interested forms of cooperation, this does not make them any less effective. Indeed, taking a good look at events in the developing countries over the past few decades, one would be tempted to give them greater credit for any growth than the more generous and altruistic forms that can be regarded as aid.

The very fact that Japan has regularly offered cheaper and better manufactured products than its competitors (which is the reason they are purchased) has given the

developing countries a broader choice of suppliers, count-less opportunities to save on specific purchases, and created a competitive market that kept prices lower in general. Japan's tremendous eagerness to purchase raw materials, which arises from its own peculiar needs, has been no less beneficial to producer countries which also have a broader range of purchasers, more demand than otherwise, and a more receptive market to sell on.

As for investment, it has repeatedly proven more useful than grants and gifts as far as economic development is concerned. The grants and gifts are ordinarily directed toward the sectors of social overhead or economic infra-structure. They help to build schools and hospitals, roads and harbors, but not shops and factories. It is the overseas investments that are channelled into the more productive sectors whose growth is essential to propel the economy. That is why countries which have received more supposed "aid" and less self-interested investments have usually fallen behind and sometimes actually been crushed under their overly burdensome infrastructures and social welfare.

It may be claimed that investment is not the only possible source of such commercial and industrial facilities, they can also be purchased or donated. Actually, there are countries, especially in the East bloc, that will gift a textile plant or a cement works and Japan itself sells turnkey factories. But then they have no vested interest in whether the project functions well or not once it is formally handed over or paid for. On the other hand, when commercial companies continue to depend on efficient operations to draw their profits or dividends, they see to it that the workers are properly trained, that the management is reasonably efficient, that the right technologies are used. This extra, which only comes with direct investment, can spell the difference between success and failure.

NOTES

1. Ministry of Finance, *Japan's Direct Overseas Investment*, 1983.
2. Kiyoshi Kojima, *Japanese Direct Foreign Investment*, pp. 84–5.
3. MITI, *White Paper on International Trade*, 1981, p. 128.
4. See Kunio Yoshihara, *Sogo Shosha*, and Alexander Young, *The Sogo Shosha*.
5. *Japan Economic Journal*, April 6, 1982.
6. For an analysis of how companies deal with overseas operations, and especially the role of the "international division," see M.Y. Yoshino, "Emerging Japanese Multinational Enterprises," in Ezra Vogel, *Modern Japanese Organization and Decision-Making*.
7. See Alan Rix, *Japan's Economic Aid*.
8. MITI, *Economic Cooperation of Japan*, 1980, p. 45.
9. See Jon Woronoff, *Inside Japan, Inc.*, pp. 194–211.

3
The Colonized

Fishing For Investment

No matter how proud they are of their nation and how intent on preserving its independence and sovereignty, there are not many places in the real world where people do not eventually start looking for additional investment. The idea that the developing countries, or developed ones, can get along on their own and that foreign investors are bribing—or even harassing—them to accept all sorts of schemes is sadly misconceived.

First of all, in the present world order in which even very small states have sufficient power to plot their own course, only the weakest have to accept anything from outside whether they want to or not. Secondly, an investor would be extremely foolhardy to impose his will on such a country... if he could. After all, he is the one bringing the capital, knowhow and other assets well before any benefits flow back. Why should he take such a risk? Finally, there is a gross imbalance between the large number of countries which seek investment and the relatively few in a position to sponsor worthwhile projects. The latter can very well afford to pick and choose.

This is quite enough to explain why, even amidst recrimination about the risks involved, just about every developing or developed country has more than flirted with the idea. The vast majority actually possess some such projects already and many are scrounging for more. Those who have uttered words in praise of foreign investment, and gone so far as to call them essential elements of international cooperation, not only represent the moderate or capitalist nations. They also come from some of the most fiercely non-aligned or economically autarchic. Even Sukarno, Nasser and Nkrumah had a good word to say for investment in their day. But a more normal approach is reflected by these comments of Malaysia's ambassador to Japan, Lim Taik Choon.

"A prominent feature of the Third Malaysian Plan is that increasing private sector investment constitutes an integral part of the program for the overall growth of the economy... On its part the Government will continue to maintain its efforts and undertake measures conducive to ensuring that Malaysia is a truly worthy centre for private sector investment, both domestic and foreign. As foreign investment is envisioned to play an increasingly greater role in the Malaysian economic development, concerted efforts have been made, including high level investment missions to overseas countries, to attract greater foreign investment to Malaysia. Japan, which is the largest source of foreign investment in the manufacturing industry in Malaysia, has been the venue for special investment promotion missions... Given the facilities for investment in the industrial and manufacturing sector, the policy of the Government of an increasing role of private investment in our development plan, the availability of natural resources and easily trained labor, investment in Malaysia will accrue benefits to the foreign investor as it has to Malaysia."[1]

While such sentiments are not surprising in a capitalist country like Malaysia, even the People's Republic of China eventually agreed that foreign investment could be useful. Prime Minister Zhao Ziyang invited the Japanese to invest in energy and natural resource exploration as well as manufacturing projects. And an official closer to actual practice, Wu Zhichao, deputy general manager of China International Trust and Investment Corp., conceded that there would have to be something in it for the investors as well. "We will see to it that you will make reasonable profits out of your operation. We all know that without attractions and the prospect of making some money, nobody will come to China and risk his hard-earned money in a hopeless venture."[2]

It is not hard to find explanations for this desire to come by foreign investment. They abound. In the host country, just as in an investing nation like Japan, they include a mixture of good and bad reasons. The only thing the two have in common is that they reinforce one another and make the goal of attracting investment strong enough to prevail in ordinary circumstances.

One frequent reason a country seeks investment is to develop its natural resources. It happens quite rarely that they are located in sites that are easy to mine and conveniently situated along whatever means of transport exist. More often than not, getting at this potential wealth can involve tremendous costs, some of which even relatively rich and advanced countries cannot afford. The developer may require huge amounts of capital to open the source, to build an infrastructure, and to get the products to the markets. In addition, some foreign companies have superior technologies that make certain of these operations cheaper or more effective.

Another good reason is to build up industry, either to replace imports or diversify the economy. Once again, this applies mainly to developing countries. But there are cases where one advanced country would be eager to gain assistance from another. Capital is a primary need, especially for major projects. Technology is another. And, for developing countries, the newness of industrialization and the many things that can, or must, be done are beyond their ability to tackle alone. They could industrialize slowly but surely, like older countries have done. But that would take decades when the process can be telescoped into much shorter periods with the right help.

A third major reason is to employ labor. Most developing countries, for various reasons, have more people than they can employ effectively and sometimes at all. One of their major problems is unemployment, especially in the mushrooming cities. But unemployment can occur anywhere and is now a regular phenomenon in most advanced nations. In addition to more gainful work, there is a hope that the people hired by foreign-invested companies will also acquire skills or simply a more modern approach.

These are perfectly good reasons to master whatever fears or misgivings one may have and allow foreign investors to help in one way or another.

The most prominent means is by providing capital. Perhaps because it appears so visibly in the word capitalism or because just about everyone is interested in money, this is usually the first thing sought. Nowadays, there is a certain amount of capital being supplied for free or on rather good terms by international organizations or through bilateral arrangements. But most of this money flows into projects that are only indirectly beneficial to a country's development, such as infrastructure, health, or education. Even if these sums were doubled, and tripled, they would still not move sufficiently into agriculture, mining and industry. Thus, today and doubtlessly in the future as well, foreign investors will be welcome if they can add their contributions. This is especially true since the capital comes in the form of foreign exchange which most countries tend to need.

However, capital invested by foreign companies comes

on terms that are rarely as generous as those of the international organizations and bilateral agencies. . . or so it seems. No company will invest on any other assumption than that the money will be returned to it one day somewhat enhanced. This is not even a question of getting the equivalent to a good interest rate since then it would be just as profitable, and far easier, to put the money in the bank. What is desired is eventually a total repatriation of the initial capital and profits taken directly or as dividends to make what is generally regarded as a fair return. Naturally, one can always quibble about what is "fair," and doubtlessly the foreign investors will opt for a higher rate than the host country. But, if he does not *expect* to earn something like this, no investor will go ahead.

This makes it look better to deal with the less self-seeking suppliers of funds. Alas, although they may get their capital on better terms, the beneficiaries are unlikely to get what they really want: effective production units. On the whole, only private or state-owned companies possess the knowhow and technology to make fruitful investments. Such investments should pay off for the host country as well in various ways. They may provide remuneration for labor, they may produce goods that otherwise have to be imported, they may provide these same goods at cheaper prices, and eventually they may be exported. Basically, these investments can promote development.

Thus, the best reasons for turning to foreign investment have nothing to do with capital. They are connected with an investor's accumulated knowledge and proven capabilities which can make the investment an effective and profitable one for all. Even the most advanced countries are eager to obtain the latest technologies and more backward countries would already be doing well with intermediate ones. This is not a question of money alone because even if a country or company has money it may not have access to the technologies. Sometimes it can buy them; frequently it cannot. And, even if the technologies are up for sale, there are any number of accompanying benefits that one cannot place a price on but are equally precious.

A technology does not exist in a vacuum, it is not a simple formula that can be memorized or fed into a computer, it is a new way of doing things with many ramifications. The technology has to be integrated in the existing productive machinery and the company selling it usually has a better idea of how this is done. It often also implies a somewhat different way of doing the same old things, techniques that engineers and simple laborers would have to learn or the technology is wasted. It can even include the whole approach to running a given business, new managerial techniques that only the owner has. A sophisticated company in the same sector could probably license or buy this outright and succeed. But developing countries are far better off if rather than a mere technology they ask their partner to come with the plant, the supervisors, and the technology, to teach novices how it is all done.

There is something else an investor may have that is even more intangible without being less valuable, namely market contacts. A country can mine its own coal or pump its own oil but, as even the OPEC nations discovered, it can be extremely useful to cooperate with companies that have built up a broad and well-organized marketing network. This sort of thing can be replicated, but only at a considerable cost. And it may not be worthwhile paying that price if it takes too long or the old network will still be better than the new. Developing countries creating totally new industries which they dream will one day also export would be wise to keep the investor around for that day.

Foreign investments are very useful and valid forms of action for such reasons. However, in the present-day mystique of economic development, there is a benefit which trumps them all because it acts as a multiplier. This is variously referred to as a ripple, or spillover, or demonstration effect. Although it can be expressed in very abstract and technical terms, the very words conjure up impressions of throwing a pebble in a big pond and watching the ripples move out smoothly in every direction. Or water is let into an irrigated field on the top of a hill and then effortlessly flows down filling field after field. Likewise, it is sometimes assumed that if a pilot farm is opened in the middle of a farming community all the neighbors will learn or if a modern factory is built in the city other factories will soon be sprouting up.

This kind of image fills a deep-felt need and admits some harsh realities. It seems obvious that the learning process is one of the most significant, if least measurable, aspects of foreign investment. No matter what he may think, the investor is expected to be a teacher of sorts. He should take the laborers, often just peasants or idle school-leavers the week before, and inculcate in them the attitudes of an industrial work force. He should improve the skills of employees at every level and show the local mangers how to do their job and ultimately how to run the factory. His factory should be a model not only in the sense of being the most modern and technologically proficient but in arousing the curiosity of others and awakening them to new possibilities.

No matter how good a case can be made for investment in general, things get much more complicated and delicate when decisions are made as to the specifics. What sort of

investments are needed? Should they be in agriculture, mining or industry? If in industry, in which line? Some governments modestly pinpoint a few sectors where strong efforts should be made and, by narrowing the field, can more readily screen the potential projects in each sector. Other countries seem to get carried away, assuming that since investment is a good thing, the more of it the better! In extreme cases, they try to introduce too many projects and disperse their efforts so widely and spread their resources so thin that little is actually accomplished.

Some other tendencies can be even more pernicious. One is a desire to "keep up with the Joneses," the Joneses being nearby rivals or even Japan itself. This leads to a demand for highly sophisticated projects that the country is not really prepared for, either because it lacks the skilled labor or supporting industries. It may also include an urge for nothing but the latest, nothing but the best, and sometimes also nothing but the flashiest. This is sought again whether the country is in a position to handle such projects or not. A "me, too" reflex leads to demands for their own steel mill, oil refinery, or automobile plant when it would be just as good (and cheaper) to import the finished products. And some leaders are badly disfigured by a taste for the gigantic, the monumental, mammoth projects that will allow them to leave their mark in history.

All of these various reasons for promoting investment involve the country's economic development as a whole and result in decisions taken at the macroeconomic level. The outcome will be a more or less open attitude toward investment in general and specific sorts of investment in particular. But most of the crucial decisions will be taken at a somewhat lower level, namely among the private businessmen of liberal economies or specialized bureaucrats of centrally-planned or strongly state-dominated ones.

Basically, investments involve at least two sets of partners, local and outside, even if the foreigner sets up a wholly owned venture. After all, mining companies or trading houses have to buy the land, prospection or exploitation rights from the owners. Manufacturers, even doing their own work, will have to fit in with the domestic suppliers, the available labor force, and existing distributors. The degree of cooperation will naturally be much greater where the investment regulations provide that foreign entrants must accept partners in joint ventures.

The local partners will have a sharper focus than the local governments or planners, since they also wish to gain a profit (or the equivalent thereof in socialist countries) and will be more or less eager to cede their rights or assets. It is less likely to be the government than the owner of mines or other natural resources that will deal with the investors and the terms will depend on relative needs. It is

Queen Elizabeth II Visits NEC Semiconductors (UK)

Credit: NEC

usually the huge cost of exploiting such potential wealth more than anything else that pushes them toward outside cooperation, although access to technologies and market outlets play a secondary role.

The interests of local partners in manufacturing ventures are even more specific. In this case, both capital and technology are usually uppermost. Capital, because it is expensive to build and equip a factory. But technology even more so because this creates a competitive edge that is vital for gaining market share. In developing countries especially, since outside companies are so far advanced, the chance to bring in such a partner makes it possible for a dynamic entrepreneur to leapfrog ahead of his own local competitors.

This means that investment policy is worked out at two different levels. Although the macroeconomic one usually enjoys the limelight and has been studied more extensively, there is reason to believe that, no matter how essential, it is not really the most decisive. It only provides the broad framework and some more specific guidelines. The actual projects result from strong lobbying by vested interests within the country. The goals of these entities, companies, state corporations, banks and others, may be quite different from one case to the next even if they all fall within the general purview of acceptable investment practice. And, depending on how they evolve, the host country will be more or less attractive to foreign investors and derive greater or lesser benefits from the exercise.

Welcome Investors!

Despite the image invoked by such cries as "the Japanese are coming," it is not as if Japanese companies were always slyly intriguing or crudely exerting pressure to get permission for investments. After all, everything they want

could be obtained through the normal mechanisms of trade. Raw materials can be bought, labor-intensive products replaced by imports, and manufactured goods sold on the international market. This is not always the best or most effective way. But it certainly is easier and involves far less risk.

Admittedly, in the case of resource-oriented investment, it was usually the foreign investor who came knocking at the door and asked for the right to procure raw materials. But the host country was hardly aggrieved by that. Many countries, including the richest, found that developing sources of raw materials was very costly. Moreover, as new sources had to replace old ones, they were frequently more remote or lower grade and required ever more infrastructural and other incidental works to be exploited. When it came to prospection, the host was even more dependent on the few companies which possessed the most advanced techniques and would accept the tremendous risks of seeking with no guarantee of finding.

The situation is more balanced for labor-oriented investment. Certainly, countries whose manpower has become expensive are eager to use cheaper labor. But there are usually some drawbacks to cheaper labor, such as a lack of education or experience, and sometimes also poor work discipline. Moreover, if the labor is cheap this almost always reveals that there is a fair amount of open or disguised unemployment in the country. This makes the host particularly eager to find jobs for these idle hands, both to bring in additional revenue to the state and wages to the workers, and to avoid possible hardship and disturbances.

For market-oriented investment, most manufacturers are willing to make minor investments to promote or distribute their goods. When it comes to actual local production, on the other hand, they are quite hesitant.

Traditionally, the Japanese system has consisted largely of importing raw materials, turning them into finished products, and then exporting them. The system is relatively simple and all the operations can be concentrated in Japan. Japanese managers can run things their own way and deal with a labor force they know and trust. Production abroad involves all sorts of difficulties that would faze any businessman and especially Japanese who are not accustomed to it.

This relative disinterest contrasts sharply with the attitude of many developing countries which have given very high priority to industrialization and are increasingly bent on getting foreign investors to establish operations in their territory. This is often necessary because they lack the capital themselves. A more significant aspect is the knowhow, which they neither possess nor can really buy. The wish for the latest technologies is even great enough for advanced countries to seek investors. They all obviously benefit from the additional local production and increased employment as well.

So, it often happens that the advances are made by the host country or a local company and not the potential investor. By now, hardly a week passes that some high-powered mission does not arrive in Japan from just about anywhere in the world, not only at the national level but representatives of component states and even cities, all clamoring for investment. Meanwhile, a far larger number of private businessmen come more discreetly to woo potential Japanese partners.

These uninvited visitors will proudly vaunt the advantages of cooperating with them and, in passing, stress how they may be better partners than a hundred other countries and a thousand other companies that could also receive investment. This is hardly a low-keyed approach and investment promotion campaigns are launched with trem-

endous fanfare and nearly incredible promises of mutual benefit. But it takes more than that to convince the Japanese. They want to know exactly what the conditions and benefits are.

One way of showing that they are in earnest, a method adopted by an increasing number of host countries, is to draw up an investment code and any necessary enabling legislation. To get the point across that the government is indeed forthcoming, some of the recent statutes were entitled for the "encouragement" or "inducement" of investment. Basically, these codes do two things. First, they announce what kinds of investment the host country wants or will accept. Then, they proclaim what special advantages are offered.

Thus, there is usually a broad indication, and sometimes a very specific listing, of the priority sectors where investment is sought. Countries with substantial natural resources they wish to have tapped will give priority to that. For industry, it will vary considerably from country to country, depending on the state of the economy. More backward countries are quite pleased to receive rather primitive industries that are highly labor-intensive. More advanced developing countries may wish to reserve that to nationals and prefer sectors offering more value added or that are more capital-intensive. Those yet further advanced will stress sectors that upgrade the skills of local labor and introduce more sophisticated technologies.

The specific industrial sectors promoted will therefore differ. In early stages, this will include textiles and garments, footwear, toys, and simple handicrafts. Later on, there will be a move to such glamor sectors as optics and electronics, although this may be nothing more than rudimentary cameras or monochrome television. But it can rise to color television, integrated circuits, and more complex articles. Also desired are electrical and precision

machinery, automobile parts, farm machinery and perhaps fertilizer. Finally come items like chemicals and petrochemicals, metal refining, iron and steel production, automobiles and shipbuilding.

However, there may also be an indication of the categories that are not desired, and sometimes quite simply rejected. This, too, will vary from country to country. The basic idea is not to induce investments to do things that local initiative and capital can handle. This may extend to a preference for projects oriented toward exports while preserving the domestic market for local talent. And nowadays more countries will be adverse to polluting or energy-consuming industries. Finally, countries with a fair amount of exporting already will reject further projects in sectors where trade restrictions have arisen.

Among the sectors often ruled out are agriculture, although large-scale plantations and ranches may be permitted, and direct mining or crude processing of local raw materials. Foreigners are frequently kept out of real estate and housing, hotels and tourism, services and distribution. Sometimes "luxury" articles are avoided, not only for imports but local production, including items like cosmetics or jewellery. Gradually, as domestic industry grows, various categories of manufactured products may be excluded, starting with garments and footwear. Oddly enough, such restrictions occur more frequently in developing than advanced countries.

Some host governments are glad to receive any size investment, counting it to the good. Others feel that below a certain level the investment is liable to be too small and primitive to make much of a contribution or of a scale likely to compete with domestic entrepreneurs. Korea, for example, used to have a minimum limit of $500,000, which was later reduced to $100,000, and Taiwan a limit of $150,000. Sometimes the capital has to be entirely in cash.

Otherwise, if appropriate, some of it can be provided in machinery, raw materials or knowhow.

Further on, the code is bound to define the degree of participation allotted to the foreign investor. Some countries permit 100% ownership for just about any investment. Others restrict the share, depending partly on how badly the investment is needed. Thus, 100% might be allowed in cases where the project involves very large capital, advanced technologies, or is entirely export-oriented. Otherwise, many hosts prefer something around a fifty-fifty split. Whether they let the outsider have 51%, 50% or 49% is far from a minor point and the actual decision is a very good barometer of the investment climate. Once again, this is also a function of what can be obtained. If investors will not come with only 50%, the host country may have to raise the level, as Korea did recently when it allowed wholly owned ventures in most fields.

Having specified what investments will be accepted, the code moves on to what are usually called the "incentives." Few of them are outright gifts as opposed to some improvement of the standard conditions. Thus, the tax incentives are merely reductions or rebates on what one would normally have to pay. The actual situation will depend very much on what the existing tax rate is. If it is relatively high, then even a handsome reduction may not mean very much. Still, in general, countries which seek investors either have a comparatively low tax base or see to it that the incentives are enough to make a difference.

Those offered by Korea and Taiwan are not necessarily typical, but they are the basic benchmark that must be matched by any countries seeking Japanese investment. For taxes, among other things, they offer a mixture of exemption or reduction of acquisition and property taxes, accelerated depreciation of fixed assets, special treatment for R & D expenses, and inclusion of special reserves. Most important, there is a five year tax holiday for corporate tax and any payments thereafter may be at a reduced rate for a while. Income taxes of expatriate staff also benefit from some relief.

As for customs, the duty on imported machinery and equipment is exempted, import duties and commodity taxes on raw materials or intermediate goods later exported are reimbursed, and there are reductions on some other customs duties that must be paid. More important is the situation for repatriation of income on production or interest, and ultimately of the initial capital, which is allowed in full but must be staggered over time. There are also a number of other incentives which are almost gifts, but play a secondary role, such as somewhat cheaper financing through government banks or loans and the provision of certain infrastructure.[3]

These incentives, rather than being a function of what the host country feels it can afford, are much more a result of the degree of competition with other countries. Thus, newcomers may have to offer more. Sri Lanka, for example, went much further in granting wholly-owned ventures, free transfer of assets, easy remittance of dividends and repatration of capital, substantial customs exemptions, and especially generous tax benefits (100% tax exemption for up to ten years and a concessionary tax rate for a maximum of another fifteen years).[4]

Even the People's Republic of China had to offer reasonably advantageous conditions to attract capitalist investors. Still, it might be remembered that countries with a liberal economy, such as Hong Kong, and to a lesser extent Singapore or some Western countries, can sometimes offer excellent terms merely by applying their existing laws which encourage investment in general.

Aside from the specific incentives, there usually are a number of other advantages of a general nature that will draw investment. A crucial one is efficient approval machinery so that projects do not get bogged down in red tape. Many countries now provide "one-stop" processing through a special agency, usually under the planning board or economics ministry, and some also have active investment promotion bodies that go out and look for investors. To this is added a generally favorable investment climate promoted and guaranteed by what is reputed to be a stable and enlightened government, a hardworking and trainable labor force, relatively low levels of wages and fringe benefits, location in or near major markets, decent living conditions and even the promise of a "good life" in a comfortable and benevolent paradise for investors.

All of this is well and good, and certainly very much appreciated by the investors. The only problem is that the investment code emanates from the host government and can be changed; what has been given can be taken away. Meanwhile, the investment climate itself may decay. For that reason, foreign investors have been urging their own governments to make this arrangement a bit more bilateral or at least provide some guarantees for them. They do not usually find the provisions in the investment code or general legislation protecting them against expropriation and the like to be sufficiently reassuring.

The Japanese government, after witnessing how the mood could change in once friendly host countries, has taken this matter up quite energetically of late. It is pressing its closest partners for the conclusion of investment guarantee pacts. This would provide, among other things, most favored treatment for investors of the respective countries, preferably as good as that accorded to national investors, freedom of transfer of earnings, protection of assets and, in the case of nationalization, swift and effective compensation based on the market price of the assets. So far, only Egypt and Sri Lanka have signed such an agreement, although strenuous efforts are being made with the six ASEAN countries. This is a rather poor showing when one considers that West Germany has concluded nearly fifty agreements and the United States well over a hundred. Japan evidently does not have as much clout as is generally assumed.

Home Away From Home

Unfortunately, no matter how tempting the various incentives, some of the most eager host countries simply could not attract much industrial investment because their economy was so backward. It was exasperatingly difficult to find a proper factory equipped with the essential utilities, obtain even rather basic supplies and components, or to have access to suitable manpower. Investors often came for a look and quickly left disappointed.

To make up for these gaps, some developing countries began establishing industrial estates, not solely in the interest of foreign investors but equally to promote their own development. But they were usually open to investors from abroad and offered definite advantages. There, on a reasonably well located plot of land, whose price was often moderate, it was possible to benefit from various common services. They included proper roads and transport, access to water, electricity and sewerage, adequate telecommunications, and so on. No less important, in the same industrial estate or nearby it would probably be possible to find essential supporting industries and suppliers.

Taiwan was among the first to construct such estates, starting as early as 1963, and eventually creating over a hundred, both general and specialized. The latest was a special science-based industrial park. Korea followed suit and now has about 39,000 acres of various types of estates dispersed around the country. Hong Kong also has excellent facilities and special estates throughout the Colony. Most other developing countries are providing similar areas. But these estates can also be found in the more advanced countries of Europe and America, while some American states and cities are actively directing foreign investors to their own facilities.

This was certainly to the good. But it was partially eclipsed by another innovation, namely the special zones established for offshore production and export. They exist under various names, free trade, free export, or export processing zones. This sort of operation originated among American companies taking advantage of cheap labor in Mexico, but it rapidly spread to Asia, at first to receive American investors. But the spectacular growth over recent years is attributable primarily to Asian host countries in their bid to attract Japanese investors. Taiwan launched its Export Processing Zones in 1966, followed by Korea's Free Export Zones in 1970. And they served pretty much as an example for what was to come.

These zones are rather unique in various ways. First of all, they promise even greater convenience for the foreign investors and are placed under a special management designed to meet their needs. They offer the same facilities as good industrial estates and more, such as packing, warehousing and shipping services. Whole factories, or parts thereof, are provided at very favorable conditions, for sale or for rent. In addition to local transport, they often lie alongside a harbor and perhaps also close to an international airport. In the zone itself are all the facilities needed to do business, such as the customs, immigration and tax offices, banks, post offices, telecommunications services, and the power company. Finally, there is an employment center.

Many of these zones are located in relative backwaters since a subsidiary goal is to provide employment for poorer segments of the population. Thus, the local cost of labor is likely to be lower even than in other parts of the country. The standard incentives may be improved upon, such as longer tax holidays and lower rates, more duty-free treatment (since most products are exported), greater ease in bringing in expatriate personnel, and better chances of getting 100% ownership. Finally, the zone's administration facilitates the investment approval procedures and helps with various arrangements, including recruitment of personnel and obtaining loans.

This means that foreign investors can come with minimal difficulty, quickly move into a well-designed and suitably equipped factory, put up their own specific machinery, recruit and train any necessary personnel and go into operation. In return, rather little is asked of them. Indeed, the basic condition is simply that they export all of their output unless otherwise authorized. This is hardly a problem for most of those which do come since they are mainly interested in an offshore production site. This may be to supply the home factory with cheaper components or to get around certain trade barriers which prevent exports from their own country.

Given the nature of the zones, namely bonded production for export and primarily exploitation of the advantages of cheap labor, the enterprises established there are limited to a relatively narrow range of sectors. By far the most prevalent branch, perhaps half of the operations, is electronics, although not usually very complex articles. Then come garments and knitted or woven goods. This is followed by plastic products (including toys), metal products (perhaps houseware or tools), and leather or rubber (often footwear). Most of these are known to be "footloose" industries which can move readily from one place to another. This is betrayed by the rudimentary, almost makeshift nature of some factories' installations. But other

companies do sink roots and progress to more sophisticated technologies and better machinery.

Given the location of the Asian zones, and the pro-
clivities of Japanese businessmen, it is not surprising to find
that the Japanese are the most prominent investors. They
represent over 40% of Taiwan's zones and about 80% of the
investment in Korea's. No zone anywhere in Asia would
even stand a chance of getting started if they did not come.
Most of the Japanese investors set up wholly-owned
operations, especially if the parent firm is a manufacturer.
But a certain number, including trading companies, enter
joint ventures with local partners. Although the Japanese
predominate among the investors, the bulk of the products
are not exported to Japan but America and Europe.

What are the advantages for the host country? Most of
them are actually indirect since, having granted very
favorable conditions for taxes, customs and so on, it will
not begin collecting anything from the investors for years.
However, then the intake may be considerable and, whatever it is, it is more than would have been collected if the
investors had never come. Much more important is the fact
that these investors, most of them in labor-intensive sectors, are employing large numbers of local personnel. They
will only be paying the going wage rate. But, in many
developing countries it is already a boon that more of the
unemployed or underemployed have a regular job.

In addition, it is faintly hoped that the export processing
zone will become a "development pole" of sorts. After all,
the local personnel are bound to learn some skills, quite
simply to do their work. Some may eventually become
technicians or managers in the firms. And some of the
foreign investors do have local partners. Meanwhile, since
the zone is not reserved exclusively for foreign investment,
other local entrepreneurs can learn by watching their
neighbors and competitors. There should also be some

spillover to the local community, first by providing wages, and also because the projects may eventually procure supplies from nearby firms or will at least purchase things like food, clothing, and other provisions locally.

This explanation does not always go down too well with academics, trade unionists or opposition politicians, who claim that the government is offering too much and getting too little in return. After all, the cost of building such a zone is appreciable and the rents, fees, etc. are relatively low. Wages are certainly not at a high level and the skills learned are few. Tax revenue will be long in coming. Instead of a pole radiating development, the zone is regarded as an enclave, cut off from contact with the rest of the country, and only concerned with its own interests. That is why the International Union of Food and Allied Workers Associations recently adopted a resolution noting that "the economic, social and political costs of free trade zones may be far in excess of the purported or actual benefits they may bring to the host countries."[5]

However, if the creation of zones offered so little, it would be hard to explain why they have caught on so well and continued spreading rapidly ever since they were introduced. Korea now has two (Masan and Iri). Taiwan eventually established three (Kaohsiung, Taichung, and Nantze) and is using the same approach for the science park in Hsinchu. In the Philippines, several already exist and a dozen more are planned, some of them reserved exclusively for Japanese companies. Zones exist in Singapore, Malaysia, Indonesia and Thailand. And they are gradually extending further to India, Sri Lanka, and Pakistan. Even the People's Republic of China is setting up "special economic zones" in various parts of the country which bear a distinct resemblance. Indeed, it is estimated that as many as a hundred zones presently exist in several dozen developing countries, the majority of them in Asia.

The number of people employed in these zones is estimated to be as high as 600,000.

Supping With The Devil

So, one of the biggest flaws in the argument that Japan is a rapacious neocolonialist power scheming to ensnare developing countries or laying plots to penetrate advanced ones through investment is that in most cases the host country allows the investors to enter. Nay, it cordially invites them to come. The Japanese have rarely had to bribe their way into a country or even sneak in by purchasing established firms. They are usually ushered in by top political leaders and influential businessmen.

Nevertheless, even as they enter, some warn that the whole thing is a mistake, that one may not enjoy their company, and there could be unfortunate consequences. Even while the news of the latest investment is loudly proclaimed by the government and heralded in the newspapers, people in the opposition make dour predictions and radicals distribute anti-Japanese tracts. Clearly, there are mixed feelings and investment can be a source of danger as well as promise.

There is an old saying that, "if you sup with the devil, you should use a long spoon." But most countries take no special precautions and instead fall all over themselves to invite such strange visitors to dinner. Evidently, many of them did not quite know what they were in for. Perhaps, they didn't even care. Although this involved serious commercial transactions, large amounts of money, and long-term commitments, the study given many projects was not really adequate. Nor was enough attention paid to what the investors planned to do, how, or why. The principal task seemed to be to round up as much investment as possible and let things sort themselves out later.

For example, some countries relaxed the conditions for investment whenever there was a shortage of ready cash. It is generally known that investors come with much of their own funds and easy access to bank loans. For a country with a shortage of capital, this is an ideal solution. One tends to forget that, to get the investors to come, it is obviously necessary to guarantee repatriation of capital and earnings. And thus, in some years' time, the desired inflow could be replaced by a nasty outflow.

A fair number of countries did not seem to have any special plan or even general concept of how development should take place. They left much of this to the investors (and local promoters) who would come up with brilliant ideas and then put forward attractive projects. Many of these projects were feasible. But, even then, there was no guarantee that all of them put together would move the country in the right direction. There were also some projects that were less good, proposed by high-class con men or put forward in good faith by decent investors who made an honest mistake.

Even successful ventures could create problems. For, the foreign investors might well be entering the same field as local investors and state corporations. In an early stage, the country might welcome all production. But, somewhere along the line, there was likely to be competition in which local companies got hurt. On the other hand, foreign investors might get into cozy relations with local politicians and bureaucrats and take advantage of their position.

Finally, the mere presence of foreigners could upset the tranquility of certain countries. The expatriate staff was almost by definition better paid, in positions of authority, and would attract attention by the way they dressed, how they behaved, and their ignorance of or disconcern for local customs. They might also hail from a different regime, capitalists in a staunchly socialist country or infidels in a highly religious society. This could make then an irritant, unpleasant if they introduced unwanted lifestyles, subversive if this rubbed off on the local populace.

There are ways of solving, or attempting to solve, many of these problems. But they have to be sought consciously and used advisedly. Some could well be included in the investment code while others required ongoing supervision by the authorities or a show of good sense in the community. If the host government took such action, investment was that much more likely to be beneficial. If not, it could be more harmful than necessary.

Basically, it is up to the host to determine the context in which investment shall take place. This can be broader or narrower, more liberal or more restrictive. The rules can go into considerable detail about what foreign investors can, and cannot do, and how they should relate to the local government, population and economy. If such rules are not laid down, or if they are poorly defined or unwise, then the host country has no one to blame but itself.

The investment code indicates primarily the sectors in which investment is sought. But, as we saw, there is no reason why it cannot also show just as clearly in which sectors it is rejected or only permitted under certain conditions. Such sectors are likely to be those that are particularly delicate, such as exploitation of natural resources, or those which should be reserved to local enterprise. This often includes agriculture, hotels and tourism, services and distribution. Even if such investment is allowed in principle, during the approval procedure it is always possible to reject specific projects or limit their number.

If there is reason to fear that foreign projects will dominate certain sectors, and that these sectors must be regulated so that local entrepreneurs can advance, that can be done in various ways. One is to limit the minimum size of investment, since it can be assumed that locals can more readily launch smaller ventures. Investments can also be excluded from specific sectors, as indicated above, or specific parts of the country. Even when physically present, foreign projects can be kept out of the domestic market in various ways. One is by simply providing that certain investors must export or can only sell domestically if duly authorized or part of a joint venture. The other is by encouraging foreign firms to locate in the export processing zones.

These zones have often been criticized as "enclaves" by those who object to investment as such. This is surprising, since they could just as well be praised as "enclaves," especially by such people. For, they make it possible to contain the foreign influence in a specific area and isolate it from the general commercial currents. This makes such investment less of a stimulus for the rest of the economy, but also keeps it from interfering with broader policies or competing with local companies. That is often why such zones were created. And it was this very advantage that made it possible for Communist China to encourage investment by foreign capitalists at all.

Another method of keeping control over foreign investment is to insist that some projects only be undertaken with a local partner. This can be a normal company with its own commercial interests or it can be, in many developing and especially socialist economies, a state corporation or semi-state body or bank. They will obviously know what is going on and this knowledge can be tapped by the government, if it does not already assume that the mere presence of a local partner will keep the project within bounds.

In the same direction, the government can encourage foreign investors to recruit more local staff as well as local managers who will thus have an idea of what is being done. Going a step further, it may provide that larger companies must take on local partners at some further stage or offer stock to the general public. From another direction this time, it is possible to keep any given company in line by seeing to it that there are other foreign and domestic investors that compete in the same sector.

But the most important aspect is the screening of projects. After all, it is the local authorities which must approve any investment before it can be made. They usually have ample time to study it from all angles, to determine whether it is viable to begin with, and then see whether it creates any special problems, some of which might be solved by granting the approval with conditions.

If, alas, things are not done properly from the outset, there is still one final resort. It remains possible for the government, as part of its sovereign rights, to admit that it made a mistake and revise the basic legislation or create an entirely new situation. The investment code can be made stricter not only for newcomers but also those projects which have already been established, tax and customs rates can be raised, and new regulations can be introduced on wages and working conditions. If specific projects were poorly chosen, or have turned out to be drastically harmful or odious, they can be expropriated. None of these measures is desirable if one wishes to encourage investment, but none of them is really excluded either.

This way at least the host country could equip itself with a long spoon. Whether it would keep the devil from spoiling the dinner remains to be seen. However, it must not be forgotten that the cook can also spoil the dinner or, if he is too finicky, there may be no dinner at all. So, the main purpose of such measures should not really be to control or tie down foreign investment so that it will not be a danger. It is more intelligent to channel and direct it so that it can make a positive contribution.

NOTES

1. *Japan Economic Journal*, September 18, 1979.
2. *Japan Times*, March 1, 1980.
3. See the investment promotion documentation of the Economic Planning Board, Republic of Korea, the Industrial and Investment Center, Republic of China, etc.
4. These are the conditions offered by the Greater Colombo Economic Commission.
5. *Far Eastern Economic Review*, May 18, 1979, p. 75.

4
Japan's Quarry

Urge For Raw Materials

There is no need to repeat endlessly a fact that every Japanese child is taught at a tender age and is regarded as self-evident by every adult bureaucrat or businessman: Japan is a terribly barren and resource-poor country. Only in the earliest days of industrialization could it meet some of its own needs, such as coal, iron and copper ore. But that period did not last long. Due to its extraordinary economic expansion, even if it had possessed much more it would eventually have depleted any domestic reserves and had to seek raw materials elsewhere.

Ever since the war, and increasingly with time, Japan has been heavily dependent on foreign sources for just about everything. It relies on them for nearly 100% of its supplies of oil, iron ore, bauxite, nickel and other minerals. Most of its coal and natural gas are also imported. It is equally beholden for agricultural raw materials like cotton and wool and scarcely less so for foodstuffs including wheat and soybean, meat and even fish. As its forests disappear, it has to look abroad for wood and paper pulp. Its degree of dependence, in most cases, is greater than that of other advanced nations.

This dependence, however, is not just the result of a quirk of nature. If Japan were a normal country, with 120 million increasingly affluent people, its needs would be substantial and growing. But its economic policy has made the demand far greater and more urgent. For, despite a lack of basic resources, it decided that the primary thrust of postwar growth should be the heavy and chemical industries. This meant numerous steel mills, metal smelters, chemical and petrochemical plants, and oil refineries. Other industries combined with this, including food processing, construction, machinery and automobiles, shipbuilding and power plants.

All of them were voracious consumers of a broad variety of raw materials, most of which had to be brought to Japan by sea. Its factories were often built along the seaside for such reasons, with massive storage areas to collect the coal, iron ore, bauxite, grain and so on until they could be processed. Later on, the finished products would be gathered for export. So, in addition to the busy factories, a huge fleet of ships also became a mammoth consumer of fuel. Thus, an endless flow of raw materials had to be channeled toward the Japanese islands.

While some sectors of the economy were designed for production, others were geared to locating, purchasing, and shipping raw materials back to Japan. Given the strict organization of industry and the incessant demands, it was necessary not only to keep the flow moving but, as much as possible, to see that there was no interruption. For, if the chain were broken anywhere, the economy could conceivably be crippled. The Achille's heel, the point that the Japanese had the least control over, was the influx of raw materials, so that is where the attention was concentrated.

For such reasons, a rather normal and matter-of-fact concern with obtaining raw materials, such as might exist in any country, was given a greater urgency and reached an almost emotional pitch because of these artificially straitened circumstances. This aroused a feeling of vulnerability and a desire to overcompensate, to be certain not only that resources were available, of a good quality and at a good price, but to be completely assured that they would be there in adequate quantity when they were desired.

It did not happen often that the flow was interrupted, but when it was this triggered what came to be known as a "shock." One of the first was the "soybean shock," which occurred when a shortfall in supplies led the United States to renege on its promised shipments. This made the Japanese very uneasy and kept them scouring markets and following production trends to see that it did not happen again. But they were alarmed even more by the "oil shock," which created a panic in the population and also among the supposedly more sensible and steadfast businessmen. Although the temporary hysteria about oil supplies being blocked subsided, it has given an almost pathological cast to the search for raw materials even today.

Another rather unexpected problem was the fact that the demand for raw materials has been growing so rapidly, quickly exceeding the supply in many cases. With this, the slow erosion in the prices of many commodities was reversed and they became increasingly more expensive. Japanese industry, or so it would seem, is geared for production on the basis of reasonably inexpensive inputs and, rather than adjust to higher costs by cutting back on production, the Japanese have done everything they could to keep raw material costs down by finding new supplies. This drive was made that much more urgent by the realization that some raw materials were actually running out, that they were finite. Thus, their prices were bound to rise. To get around this deeper threat, alternatives had to be sought.

Fortunately for Japan, in most cases—but far from all— its own needs tied up with the needs of certain countries which had relatively abundant raw materials and sought to develop and sell them. Many of them were developing

Degree Of Dependence On Overseas Resources

(%)

	Japan	U.S.A.	West Germany	United Kingdom	France
Energy	87.0	20.6	57.7	9.3	80.3
Coal	79.2	△ 9.6	△ 8.7	1.6	57.0
Oil	99.8	42.3	95.8	18.9	99.0
Natural gas	88.7	5.8	65.8	19.5	68.8
Iron ore	98.6	29.7	96.9	80.7	44.4
Copper	95.6	33.5	99.9	100.0	99.9
Lead	82.4	59.9	90.9	99.3	86.0
Zinc	68.7	70.6	71.9	100.0	87.2
Tin	97.7	100.0	100.0	81.8	100.0
Aluminum	100.0	63.6	100.0	100.0	△ 230.5
Nickel	100.0	93.0	100.0	100.0	100.0
Lumber	69.2	3.8	20.7	72.9	16.0
Wool	100.0	23.2	92.3	51.4	73.3
Cotton	100.0	△ 84.4	100.0	100.0	100.0
Soybean	95.4	△ 51.2	100.0	100.0	97.2
Maize	100.0	△ 42.9	79.1	100.0	△ 30.0
Wheat	93.0	△ 147.1	△ 0.8	25.4	△ 80.2

Source: *White Paper on International Trade*, 1981, MITI.

countries, largely because they had little domestic industry to consume them. But some more industrialized ones, which happened to be unusually lucky in having large reserves, were also willing to cooperate. Since the decisions, in liberal economies at least, were taken by private businessmen and not the government, the situation was actually much simpler since most owners of raw materials didn't particularly care who they sold their goods to, whether domestic or foreign buyers, as long as they get the going rate.

The essential point was quite simply to turn the potential wealth into hard cash. Coal and iron mines were in business to sell their output just like any other commercial establishment. Nations, just like companies and families, needed sources of revenue in order to function and prosper. So they were quite willing to permit, or encourage, such transactions as long as they, too, benefited. As it happens, raw material sales is one of the easiest forms of economic activity to supervise, and the government has less trouble knowing how much is sold, at what rates, and thus taxing it. During the early stage of development, resource-related fees, royalties and taxes can be a major source of income.

However, the benefits can reach much further than this. When a source of natural resources is tapped, it is often necessary to build all sorts of development and infrastructural works to enable smooth operation. This means not only opening a mine or well but sometimes providing a pipeline or railway to evacuate the products. Roads and harbors have to be constructed. Electricity is brought in. All of this is basically intended for the raw material project, but it can also be used by others. If the activity generated is sufficient, it can give a boost to the whole region.

These undertakings will also increase employment. Some natural resource projects require vast numbers of relatively unskilled workers during the construction phase, to lay the pipelines, open the mines, build plants and houses, etc. For underground mines, the operation may continue to demand many miners and other workers. Even for more mechanized open cast mining, there are jobs as truck drivers to transport the ore. Thus, throughout the life of the project there will be work and, as time goes by, some of the more sophisticated jobs requiring more training may eventually go to locals.

Finally, it is hoped that even a project in the primary sector will be a springboard to other things. It is assumed that there will be some transfer of technology, allowing the country to progress more on its own in future projects of the same sort. It is conceivable that the raw materials extracted locally can also be used by domestic companies and help promote national industries. In other cases, rather than exporting crude raw materials, they may be processed locally and this would create new branches that could also have spillover effects.

Normally, foreign investors, and the Japanese are no different here from any others, would be uninterested in the possible spinoffs for the host country. All they want is to obtain the raw materials. However, if they want this badly enough, which is often the case, they may be willing to go much further than they would for any other sort of project. Whereas they would hesitate to advance loans for the country's agricultural or industrial development, and are otherwise unconcerned by its lack of basic infrastructure, they would gladly put up substantial sums of money to get at raw materials that are being produced and even some that are merely presumed to exist.

This means that it may be possible to launch projects that would not be conceivable otherwise. Even if the host country, or a local company, does not have adequate funds to carry out extensive prospection, to open new mines or expand old ones, to risk the tremendous sums necessary to bore test wells for gas and oil, it can usually find partners who will help. And these partners will be the very same ones who eventually buy the raw materials that are extracted.

While Japanese interests are not basically different from those of other investors, their needs are certainly more pressing for the reasons mentioned. Their home country is entirely bereft of local resources and more dependent on the outside world. Their industry is more voracious and consuming at a faster rate. And, because they are latecomers, having lost their earlier holdings during the war, the Japanese are even more inclined to enter new projects than the Americans, British or French. Finally, they have the money. If this does not create an ideal partner, certainly it makes for a very eager one.

Let's Dig Here

Given a definite receptivity in the countries possessing
natural resources and the frantic efforts of its entrepreneurs
to obtain a steady and usually growing supply, it is not
surprising to find that Japan quickly became one of the
world's biggest consumers of most raw materials. In fact,
there was hardly anything for which it was not among the
top five and, for a fair number, it ended up as number one.
It is by far the largest importer of coal, iron ore, copper and
wool and, by somewhat smaller margins, of lumber and
foodstuffs. It ranks high for many other items, including oil
and gas. While it is not quite as big an importer of some
articles as the United States, whose economy is twice as big,
it easily surpasses the levels in most European countries.

While these figures show its success as an importer, they
could never have been attained if Japan had merely
remained on the sidelines and been supplied by foreign
multinationals or bought what it needed on the spot
market. Direct overseas investment of one sort or another
was essential. Actually, mining was among the first sectors
to receive substantial investment and the amount has not
ceased growing, reaching a cumulative total of $10,291
million in 1982. Timber and pulp projects also got off to
an early start. And, more recently, investment in extraction
of raw materials is being eclipsed by massive operations
to process them. If we take only the sums related directly
to mining, agriculture, forestry, and fishing, they represent
about 22% of total investment to date. However, if we add
the projects involved in processing some, such as aluminum
smelters, pulp and paper making, and petrochemicals, the
figure is much closer to 30%.[1]

Over the years, Japan's needs have varied considerably

and investment has also varied as a function of those needs. The very first area to be tapped was timber, partly because wood was necessary to reconstruct a warworn country whose houses are to an exceptional extent still made of wood. Timber and paper are still consumed in large amounts by its consumers although an early export, plywood, has since faded. But this investment has not been entirely exploitative. In some cases, as for Brazil, it consisted of reforestation and harvesting of high-yielding eucalyptus trees, just like any other crop.

As its heavy industry developed, the needs shifted to just about every mineral ore in existence. Japan needed massive amounts of iron ore for its steel mills, bauxite, zinc and copper for its smelters, and so on. Other minerals like titanium have become important of late. Coking coal was also necessary for steelmaking. For the chemical industries, petroleum was crucial as a feedstock. Whereas the original investments were largely in mining, more and more projects have been launched to process some goods prior to shipment.

Even before the oil crisis, petroleum was important as a fuel and for industrial purposes. Since then, its value as a source of energy has been greatly enhanced and every effort was made to obtain it. However, investment here is still relatively small. In the early days, much of this trade was monopolized by the international majors; now a big chunk has fallen into the hands of the oil producers themselves. Meanwhile, alternate sources have become vital, including liquefied natural gas. There has also been more interest in uranium for nuclear reactors and steaming coal for power plants.

Throughout this period, although far less noticeable, there has been some concern about Japan's other vulnerability, an inability to produce enough food. While most foodstuffs have simply been imported, there were attempts

Major Countries' Share Of Total Resource Imports

(Unit: %)

	Japan	U.S.	West Germany	U.K.	France	Italy
Energy	13.7	18.9	7.4	3.6	6.8	6.0
Coal	26.9	1.5	4.1	1.1	11.3	5.5
Crude oil	14.6	18.3	5.9	4.2	6.9	6.6
Natural gas	9.3	17.5	19.5	2.3	10.4	9.5
Iron ore	40.5	14.0	16.2	5.4	4.4	4.6
Copper	23.9	11.4	15.5	8.8	6.6	7.7
Lead	5.0	18.4	10.8	20.6	3.2	10.3
Zinc	8.5	26.5	10.1	8.2	8.2	3.9
Tin	19.8	31.7	10.7	5.6	8.0	4.5
Aluminum	17.6	22.9	11.4	4.8	8.2	5.6
Nickel	9.5	28.6	12.6	14.9	7.1	4.0
Lumber	21.6	18.7	6.1	7.2	4.0	5.7
Wool	17.5	2.2	6.7	12.9	9.9	8.0
Cotton	16.3	0.0	4.9	2.3	4.6	5.2
Soybeans	18.4	0.0	15.6	5.3	3.4	5.5
Corns	15.6	0.1	4.4	4.9	1.3	5.6
Wheat	7.7	0.0	1.8	4.3	0.8	4.9

Source: *White Paper on International Trade*, 1980, MITI.

at agricultural investments to grow some of the food, including grains, coffee, and cattle. Using its expertise in fish farming, there have also been projects to cultivate shrimp or other species. Some of the resulting produce was then frozen, canned or processed before being exported back to Japan.

Over the years, the range of host countries has not stopped expanding, although there are clearly places which receive higher priority. Naturally, investment has flowed more readily toward countries with which Japan has good or traditional relations. But it does not hesitate to invest in others where the risk is a bit greater or conditions somewhat more complex if it feels it can get what it wants.

Actually, the only real common denominator would seem to be whether the host has the desired products and is willing to part with them on reasonable terms.

The biggest share of this investment has been made in Asia, but it is largely concentrated in just a few countries and sectors. Many of the projects are located in Indonesia, and they involve mainly oil or LNG. Others are located in Brunei and Sabah, Malaysia, once again for LNG. Between them, Indonesia and Brunei provide about 80% of Japan's total LNG requirements. One of the biggest single investments is for the Asahan aluminum smelter, a top priority of Indonesia. Other processing operations include a copper smelter and an iron sintering plant in the Philippines. Asia is still a major source of tropical woods as well.

A fair amount of investment has also been made in Oceania, this time meaning primarily Australia, although there is growing interest in Papua New Guinea. Relatively closed under the Labour Party, it was hard to invest in natural resource projects and sometimes even difficult to export raw materials until a more forthcoming approach was adopted, and then amplified by the conservatives. By now, Japan draws nearly half of its iron ore, coal and salt and even more of its bauxite, wool and beef from this very close partner, Australia.

The other major site is Latin America. Here, there is a particularly strong concentration, since most of the projects are located in Brazil. Even in Brazil, the bulk of the money has been put into a few large ventures including farming and ranching, a paper and pulp scheme, and especially another giant aluminum smelter. While investment in most other countries seems to have passed its peak, there is a chance of further growth in oil producers like Mexico amd Venezuela.

North America, which was the first site to be tried, has gradually fallen behind as compared to other regions. This included timber ventures in Alaska and Canada, various mines in Canada and the United States, and more lately some oil deals. However, with the shift to coal as a source of energy, the region is bound to benefit and many new projects are being studied.

Africa comes in for a relatively small share, and this is spread widely. There are some oil operations in North Africa, copper and other mining in Zaire, a uranium project in Niger, and so on.

More surprising is the small amount of investment in the Middle East. This may be, as already indicated, because much of the area was already staked out for oil prospection and extraction. However, for petrochemicals, the Middle East has a major share of the Japanese investment and this is likely to grow.

Europe, according to the statistics, has a somewhat greater share than either. This is only because the Soviet Union is included and Siberia has long appeared as a new frontier for Moscow and Tokyo. During the 1970s, there was much talk of joint development to obtain mineral ores, wood chips and oil. Some of the projects went ahead, especially the drilling for natural gas and oil off Sakhalin. But the rest is on ice.[2]

This lack of progress was not only due to political friction but the fact that a considerably more attractive partner suddenly appeared in the form of a new Chinese regime. While the People's Republic sank into economic chaos during the Cultural Revolution, little could be done. The more rational policy of Deng Xiaoping, despite some setbacks, has offered a glimpse of almost unprecedented possibilities of cooperation in oil prospection, development of vast coal reserves, and numerous other mining ventures.

Natural resource-related investment has always been important for Japan and this is not likely to change.

However, as indicated, the exact composition with regard to specific types of raw materials and specific host countries may change rapidly and radically. Also, on the whole, the coming period may see a relative tapering off of such investment. The growth was swift as Japan's heavy and chemical industries grew, and there was another desperate spurt just after the oil crisis. Now that a worldwide recession has set in, and Japan is trying to convert from energy-intensive and raw material-intensive industries to higher technology, knowledge-intensive ones like electronics and robotics, the growth could well be slower.

The Japanese Team

Given the vast amount of raw materials absorbed by the Japanese economy, it was not an easy matter to organize the many complex channels needed to keep the flow moving smoothly. Any number of problems could arise. There was a need for considerable commercial knowhow and technical expertise, tremendous funds had to be raised, a receptive market prepared, and there were still the external risks. Yet, gradually the Japanese put together a team that did an exceptional job. However, given the very different structure of Japanese industry, this team had a number of characteristics not usually found elsewhere.

In most other countries, it was the major processing companies that looked after their own requirements. Steelmakers would locate and import supplies of coal and iron, aluminum smelters would get the necessary bauxite, the oil refiners were also in the business of prospection and distribution. In Japan, obviously the manufacturers *could* have done the same thing. But, in the early postwar years they were much too involved in other activities that were more vital, such as rebuilding and expanding their factories or facilities, introducing new technologies and improving on them, upgrading their products and making savings on production, and so on.

Thus, much of the burden fell on the trading companies again, just as they had been the principal vehicles ever since Meiji days. Their field of expertise was buying, buying anything and everything in just about every part of the world, and they could not be matched by an individual company no matter how big. Moreover, in Japan, most of the major trading companies are related to the leading manufacturers and users one way or the other. This arises from the existence of groups or *keiretsu* and other forms of integration. So, it was perfectly normal for Mitsubishi Steel to turn to Mitsubishi Corporation, or Mitsui Aluminum to Mitsui & Co., the trading arm, to handle most of their needs.

Actually, it was this possibility of making massive purchases of bulk goods and raw materials which gave the trading companies the chance to expand and become the giants they are. In so doing, they were able to keep their overhead and other expenses low and thereby demand rather small margins. The 1% or 2% they charged on huge deals was hardly enough to put off the buyer and, even if it engaged in its own procurement, it was not likely that it could obtain the raw materials any cheaper. For, the trading companies were also experts on related operations like transport, insurance, handling, distribution and so on.[3]

Up to the present time, it has been the trading company which took the initiative in most transactions. However, it only assumed full responsibility on rare occasions or for relatively small projects. Otherwise, the trading company usually appeared together with its partners which were basically its customers, the actual users. Both parties would put up whatever financing was necessary and take equity, with the trading company sometimes playing a leading role, sometimes a more modest one. This way, the trading company knew that it would be able to handle the commercial aspects of the deal, what really interested it, while the user knew it would have access to the essential inputs. In return, the trading company could draw on the user's expertise regarding the quality of the product or feasibility of mining.

Still, in recent years, there has been a trend for some final users to play an increasingly active part, either alongside the trading companies or sometimes excluding them. This is because their interests were not always exactly the same. The trading company often derived its profits as a function of the price of the goods. If they rose, it would earn more. The users, to the contrary, wanted the lowest possible prices and they were more interested in keeping their own costs down than any gains from investment in raw material production. Thus, they have increased their share of the action and, at the same time, the range of investors has broadened. They now include steelmakers and metal smelters, power plants and oil companies, food processors and paper manufacturers.

Occasionally a further member joined the team, namely the banks. Even when they did not appear directly, obviously it was necessary to obtain solid financial backing. This could take the form of loans to the trading or processing companies and sometimes also to the overseas venture itself, with the Japanese parent company or partner providing the guarantee. However, if the amount of funding was substantial or the risk greater than usual, the banks might become full-fledged participants.

In some of the larger, or riskier ventures, the Japanese team was expanded yet further. It would include a state-run corporation established specifically to encourage activities in the sector. Among them are the Japan Petroleum

Development Corporation (JPDC), the Japan National Oil Corporation (JNOC), the Power Reactor and Nuclear Fuel Development Corporation (PRN), and others. Another partner in some projects was the Overseas Economic Cooperation Fund (OECF) which could advance funds or actually take an equity position. The Export-Import Bank was also enabled to supply low-cost loans that might be necessary to get a project moving. And, if the investment was regarded as being of exceptional importance, the government could turn it into a "national project."

There were several reasons for setting up such a "team" rather than going into ventures on their own, as most foreign multinationals not only tended to do but actually seemed to prefer. One of them is that Japanese companes, just like Japanese people, prefer cooperation where possible and this sort of cooperation is greatly facilitated by the network of relations that already exist. Trading companies have long and close links with their customers and there is nothing surprising in both joining the same project. Relations with the government are also much closer than elsewhere, and the government has a long tradition of backing or participating in particularly important or sensitive ventures or those which the private sector is not willing to attempt on its own.

By bringing in more participants there is a possibility of increasing the total amount of funding available and pooling more expertise, so that projects which would otherwise be unfeasible can more readily be launched. It is also possible to spread the risks. Since there are so many participants, they all face the same benefits and dangers and will support one another. If the project is a success, they all succeed equally; if a failure, the losses are fairly and broadly spread and no one is strongly disadvantaged. Also, by keeping its participation in any given project to a minimum each partner can enter into many more projects, a second way of spreading the risks.

But another benefit can be even more crucial. By assembling a broad array of participants, whether trading companies, users like steelmakers and smelters, or consumers like the power companies, it is possible to absorb much larger quantities of the raw materials offered. Increasing the size of the purchase is an excellent means of cutting costs, whether through commercial economies of scale or by exerting pressure. This sort of leverage is even more significant when much of the Japanese market is tied up in such arrangements. By sticking together, rather than competing against one another, the Japanese purchasers can bring down the price.

In most commercial projects, the Japanese team as already outlined is fully sufficient to handle the operations. Despite this, there is still a tendency for the Japanese side not to wish to assume too prominent a position. Thus, they may seek further partners. In the private sector, they are quite willing to work with local mining companies in the host country and they often also include other foreign multinationals. They would not even hesitate to join up with what is normally a competitor. This is partly to obtain its expertise, which may be necessary for prospection and development, and partly again to have a broader front of purchasing interests.

In yet other ventures, either because they are too big to handle otherwise or because the host country has some specific interests it wishes to protect or has publicly committed itself to the success of the project, the host government will also play a role. This is increasingly frequent in the oil and natural gas sector, since most producers have already set up national companies to supervise operations and participate in as many as possible.

In other projects, a special government corporation may be established as a partner, one which usually takes a majority of the ownership and control.

The differing degrees of teamwork will be noticed when examining the various projects that exist or are being put together. A surprisingly small number of them consist of just one Japanese company joining with some local producer and there are even fewer where a Japanese company undertakes more than mere purchasing on its own. More typical is the case where a trading company ties up with a user and also a local partner. Some align several trading companies, users, processors and banks, as many as a dozen or more partners on the Japanese side alone. And the biggest seem to bring in just about everyone involved in a given sector, as well as the government, in a striking display of solidarity by Japan, Inc.

Guaranteeing Supplies

Japan was not only eager to step up its supplies of all sorts of raw materials, it sometimes became almost paranoiac about it. The reason is quite simple. More than any other country, its steel mills, smelters, refineries, power plants and so on were built to economies of scale, usually attaining an exceptionally large size and also presupposing a very steady output. If, for one reason or another, there were an interruption, these mammoth and highly efficient operations could be idled or forced to work under capacity. It was essential to avoid such an occurrence at all costs.

The Japanese therefore began seeking new sources of supply and increasing purchases from all suppliers so that a constant flow could be maintained. However, they soon encountered another barrier which annoyed or worried them. As a latecomer, in most cases the Japanese purchasers could not even enter into direct contact with the country of supply. Rather, they had to pass through major multinationals which had already staked out most of the raw material operations. They had to make a deal with Kaiser or Alcoa for bauxite, Kenneco for copper, or the "seven sisters" for petroleum.

This meant that, for all practical purposes, it was not only a question of dealing with a dozen or more producing countries and perhaps hundreds of individual companies, some of which were bound to accept cooperation with Japan, but rather a much smaller group of MNCs whose wishes might be contrary to those of the purchasers. The most obvious bone of contention would be price, something the majors could control partially. After all, they often formed an oligopoly. Higher prices would definitely hurt the Japanese users, smelters, refiners, steelmakers, etc., then further on, manufacturers and consumers. Worse, there was always some risk that the majors would not sell to Japan if there were a shortage.

To get around this barrier, and diversify sources, the Japanese purchasers, whether direct users or trading companies, developed various strategies. One of them was quite simply to enter into closer relations with the companies that controlled the supplies. Some of them tied up with oil majors or mining companies. In Australia, they joined with foreign MNCs like Kaiser and Rio Tinto for aluminum. In Canada, major steelmakers went into cooperation with Kaiser Steel and the smelters with Alcan. The Japanese have a minority share in iron mining in Liberia, along with Amax. Mitsubishi shared the natural gas project in Brunei with Royal Dutch Shell.

Another policy, a considerably bolder one, was to get around these companies and work directly with the producers. This move, which grew during the 1960s and 1970s, came at just the right time, for that was when many Third World countries were themselves trying to break away from the Western multinationals and assume greater control of their own natural resources. Some countries, like Chile for copper and Mossadegh's Iran for oil, simply nationalized the holdings. Others were trying to slip out more discreetly. Japan, as a newcomer with no objectionable practices yet, was seen as a potential partner and proved willing to cooperate. It was, in fact, the only major capitalist country which had a vested interest in change.

The prime example of this process arose for oil. Whether it was because the oil majors were doing such a good job, or its own companies were busy in other sectors, the Japanese depended on foreign multinationals, mainly American, for about 90% of their total supply of crude at the time of the oil crisis. When this struck, in 1973, purchasers were aghast to find that the majors could not always meet their needs and were giving preference to older, more important customers, usually in their home country.

With this, the government decided that Japan must make its own arrangements to avoid a repetition. One step was to reinforce the publicly owned Japan Petroleum Development Corporation and Japan National Oil Company and the national refiners so as to conclude direct agreements with the producers. The other was to gradually raise the share of oil provided to the Japanese government in one way or another. To this end, Japanese companies did not hesitate to deal with producers that had squeezed out, or nationalized, foreign companies. They were among the first purchasers of such oil from Oman, Abu Dhabi, Kuwait, Saudi Arabia and Iran, both under the Shah and after the Islamic Revolution. Although MITI's goal was only to raise imports from autonomous sources to 30% of the crude by 1980, the actual amount of direct-deal (DD) and government-to-government (GG) imports reached 47% and imports by independent Japanese oil companies and developers another 8% by then.

Having established closer relations with the producers or the multinationals handling production, the Japanese could approach their broader goal which was basically massive and regular supplies of raw materials. To do so, they went into a series of arrangements with as many partners as possible, often taking just a minor share in any given operation so as to be able to participate in more different projects. This could be seen in Australia, for example, where the Japanese soon became the top purchasers, and sometimes also partners, in many of the new projects being launched.

But it was not enough to buy what was needed when it was needed. The Japanese much preferred tying this down well in advance through long-term contracts. These contracts had advantages for both sides. By knowing it could purchase a given amount at a reasonably fixed price, the Japanese were approaching their goal of stability and regularity of supplies. They did not appear to mind terribly if the price they paid was sometimes slightly above the going rate, for at other times it might be lower, and the important thing was long-term planning and implementation. On the other hand, once a mine owner had a long-term contract with the Japanese, he could use this as collateral to borrow money from the bank to finance any necessary expansion.

Long-term contracts have already been concluded for most essential materials including coal and iron ore, copper and bauxite, natural gas and oil. The specific terms vary greatly, some only being for a few years, others running into a decade or more. In Australia, which has favored this sort of transaction, Japanese interests have one 15-year contract for coking coal with Thiess Dampier and another for steaming coal with Blair Athol. The Mexican state oil company, Pemex, offered a 10-year contract while Indonesia's Pertamina recently extended an earlier 10-year agreement for an additional 20 years, up until the year 2002. In all cases, the amounts covered are substantial, 3 and 5 million tons a year for the first two, 100,000 barrels of crude a day for the latter.

But this arrangement was not always adequate. It was fine when dealing with going concerns, especially prosperous ones that could expand production quite easily. However, as demand kept growing and completely new sources had to be tapped, they were not always ready to meet Japan's demands. It is terribly expensive to open a new mine or drill a well. And, if they are not suitably located, there may also be all sorts of development and infrastructural costs. This will probably involve financing that is beyond the reach of the local company, or even the host government, and which Japan would have to share if it is to get the desired raw materials.

Thus, Japanese companies and the government itself have repeatedly been obliged to offer some kind of financial aid. For example, a counterpart to the first Pertamina deal was a loan of $200 million by the government and another $100 million by the private sector. Pemex, in return for its oil sales, obtained a $500 million loan, 70% by the Exim Bank and the rest by a syndicate of commercial banks. A group of power companies will help finance the world's largest natural gas project in Qatar. The government will lend $500 million to Brazil to launch the world's largest iron mine in Carajas. And the biggest offer yet was made by Prime Minister Ohira on his historic visit to Peking. Credits, estimated to total ¥10 trillion, were offered for six major projects including railway lines and port facilities to help open China's natural resources to Japan.

In some cases, the local company did not want to run the risk of making huge investments without a firm guarantee that the Japanese would keep on buying the output. Also, for most ventures, it was necessary to obtain normal

Coking Coal From Bowen Basin

Credit: Mitsubishi Corp.

operating capital which could just as well come from the purchasers. At first, the Japanese were reluctant to take equity in such companies and be tied down. However, they ultimately realized that there were also advantages for them. If they held a share of the ownership, they could also be sure that they would get preference on sales and prices. The end result was to make both parties the captive of one another, and to ensure closer cooperation in both their interests, if the venture were to succeed.

The equity position was sometimes quite modest, as when Nippon Steel, Kawasaki Steel and Marubeni took a slim 6% slice of Hamersley Holdings. But it could be much higher. Mitsui & Co. and C. Itoh held 10% of the huge Mt. Newman iron mine and Mitsui & Co. some 20% of what became the Thiess Dampier Mitsui Coal Pty. Marubeni had 25% of the Silver Valley mine and Mitsubishi Corporation a 49% interest in the Ulan Coal Mines. There was a tendency, in Australia and elsewhere, for the share to be relatively larger in smaller operations and also to increase gradually with time.

The trend toward long-term contracts arose during the 1970s especially and by the 1980s the further phase of buying into existing mining companies became dominant. Indeed, about then the Japanese purchasers began insisting that they be given a reasonable equity participation before they would enter into long-term purchase agreements or advance substantial funds. With this, the relatively shallow involvement of the 1960s was being replaced by full-scale participation of the Japanese in the hope of firmly guaranteeing their access to raw materials.

From afar, it looked as if Japan had been enormously successful in this effort. The share of various raw materials purchased directly from local sources without passing through foreign multinationals grew, the share of purchases made on a long-term basis also increased, and more and more often the Japanese held equity in the producing companies and could influence their operations. But this did not really exclude certain dangers.

Even when the long-term contracts provided, for example, that coal or iron ore would be shipped at a given tonnage per year for five, ten or twenty years, this did not guarantee that that would actually happen. Repeatedly in the past, and doubtlessly again in the future, the Japanese found that the contracts could be cancelled or simply ignored. In China, the targets indicated for export of oil and coal were quite simply unrealistic and could not be met with the best will. Oil producers in the Middle East did not hesitate to hold back if they felt the terms were disadvantageous. Even Malaysia, a friendly Asian country, could cut its promised delivery to Japan to supply a closer partner, Thailand.

Of course, in more serious cases, the longest-term contract, with the most formal guarantees, was little more than a scrap of paper. It became very difficult for American or Australian mines to meet some of their obligations because of lengthy strikes in the mines or by dock workers. It was quite impossible for Iran to fulfill earlier pledges when production declined sharply after the fall of the Shah, whose undertakings hardly interested the new regime anyway. When the Iraq-Iran war broke out, not only were many oil supply contracts rendered invalid, even ships filled with oil were blocked in the harbor. Nor was nationalization of Japanese-invested companies excluded.

On the other hand, Japan might occasionally have to renege on its own pledges. Its leading companies had rushed headlong into contracts and commitments of all sorts to obtain tremendous amounts of raw materials. The amounts actually contracted for were usually a function of forecasts of future requirements worked out by the industries concerned and MITI. Yet, there is not the slightest doubt that both industrial and government circles tended to exaggerate needs. This was due to a mixture of concern about getting enough and a tendency to order more just in case, given the general dynamics of Japanese business. If the demand fell, as happened recently due to the worldwide recession, the actual needs could be much lower than predicted. Thus, Japanese interests periodically had to bow out of purchases they had already promised or more vaguely hinted at.

Problems over the prices paid were even nastier than those related to the quantities ordered. With the massive amount of investment that was going on, and also normal or less expected slumps, the prices of certain raw materials could slip below the agreed level. The most memorable case arose in connection with purchases of raw sugar from Australia. In 1974, the Japanese entered into a long-term contract to buy Queensland sugar at a price considerably under the market price. Within a short time, alas, the market price fell drastically, and the Japanese ended up paying twice the international rate. Japanese refiners complained bitterly and tried to revise the contract to a lower rate, only to meet strong resistance from the producers and Queensland government. The final settlement only gave them partial satisfaction, and they had to pay well over the market price to the end.

By the same token, the prices of raw materials could also rise. The most significant example is obviously oil. But this has happened to other products such as uranium and, once again in Australia, coal and iron. In all these cases, the coverage of a long-term contract offered very little protection for the Japanese once the suppliers decided that they were getting a raw deal and imposed their will. This they could readily do since the products, which they held, could always be sold to someone else for more. To avoid such conflicts and increase flexibility, escalator clauses and other formulas have been tried. But this makes the very concept of stable prices even more illusory than that of guaranteed regularity of supply.

Upstream To Mining

Slowly but surely, the Japanese purchasers were being drawn further into the process of producing raw materials. Rather than buy on the spot market, they went into long-term contracts. Rather than remain purely buyers, they took equity in producing companies to guarantee access to output. And it soon happened that they were induced to go a step further. To ensure that there were enough supplies on the market whenever they wanted them, they launched what were called "develop and import" projects.

Under D & I arrangements, the Japanese would take various measures to encourage production. This could be little more than granting or guaranteeing a loan to permit a going concern, of which they might or might not be a shareholder, to expand existing operations or make them more efficient. It might be to help such a company open new seams or veins or have more wells bored. But it could also go as far as joining a venture for the specific purpose of seeking entirely new sources including the necessary exploration, prospection and extraction.

There were various advantages to this. Among them, one had a very broad nature, namely to ensure that the supplies did keep coming. During the 1960s and 1970s, Japan's steel and metal production, electricity generation, and foodstuff consumption were growing so rapidly that it had to race ahead just to keep up with needs. Naturally, the supplies were also expanding, but never at quite the same pace. Moreover, most of these supplies had to be prepared well in advance, since it might not be for years, or even a decade, that they would actually come on stream. To be certain that they were there when they were needed, the Japanese had to intervene to help the process along.

In addition, if production could be expanded rapidly enough, this would correct the imbalance with demand and perhaps even reverse it so that supply would become relatively loose and perhaps excessive. This meant that, in the worst hypothesis, the prices of the various raw materials would not rise as quickly as otherwise. In what, for Japan, could be regarded as the best hypothesis, there might actually be an oversupply, conceivably even a glut, which would cause prices to slip back or decline. This would be to the good of its industries and consumers.

On this particular point, however, there is an intriguing divergence of interests among the usual partners. Local companies wanted to bring in Japanese buyers as investors to know they would have a good market and, of course, also for the capital and loans they provided. But they certainly did not want to have the buyers dictate low prices. Between the Japanese companies, an even more subtle difference crept in. The direct users and consumers naturally wanted low prices. The trading companies and distributors, to the extent they earned a percentage-based commission, could do better on higher prices. Moreover, all the Japanese investors stood to gain if the products sold for more as long as these higher costs could be passed on to the consumers. This often left the Japanese side with more divided interests than might at first appear.

The more specific and concrete advantage was simply to participate in a broader range of activities in the same sector. This would give the trading companies, or refiners and smelters, or other users, some control over the upstream operations. They would have a greater say on how, or when, products were extracted, what quantities were taken, and especially what they were sold for. More to the point, they would be able to share in the value added derived from these operations and the profits accruing from the sales of the resources. In earlier days, these profits were—or at least appeared—quite substantial.

Of course, there was a counterpart to this. It was necessary to accept the inherent risks of the trade. For example, there was no guarantee that a new mine or well would be found or that, if discovered, it would be of very great value or even exploitable. Nor did anyone really know until the products were put on the market what they were worth. Yet, from the outset, it was clear that the costs would be tremendous. All of the various operations, exploration, prospection, actual sinking of wells or opening of mines, cost a fortune. If per chance the sites were not conveniently located, this could be compounded by equally fantastic costs of infrastructure, transport, and handling facilities.

Given these considerable expenses up front, it was not

surprising to find that the Japanese partners played a rather minor role in the beginning, although they tended to raise their investment and equity in ventures with time. Moreover, to play it safe, they rarely appeared singly but in teams, trading company plus users or several users forming a consortium or joint company. And this company would then join with local companies or yet broader consortia. For the Japanese, in addition to risk, there was sometimes the problem of a lack of expertise and experience, since most of these companies had engaged in little mining of certain minerals and almost no oil prospection before.

The first of the D & I projects were quite modest. They were also a bit sporadic, occurring in various sectors and various countries as the opportunities arose. Already in 1953, Mitsubishi Metal Mining made a loan to Atlas, an American company, to develop a copper mine in the Philippines for which it had the right to purchase most of the output. For the Mt. Newman iron ore project, in 1969, the Japanese partners granted a loan and also took an equity position. This pattern was then followed for other major ventures like Hamersley, Robe River and Mitsubishi Development's Bower Basin venture, the world's largest opencut coal mine. Similar projects materialized for iron ore in Liberia, copper in Zaire and bauxite in Canada. But they could be hardier. Marubeni, Nissho Iwai and C. Itoh took a 35% share in Dampier Salt of Australia. In Sabah, Malysia, Overseas Mineral Resources Development took the initiative, and a 51% share, in opening a copper mine.

But Japan was still only whetting its appetite. Over the years, its companies entered more and more projects and by the early 1980s they climbed into some of the most ambitious. Mitsubishi Corporation operated the world's largest salt farm jointly with the Mexican government in Baja California. Mitsui Mining, Tokyo Boeki, Mitsubishi Chemical, Sumitomo Corporation and eight major steelmakers took about a third of the equity in Quintette Coal Company of British Columbia, Canada. To finance this huge colliery which will eventually provide over 6 million tons of coal a year, a consortium of 55 Japanese banks had to advance a C$950 million loan. Meanwhile, seven leading steelmakers, headed by Nippon Steel, will participate in the Carajas iron mine in Brazil. In keeping with Prime Minister Suzuki's promise, made during his trip to Brazil in June 1982, they will bring with them nearly $500 million in credit from the Exim Bank and various city banks. By 1985, Japan should be procuring 10 million tons of ore a year from the biggest such development project in the world.

For many of the metal ore and coal mines, the sources had already been located and only a development effort was necessary. But, for uranium, it was often necessary to get in at the prospection stage. While four Japanese power companies were able to acquire a share of Energy Resources Australia, which wanted to expand the Ranger mine, the state Power Reactor and Nuclear Fuel Development Corporation had to undertake prospection along with Continental Oil in Wyoming. And even deeper involvement arose for the Overseas Uranium Resources Development Co., a consortium of 32 Japanese mining and power companies, in hunting for uranium in cooperation with the Niger government and French and Spanish companies. This time the search was a success, encountering major deposits that should be able to meet more than half of Japan's total needs.

This effort, in turn, was less extensive and apparently less risky than prospecting for oil and natural gas. The process began very timidly in the 1960s and gained strength during the 1970s. It was undertaken by Japanese oil companies like Arabian Oil and Idemitsu which engaged in work in Saudi Arabia, Kuwait, Canada and Alaska. Trading companies also participated, with Mitsui in Iran, Sumitomo in

Iraq, C. Itoh in Indonesia, and Mitsubishi taking natural gas from Brunei. Sometimes joint operations were formed for specific projects, like the Egyptian Petroleum Development Company that is hunting for crude near Suez and the Japan Oil Development Company that has been active in Abu Dhabi. In Qatar, nine electric and gas companies are participating in the world's largest natural gas development project. These companies can often count on backup from two government agencies. The Japan National Oil Corporation helps finance exploration and development costs, up to about 70% or 80% of the total, either through loans or investment. JNOC has been supporting operations in China's Bohai Bay, Sakhalin and Abu Dhabi. The actual funds come mainly from the Export-Import Bank. Thus, the private promoters sometimes only carry the smaller part of the financial burden.

This sort of investment is naturally a big gamble. Costs are high, at least ¥100 billion for a minor project and as much as ¥1 trillion for Bohai Bay. Yet, there is no guarantee that oil will be struck. The Japanese were lucky in Abu Dhabi, Saudi Arabia, Kuwait, China and Gabon, but Idemitsu pulled out of Alaska and Mitsui gave up in Iran. Even the prospective returns on good wells, which should compensate for the bad ones, are being whittled down by the host countries. Indonesia, a particularly close partner, is a reasonably instructive example. Back in 1972, for the right to prospect, the OECF had to grant it some $200 million in soft loans and private oil companies added another $100 million. Alas, they never struck oil, but Pertamina kindly allowed them to buy some from other fields. Another attempt was decided on recently and JNOC agreed to put up 70% of the $110 million needed. The terms the Japanese oil companies were offered are not terribly generous, namely 15% of production... assuming they find something. If not, the whole investment is lost. And this deal is no worse than they are likely to get elsewhere.

In the hope of escaping from dependence on oil, some projects are being promoted that may end up involving even more difficulties. The Japanese wanted to enter one of the oil shale projects in Australia, either at the Rundle or Condor deposit. While the shale is manifestly there, the economics of crushing and any cost advantage over conventional sources are uncertain. For coal liquefaction, it is still necessary to perfect the techniques as regards cost and capacity. To this end, the Japanese and Australian governments agreed to build a demonstration plant when Prime Minister Masayoshi Ohira visted Prime Minister Fraser in Canberra, in 1980. Although this "national project" will have a rather small capacity when it is completed in 1985, it was interesting enough to induce Kobe Steel, Mitsubishi Chemical and Nissho Iwai to become sponsors.

While most of these operations are extractive, some others which attract less attention are more clearly productive. This arises especially for agriculture and, to a lesser extent, fisheries. There are a multitude of such projects, many of them quite small, and a majority run by various trading companies. Sumitomo grows bananas in the Philippines, C. Itoh cultivates maize in Indonesia, and Mitsui and Mitsubishi can pineapples in Thailand. Marubeni handles coffee beans and instant coffee in Brazil while a small coffee distributor revived the famous Toraja blend in Indonesia. Cotton is grown in various places and a knitwear firm recently decided to raise sheep in Australia. Mitsubishi and C. Itoh engage in cattle breeding in Australia, Itoman is growing hogs there, and C. Itoh has a ranch in Brazil. While many trading companies, and fishing firms like Taiyo, have joint ventures abroad to benefit from the 200-mile limit, others are cultivating trout in Australia or shrimp in the Philippines. The most publicized of these projects, however, were three large farms carved out of the jungle in Indonesia by Mitsui, Mitsubishi and C. Itoh in an attempt to teach the locals modern agricultural techniques.

These various operations have taken the Japanese quite far from the early days when they merely appeared on the market to buy or collect the ore or crops they needed at the dock. They now have to go out and prospect, develop or grow them before they can even be shipped to Japan. And this can take a considerable time. It is not unusual to spend several years before striking oil or uncovering a viable deposit, then another few years before the find can actually be exploited, and many more years until the original investment has been paid back. The amount of time this will take naturally depends on the type of project and price of goods, but it is not at all infrequent for major projects to require as much as twenty years to pay for themselves and then start bringing in real profits.

To grasp what this involves, it is worthwhile taking a quick look at the cost side. It has been estimated that in Australia, a relatively stable and civilized place, even a small ranch or fish farm costs $1 or $2 million. Dampier Salt is capitalized at about $35 million. When you get into mining, the figures shoot up immediately. It takes something like $300 to $400 million to develop a modest coal or uranium mine. But the Quintette coal mine would require over $1 billion, the Rundle oil shale development project some $2 billion, the vast Carajas iron mine in Brazil nearly $5 billion, and the natural gas on Australia's northwest shelf as much as $10 billion. Since much of this money must be Japanese for the development even to happen, it is almost miraculous that there have been so many ventures to date.

Of course, the costs may seem less daunting if one considers the potential profits which derive from the operations or sales of the final products. But this is rarely known in advance with any accuracy. Unlike the actual costs, which tend to snowball and exceed the estimates, the actual proceeds have a nasty tendency to shrink or dissipate due to unexpected complications. Some are natural risks like striking dry holes or finding that prices have slumped. Others arise from the fact that nowadays few owners of natural resources, whether capitalist enterprises or socialist governments, are willing to let their partners get away with much of the loot. The biggest problem has thus been political intervention. No sooner does the outside developer seem to be doing too well than the politicians, businessmen and newspapers start complaining. Depending on their influence, and the kind of regime, an "amicable" settlement or official constraints may be imposed ranging from higher prices to higher taxes and not stopping short of expropriation. So, no matter how fabulous the returns may seem when the plan is first being mooted, the day when foreign investors could make a killing on natural resources is rapidly passing.

Downstream To Processing

While the Japanese companies were gradually moving upstream toward mining and prospection of raw materials, largely of their own volition although sometimes coaxed by their partners, they were much more reticent about moving downstream to processing. In this direction, however, they came under much stronger pressure in the host countries, particularly from the government, to play a more active role. But they had more then enough reasons to resist it.

The primary ones were quite obvious and terribly convincing, for the Japanese at least. After all, the major potential investors had a definite vested interest in leaving the situation pretty much as it was, with the host countries merely providing raw materials while an advanced and industrialized Japan handled all further processes. The mining companies, for one, had major investments in downstream operations back in Japan. They ran smelters and refining companies. Meanwhile, the oil companies had their own refineries and related petrochemical plants. All they wanted were raw materials to feed them. The trading companies' interests converged, if for somewhat different reasons. They lived off what they bought and shipped, and they could certainly carry more raw materials than processed products.

Thus, during the 1950s and 1960s, Japan stuck to the consecrated pattern of importing raw materials, processing them and then passing them on to manufacturers to be turned into finished products. Many of these products were then exported to earn revenue with which to purchase yet more raw materials. Thanks to the tremendous advances in sea transport, it was increasingly inexpensive to ship vast amounts of coal, metal ores or crude petroleum to Japan for processing, often in facilities built just alongside the port. Due to the tremendous economies of scale and very sophisticated technologies, Japanese smelters, refiners and steelmakers were able to remain competitive for a long time.

Alas, the 1973 oil crisis changed much of that and began altering the whole economic basis of these industries. No matter how cheap transport was relatively, even in the best circumstances it was quite costly. It was necessary to import many times more ore then was obtained as finished metal after processing. And, to actually process the metals, it was also necessary to carry huge quantities of coal for steelmaking or crude to generate electricity for refining other metals. When energy costs went up, the overall costs rose substantially for two reasons: oil was used for production, oil was also used for shipping.

It therefore became comparatively more advantageous to process the raw materials on the spot when they were suitably combined, or to simply move one ingredient or another and not all of them as for Japan. Thus, a country with both iron ore and coal located in reasonable proximity had a definite advantage. Even having one or the other meant that much of the transport was unnecessary. Water power to generate large quantities of electricity, if sited near a source of aluminum, zinc or copper had the same effect. For petrochemicals, the situation was even more decisive. Not only was it expensive to ship naphtha abroad, it was inherently cheaper to use the associated natural gas from oil fields which would otherwise be wasted.

While these new circumstances were already making Japanese investors think, with longing or regret, at the shifting comparative advantages that were making operations back home less rational than abroad, some host countries became very eager to move in that direction. In some cases, they offered considerable incentives to introduce processing operations. In others, they applied moral persuasion or even arm-twisting to get Japanese purchasers of raw materials to venture into local processing. At the extreme, they simply announced that henceforth raw materials would not be exported and the only way to have access to the country's natural resources was to process them first.

This national policy was not enough to make the Japanese, or anyone else, comply without looking into the situation very carefully. Prospection and mining were already rather complex and costly operations. Processing turned out to be even more daunting. The processing plants, especially if they were to benefit from economies of scale, had to be extremely large. They were also quite sophisticated involving very advanced technologies, some of which the company regarded as trade secrets. The personnel in certain categories had to be highly trained and could not always be found in developing countries. And the

Mitsubishi's Salt Farm In Mexico

Credit: Mitsubishi Corp.

costs were bound to be tremendous. So much so that a developing country might not have the necessary funds and, no matter who put up the money, it would take many years for it to be paid off and for the plant to start making profits.

As if this were not bad enough, there was also the problem of infrastructure. It was not just a matter of building a railway to carry the ore to the coast and a port to ship it. They were often necessary. But this was a long-term proposition that would require the establishment of a whole town to accomodate those who built the processing plant and other installations and then those who ran them later on. And the biggest expense was yet to come. For, it was necessary to provide enough electricity to refine certain metals. This could well involve a huge coal-fired power plant or an even more massive hydroelectric power plant built onto a ponderous dam. In this case, it was not unusual to find that the related infrastructure cost more than the processing facility itself.

This will explain why the number of such projects, aside from relatively simple and small ones, did not grow very rapidly. It more than explains why foreign investors, including the Japanese, were hesitant to be drawn in. For such reasons, many of the projects that reached fruition were actually a result of local government—and not private sector—promotion and required a strong moral commitment and financial support from the Japanese government to be launched. Although the private mining or other companies played a crucial role, there was always a backup on both sides fron the highest political level.

Admittedly, some of the projects are so fundamental as to be almost a matter-of-course. There are a few natural resources which simply could not be transported without preliminary processing. Among the most obvious is natural gas. This has to be turned into LNG, usually by a rather large unit, before it can be put on carriers and directed toward Japan. More recently, technologies are being developed to turn coal into liquefied form that is much easier to transport and takes much less room. Oil shale also has to be crushed in a nearby plant so that the liquid can be collected.

As we saw, Japan is engaged in a coal liquefaction project, and may also join in oil shale development, both in Australia. For liquefied natural gas, however, it has already become one of the world's major promoters. It helped build facilities in Brunei and Abu Dhabi, without which it could not get LNG. In Indonesia, it went much further. Back in 1974, the Japan Indonesia LNG, Co. (Jilco) was established by 32 firms including 5 users, 16 banks, and 7 general trading companies to help fund two plants, one in Badak, the other in Arun. The total cost of the project was initially reckoned at $1,180 million and later revised to $1,638 million, the bulk of which was supplied in credits and loans from Jilco to Pertamina.

Something of the same nature, although differing in method, applies for most other raw materials. Just about any ore represents a tiny fraction of the vast amounts of rock that are mined and have little, if any, worth. It is much easier to get rid of most of the rubbish near the mine rather than shipping it. Thus, for copper, bauxite, uranium, etc. the rock will first be crushed and then sorted. One may go a step further for iron, pellitizing it. A rather unusal approach to this arose when Kawasaki Steel built a major sintering plant in Mindanao, Philippines, where iron ore is mixed with limestone and burnt. The limestone is produced locally, and substantial amounts of fresh water and electricity are tapped, but the iron ore comes from Australia. It therefore made less sense than the huge sintering plant in Brazil that Kawasaki and six other steelmakers may participate in. For, this would process the massive iron ore resources of Carajas.

A similar economic rationale applies to timber and wood products. Logs are clumsy and bulky items to transport, although that is not the primary reason why many developing countries, including Indonesia and the Philippines, first restricted log exports mainly to nationals and then banned it altogether. More important is to increase local value added by turning out timber in sawmills and also producing plywood. In many cases, Japanese logging ventures have had to cease operations and enter such ventures, often with local partners. But others were stubbornly attached to importing only logs and producing finished products at home, preferring to withdraw instead and move on to whatever countries still allowed logging.

The attitude among pulp and paper makers has been

much more enlightened. At an early date, they saw the writing on the wall and also realized the tremendous savings that could be made by importing wood chips or even pulp and restricting themselves to paper production in Japan. In addition, they admitted that if urgent action were not taken for forest development, there might not be any trees left ere long. Two Japanese paper manufacturers' associations are now engaged in planning afforestation plus woodchip production projects in Indonesia, the Philippines, the Solomon Islands and elsewhere. Other companies are finding it wiser to buy into going concerns in Canada or the United States. The most striking move so for came when Oji Paper, Japan's largest, went into a tie-up with the world's top maker, International Paper, to produce printing paper and ultimately newsprint and other types in the latter's factories. This followed a somewhat less extensive tie-up between Jujo Paper and Weyerhaeuser.

Far more ambitious is the Japan-Brazil Paper and Pulp Resources Development Project (JBP) formed to plant eucalyptus trees in various parts of Brazil for later processing into woodchips or pulp. Established in 1973, JBP includes 18 paper and pulp manufacturers, a trading company (C. Itoh) and the OECF, which holds 38% of the stock. It then entered into two joint ventures in which its Brazilian partner, the government-related Companhia Vale do Rio Doce, held just over 50%. The first is the Cellulose Nipo-Brasileira S. A. (Cenibra), capitalized at $163 million, and the second Empreendimentos Florestais S. A. (Flonibra), capitalized at $431 million.

Cenibra was to construct a pulp factory to use eucalyptus trees grown in existing forests in Mina Gerais state. But the raw material supply was inadequate and it was subsequently decided to plant more eucalyptus in Espirito Santo state which would also have a wood chip factory and a pulp factory, this one three times as large.

Alas, the Cenibra plant had teething troubles and it proved impossible to grow as much eucalyptus as planned for Flonibra. Worse, there was a worldwide oversupply in the late 1970s so Flonibra's wood chip production was temporarily postponed while Cenibra's pulp production became uprofitable. Meanwhile, costs had been escalating, both for equipment and especially land. To put things right, the initial funding of $1,649 million was considerably expanded and renewed efforts were made to rationalize operations. Even then, funds were running out and the Japanese partners began having serious misgivings about proceeding any further.

Electricity and ore are the crucial elements in refining aluminum, copper, zinc, lead and various other metals. Countries which possess both in abundance have naturally tried to move into processing. One of the more interesting projects is the huge copper smelter built in Leyte Province, Philippines, in 1983. It is one of the few major industrial projects the government managed to launch, but it does make sense and could stimulate regional development. The $350 million smelter should eventually be processing two-thirds of the country's copper production. It will also produce sulfuric acid to be used by a phosphate fertilizer plant nearby. And, if all goes well, a $200 million copper fabrication plant, one of the ASEAN industrial projects to be financed by Japan, will turn the copper into rods, sheets and bars. While the smelter was a brain child of the government, whose National Development Company is a main shareholder, 32% of the equity is held by Marubeni, Sumitomo and C. Itoh, who will be marketing much of the output.

Big as this is, it is still small compared to some of the aluminum ventures. The first was located along the Asahan River in Northern Sumatra. It will consist of two massive hydroelectric plants on the upper reaches of the river and a

huge aluminum smelter further downstream with a capacity of 225,000 tons a year. Although originally suggested
by a Japanese company back in 1967, and only taken up by
the Suharto government a few years later, it was ultimately
given top priority for Indonesia's second Five-Year Plan. It
was hoped that the project would upgrade the economy by
bolstering industry, mainly through processing national
resources (i. e. bauxite from another island) and by
providing cheap aluminum for local manufacturers. It
would create employment for as many as 10,000 workers
during construction and 2,000 when in operation. The fact
that it was being implemented in a somewhat neglected
area was an added reason, since the whole region would
benefit from the new infrastructure, roads, port, housing,
jobs, etc. Finally, since most of the aluminum would be
exported, this would bring in much needed foreign exchange and help finance the project.

The basic advantage was the cheap electricity of the
Asahan dam to refine the ore. However, while very promising at first, the whole scheme became less attractive as costs
rose swiftly and demand for aluminum slumped. In fact,
two American multinationals which were once quite interested pulled out and Japanese companies were a bit
hesitant to replace them. The preliminary studies therefore
dragged on and the project was only reactivated when
President Suharto obtained a pledge of Japanese financial
support from Prime Minister Tanaka during his visit to
Djakarta in January 1974. By July 1975, the Japanese
cabinet formally elevated this to a "national project" and
provided enough guarantees for the private sector to
proceed. A consortium of 5 aluminum companies and 7
trading companies was formed, thereby involving much of
the industry in the project. Moreover, the Overseas Economic Cooperation Fund became a major partner and huge
loans were provided by the Exim Bank and commercial

banks. In the end, the Japanese provided some 75% of the total investment and 90% of total loans. This made the stake in Indonesia Asahan Aluminum (Inalum) exceptionally high.

Unfortunately, prices kept rising and it soon became evident that the original cost estimate of ¥250 billion was much too low. In 1977, it was revised upward to ¥411 billion and it may well climb higher. This naturally caused some trepidation among the investors and the anxiety was only calmed by further assurances from both governments. To help ensure the viability of the smelter, the Indonesian government agreed to charge reasonable rates for electricity, the key cost in operation. It also decided to levy low taxes. In addition, most of the plant equipment orders were placed with Japanese firms, usually through the trading companies involved. Thus, the construction, which began in 1976, continued and a first phase was opened in 1982 with total completion scheduled for 1984. Meanwhile, much to the annoyance of the Japanese partners, the Indonesian government decided to handle the closely related operation of producing alumina itself. Since this would then be sold to Inalum, the smelter would be dependent on the alumina plant on Bintan island for its raw materials and the price would strongly affect its own profitability.

Although it was already involved in this exceptionally large project, Japan was being drawn into a second one in Brazil that was even more ambitious. This was expected to become the world's biggest complex producing 320,000 tons of aluminum and 800,000 tons of alumina a year by 1988. It is located near Belim in Para State and will derive its bauxite from the Amazon region which boasts the most extensive reserves and 80% of the alumina produced will go to the smelter. Low-cost electricity will come from the hydroelectric plant at Tucurui. This time, the proposal came from the Brazilian side and, while it was agreed that the project was viable, the Japanese investors were again fazed by the tremendous scale and immense costs involved. Not until September 1976, when President Ernesto Geisel visited Tokyo, was the project endorsed by a joint communique with Prime Minister Miki. The result was that an even broader consortium was formed among 32 smelters, banks, trading companies and aluminum users, in fact just about everyone interested in aluminum, which created the Nippon Amazon Aluminum Company (Nalco), 40% of whose equity came from the OECF. Nalco then took 49% of the two joint Brazilian-Japanese companies set up to operate the project, Alunorte for alumina and Albras for the smelter. The Brazilian partner was the state-run Companhia Vale do Rio Doce.

However, even before construction began and repeatedly thereafter, the Japanese investors were alarmed to find that the costs were escalating, largely due to rampant inflation. From the initial estimate of $1,364 million in 1976, it rose to $1,914 million in 1979 and may hit $3,000 million or more by completion. In face of these incredible overruns, some of the Japanese investors doubted that the project would remain viable and a few trading companies actually hinted at dropping the smelter part. But the Brazilian government offered further inducements and loans and revamped the project to enhance its profitability while the Japanese government accepted to provide additional assistance. Meanwhile, some Japanese companies were already benefiting through sales of plant and equipment. For a while the problems seemed to have been overcome. Then, in late 1982, the Japanese side agreed to suspend construction of the alumina plant due to Brazil's financial difficulties and a worldwide glut.

Despite two such massive projects, Japanese companies entered several more, most of them in the private sector.

They were located in Canada, the United States, Venezuela, New Zealand and Australia, with capacities ranging from 90,000 to 280,000 tons of aluminum a year. In these ventures, the Japanese held from 15% to 50% of the total equity and were presumed to be the major purchasers. Among the companies involved were Sumitomo, Mitsubishi, Mitsui, Kobe Steel, Nippon Light Metal, Showa, and YKK. These various projects presage a basic shift in Japan's aluminum industry from one where most of the metal is refined locally to one where only a third will come from domestic smelters, another third from joint ventures abroad, and the rest from imports.

The only other projects that can compare with these are being launched in the petrochemical sector. The most extraordinary one is the huge complex undertaken by the Mitsui Group at Bandar Khomeini in the Persian Gulf. Originally, Mitsui's interest had been oil development. In return for prospection rights to an area where, alas, no oil was found, in October 1971 it agreed to construct a major complex producing 300,000 tons of ethylene a year as well as polyethylene, polypropylene, and caustic soda. The leader was to be Mitsui & Co., the trading company, but four other group members joined to provide technical expertise or as ultimate purchasers, Mitsui Toatsu Chemicals, Mitsui Petrochemical, Toyo Soda and Japan Synthetic Rubber. Between them, they formed the Iran Chemical Development Co. (ICDC), with a capital of ¥74 billion. In April 1973, ICDC joined the Iranian National Petrochemical Co. in establishing the Iran-Japan Petrochemical Co. (IJPC), a 50–50 joint venture with a capital of ¥100 billion. Things were booming in Iran and the project moved ahead rapidly.

Then, most unexpectedly, the Shah was overthrown by the Iranian Revolution and an Islamic regime came to power in February 1979. Almost immediately, difficulties began cropping up including trouble with the workers and tension with the authorities as well as serious differences of opinion between the partners in IJPC. Although the plant was already 85% complete, work was interrupted or proceeded fitfully. Then, in late 1980, the Iran-Iraq war broke out and the unfinished plant was bombed repeatedly. Bad as this was, it only represented part of the problem. For, due to extensive delays and skyrocketing prices, the cost of the project kept rising. Initially estimated at ¥130 billion, it rose to ¥550 billion in 1975, and then ¥730 billion by 1979. If it were ever to be completed, it might run into ¥1,500 billion or more. At such a cost, the operation would never be profitable. Worse, even at the lower figures it was hardly viable. The basic idea was to use associated natural gas from the Abadan oil field. But this possibility was subsequently ruled out by the new Iranian government.

Although there was already no hope of profitability, and indeed little chance of completing the plant, the Mitsui Group had to continue payments for personnel and work that was going on and, more so, for substantial interest on loans made to it by various Japanese banks. These banks, with Mitsui's guarantee on occasion, had also made loans to the Iranian side. Thus, to meet the costs and keep the project afloat somewhat longer, Mitsui turned to the Japanese government. Whereas it had previously insisted on going it alone in a "private and independent" venture, now that it was in trouble it urged that the complex be upgraded to a "national project." To maintain decent relations with Iran, and to help Mitsui out, among other things, the government agreed in October 1979 and the OECF made an initial payment.

This increasingly looked like throwing good money in after the bad and the Japanese side steeled itself to break the noose. In mid-1981, the Mitsui Group said it would not put up any more funds although it was not going to withdraw from the project. By then, the Japanese had sunk ¥322 billion into the project. Yet, despite the strong words, ICDC kept advancing more money to IJPC and, by mid–1983, the Japanese investment had grown another ¥125 billion. Of the total, ¥185 billion came from the Exim Bank and OECF and the rest from the Japanese companies, most of it borrowed from commercial banks. The only positive sign then was that the Iranian government promised to finance the completion of the petrochemical complex. But the collapse of the long heralded "symbol of Japan-Iran friendship" and the related losses were extremely traumatic for the whole business community.

Nevertheless, or perhaps all the more eagerly because Mitsui's attempt had failed, a consortium of about sixty companies led by the Mitsubishi Group signed up for one of several petrochemical projects being promoted by Saudi Arabia in May 1981. This move grew out of a promise of cooperation made by Takeo Fukuda during a trip to Riyadh in 1978. The complex was to be located at Al Jubail on the Arabian Gulf and would hopefully go into oper- ation by 1985. The largest in the world, it should produce 500,000 tons of ethylene a year as well as ethylene glycol, polyethylene, etc. The feedstock would be nearby natural' gas. To this end, the Japanese investors formed a Saudi Petrochemical Development Company (SPDC) with a capital of ¥48.5 billion, 45% of which is held by the OECF. It in turn entered a joint venture with the Saudi Basic Industries Corporation which will provide 30% of the total investment of ¥330 billion, the rest being low-interest loans mainly from the Saudi government. This financial arrangement already limited Japan's risks and, having learned its lesson, Mitsubishi negotiated more guarantees into the contract. It also got Japanese government backing for what became a "national project." The only eventuality it could not cover, however, was the crucial one . . . the stability of the Saudi regime.

But this was not all. Back in May 1977, when Prime Minister Lee Kuan Yew visited Tokyo, the Japanese government agreed to support a petrochemical project in Singapore. A plant with an annual output of 300,000 tons of ethylene as well as several smaller plants for derivatives would be built on the island of Merbau. The Japanese side set up a Japan-Singapore Petrochemical Company (JSPC), capitalized at ¥10 billion with 30% coming from the OECF and the rest from 11 petrochemical firms, 3 trading companies and 4 commercial banks. JSPC then joined the Singapore government in the Petrochemical Corporation of Singapore (PCS) with a capital of ¥20 billion. But the total cost was estimated at ¥103 billion, of which ¥74 billion would come from Japan, most of it as loans and suppliers' credits. The same would apply for the three derivative plants expected to cost ¥78 billion.

The project progressed slowly, but far from surely. The main Japanese backer, Sumitomo Chemical, which initiated the joint venture with the Singapore government, decided it could not go it alone on the oil cracker due to difficulties arising from the oil crisis. It was therefore replaced by the broader JSPC and the complex was made a "national project." Then, in 1982, Mitsui Petrochemical withdrew from the ethylene glycol plant after the losses suffered in Iran. To keep the project moving, the Singapore government agreed to assume half the cost involved. But that was not the end of the trouble. Since the Merbau complex would use imported naphtha it could hardly compete against plants based on cheaper associated gas on what had become a very congested market. Sumitomo Chemical, fearing massive losses from the start, asked the Japanese government to increase its funding of JSPC and the Singapore government, through PCS, to raise its ownership from 50% to 75%. Still, in 1984, it was put into operation.

One reason the Singapore complex and the much larger one in Saudi Arabia were bound to encounter such a crowded market was that the Japanese, and others, were launching or participating in many other projects as well. Among them was the construction of a large petrochemical complex in Alaska to use the associated gas in the North Slope oil field, which attracted Mitsubishi Corporation and Mitsubishi Chemical. Along with Mitsubishi Petrochemical and Asahi Glass, they were also interested in a similar project in British Columbia. One group of chemical companies wanted to launch an ethylene dichloride plant in South Australia to get cheaper raw materials for their polyvinyl chloride while another group actually joined one in Alberta, Canada. Still, by the 1980s, the Japanese finally realized that there must be a limit and fewer projects were mooted while some formerly planned had to be discarded.

Facing Counter-Currents

That Japan has entered an increasing number of projects around the world, and that its total amount of investment in raw material sourcing keeps rising, should not blind us to the fact that this was not always easy and some of the difficulties have only grown with time. The problems have not even been as simple as sporadic revolutions or the sudden appearance of radical regimes. More significant are a number of broad and pervasive trends which are still spreading.

Often they spring from a mixture of economic and political causes, sometimes with a thick ideological overlay and deep emotional commitment, which make them very hard to counter. The most striking phenomenon of this sort has been the rise of economic nationalism and in particular natural resource nationalism. This has been strongest in many of the newly independent states which felt that they had been exploited by their former colonial masters and were extremely suspicious of those they needed to help them. But they were not the only ones. An eruption of this occurred in Australia, strongly infecting the trade unions and Labour Party, which completely ruled out many mining activities for a while.

The essential leitmotiv is that the country which possesses the raw materials or basic commodities is getting a bad deal. It is not paid enough for these precious resources which are assumed to be worth much more. One variation on this theme was developed by Raul Prebish and disseminated through UNCTAD to the effect that there was a long-term trend toward a degradation of the terms of trade. Not only were many basic commodities underpriced to begin with, they were steadily losing value in terms of the manufactured products or capital goods they could buy.

This has been heightened by the tardy realization that most natural resources are finite. They are non-renewable and once they have been sold they cannot be replenished. Although the country involved may need the money they bring in now, it may need the resources itself just as badly later on. This causes many to consider the alternative of leaving their ore or their oil in the ground. This tendency is reinforced by the expectation that the value of finite resources should increases as the supply shrinks. This offers a bonus for holding on to resources.

Obviously, it is not easy to determine the value of any good in abstract terms and the task is usually left to market forces. This solution, however, is not feasible when it comes to long-term projects where one must calculate well in advance the expected value of ores that may not be mined for years to come or a processing plant whose useful life runs into decades. Many things can happen in between to change their value. And investors also have to think of alternative uses of their capital.

In negotiating such projects, there is an almost endless range of values that can be set. The ore or oil is not worth anything until it has been discovered, mined and extracted, and then brought to the market. Depending on the supply and demand, it can be precious or superfluous by then. It is therefore not surprising that there should be more than slight differences of opinion among the owners and outside investors. And, no matter what the final decision is, there will be reasons for one side or the other to feel that it has not done as well as it might and to question the results.

Others will doubtlessly go much further and talk of rank exploitation. They question the whole concept of leaving the decision to the market (either the actual spot rate or an anticipated one). They insist that there cannot be fair bargaining between a relatively small and poor country, or the rather insignificant owners of mining properties, and the huge multinationals from the predatory imperialist nations. Not only are they stronger and more capable of waiting, and thus able to drive the price down. In many cases they form, with a few other multinationals, a cartel of sorts that fixes the price rather than letting it settle naturally.

It is impossible to judge these arguments abstractly. Doubtlessly, in many cases the multinationals actually are stronger. However, if they are in serious need of the material concerned to carry on their operations or are pitted against one another in competition, they can have a much weaker position than is claimed. Indeed, it often happens that a developing or resource country can, and will, play several multinationals off against one another. With OPEC, we have also seen that raw material suppliers can form cartels and in other cases are certainly influencing prices to their own advantage.

At any rate, the addition of extraneous political and

philosophical elements has not really helped either party. It makes it even harder to strike a deal by widening the gap between the sides and making too many decisions a question of principle and not practice. The result may well be that, rather than benefiting from its natural resources, the country simply cannot reach any agreement and they lie sterile. Due to overreactions when it later decides that perhaps it has been taken advantage of in the past (knowingly or by accident, since no one can really calculate future prices), it may resort to expropriation or nationalization. This very possibility reduces the chances of cooperation because the investors will see their risks rise sharply and hesitate in many more cases than before.

Another trend is more diffuse and, at first sight, does not seem to have as serious implications for investment. That is the general worldwide move toward conservationism in the broadest sense. This can imply simply cherishing and preserving nature or wishing to avoid unsightly, or dangerous, pollution. In their positive aspects, such goals are too attractive and inherently good to reject. However, as with anything else that becomes an ideology, they can go too far.

One side effect has been to rule out an increasing number of development projects which would have been permitted in earlier days. There are objections to developing oil shale in Wyoming, prospecting for oil off New England, or mining copper in Cebu, Philippines. Many forests are now protected and a campaign is directed against whaling. In other cases, the project would be permitted if the damage or disfigurement could be reduced or made up for. This can be done through underground mining, landscaping works, reforestation, and other techniques.

Whatever the outcome, whether the project is rejected or only allowed under restrictive conditions, there will be less investment than otherwise. While the second alternative does not exclude projects outright, by making the preparatory work, the infrastructural costs, or the clean-up tasks so onerous, the investors will have to reconsider the project. Sometimes, they will find that it is no longer commercially viable. As a matter of fact, there have not only been individual and sporadic examples of this but much broader trends. All countries which have introduced particularly strict conservationist or environmental codes have subsequently cut down substantially on mining and related activities.

The fact that so often it is the advanced countries which have already polluted their environment most, and thus been forced to adopt the strictest legislation, adds a further otherwise extraneous dimension. It is passionately argued in some quarters that one of the primary motives of investment at present is to "export pollution." There is no doubt that there has been much more willingness than before to process raw materials or commodities abroad, where they are produced, not for rational economic reasons but to avoid pollution back home. This additional incentive was created by the gap in environmental regulations.

But, this gap was not really the doing of the advanced countries. The backward ones are basically free to adopt any legislation they desire and can be as strict on pollution as anyone else. They may not do this because they are much poorer and desperately need the extra money that can be earned. They may also not do it because local industrialization still has not proceeded far enough to create major pollution hazards. Whatever the reason, raising this also to a matter of principle makes it harder to deal with than by considering the trade-offs. If economic development will imply some pollution, and it almost always does, which is more important: improved financial conditions and growth or a finer natural environment?

It is evident that some developing countries have chosen the former, although there are a fair number that have opted for the latter (often on the advice of outsiders) and a much larger contingent that want both and never make up their mind. It is only the former that are likely to launch the projects leading to international investment. But even they should be divided into two categories. Most engage in mining or processing largely at the behest of foreign interests that are eager to purchase their raw materials and accept to take them in processed form for economic reasons or to avoid pollution. Relatively few are really engaged in a conscious long-term policy of economic development.

This select group usually goes about dealing with investment in a relatively businesslike manner and rarely makes wild charges of exploitation or exporting pollution. It knows that there are certain counterparts to any assistance and they are generally accepted, even while trying to reduce the burden as much as possible. Applications for investment are screened more carefully and, rather than wait for the investors to come to them, the government often seeks out the kind of investment it wants and the best partners. Then it introduces a number of measures designed to move from raw material production to processing and ultimately manufacturing.

Much of this is done voluntarily. As we saw, there are many valid reasons for foreign companies to move into mining or prospection. Local processing may also be cheaper because of lower transport or labor costs, for some products due to cheaper energy costs as well. Otherwise incentives may be offered. Sometimes, however, more forceful measures are taken which push the investors in the desired direction. Quite simply, the government may prohibit the export of crude raw materials or insist that an increasing share be processed locally. Or it may go into processing itself either on its own or as the essential partner for foreign firms.

This scenario is far from theoretical and has occurred in various countries for various products. Many places which once provided tropical wood in log form have since gone over to demanding that it be exported as timber or turned into plywood. More countries are processing their agricultural commodities, such as coffee and cocoa, rubber, or jute. More and more lead, zinc and aluminum are being sold as ingots. The biggest shift is occuring with petrochemicals since oil producers can take advantage of cheaper naphtha or natural gas.

It is only a step further from processing to manufacturing. With cheap sources of plastic base material, there is no reason the more competent oil producers should not also begin making many articles they presently import. The aluminum, rather than just forming ingots, could be cast into more intricate products. Wood, which already fetches a high price abroad, can be fashioned into furniture locally. And so on down the line.

These various policies, unlike the more erratic movements first mentioned, frequently result in investment because they meet some needs of both the host country and the investors. Many of the projects are therefore carried out as joint ventures. But, even when the investors are less eager, more resolute governments have brought the necessary political pressure to bear. Others have just drawn on their earnings from raw materials to move further up or downstream on their own by acquiring the necessary plant, equipment, technologies and personnel. Indeed, some Arab oil producers are now trying to invest in Japanese oil refiners. Thus, certain countries do know what they want and how to get it and may well end up as major competitors in the future.

NOTES

1. Ministry of Finance, *Japan's Direct Overseas Investment,* 1983.
2. See Allen S. Whiting, *Siberian Development and East Asia.*
3. See Young, *The Sogo Shosha,* pp. 145–66.

5
The World Factory

Quest For Markets

Obviously, if Japan was going to import tremendous quantities of raw materials, as well as foodstuffs, and with affluence even luxury goods, it would be obliged to export considerable amounts of its own products to pay for them. This led it to seek more and more markets. It also led it to seek them ever more actively. For, if Japan ceased earning the wherewithal to pay for its basic inputs, it would be unable to keep its busy productive machinery running.

Since the Japanese usually do things with a vengeance, it is a bit hard to tell which comes first, the imports or the exports. When one considers the positive trade balance it has run so often in the past it would seem that it often put exports first, selling them as aggressively as it could and finding that in some years it had more than enough cash flow. Meanwhile, its population, and especially the businessmen, were hooked on the simplistic notion that Japan is a country poor in resources that must export to live. And, export they did!

Over the years, exports shot up at a terrific pace, rising from just $1 billion in 1950 to $130 billion in 1980. This was an extraordinary rate of expansion that far exceeded anything in the rest of the world. It gave Japan an ever larger share of total world trade, reaching something like 8% by 1980 although it was only 3% in 1950.

During this progression, it drew an increasing number of countries into its circle of trading partners. Foremost among them was the United States which took about a quarter of all exports. Asia as a whole absorbed a third. A goodly share of this went to its closest neighbors, Korea, Taiwan, Hong Kong, and Singapore. The rest of Southeast Asia also figured prominently. Exports to Europe were substantial and growing rapidly. Latin America, Africa and Oceania were more stagnant. Japan, which did not let politics get in the way of trade, also sold what it could to the Communist bloc, including both the Soviet Union and the People's Republic of China.

Given this large and growing trade with the outside world, the imports and even more the exports, Japanese companies made repeated investments in facilities and premises in foreign countries. This frequently started with a branch office and a rather minimal staff. But it gradually spread to other related items such as delivery vans and trucks, warehouses or other storage facilities, and sometimes shops and stores. The initial office might grow and several branches be established in different areas. And the sales network could expand from a staff at the main office to agents scattered around the country and even full-fledged dealerships for products like motorcycles, tractors and automobiles.

All of this was regarded as a valid contribution to expanding sales and maintaining relations with the distributors, retailers and also the final consumers. The offices could handle sales contacts and conclude deals, they could look for outlets or create their own, they could engage in any necessary advertising or public relations. They also arranged a myriad of incidental services such as sea, land and air transport, storage, insurance, and financing. Even prior to sales, they might scan the market, see what products were desirable, decide if existing products had to be altered, and look into problems that could arise from environmental, safety, or other regulations.

The Japanese investors came at different times. The first group to arrive were the trading companies. The biggest presence was naturally the major *sogo shosha*. But there were many more specialized trading houses as well. They formed advanced posts of a sort to scout the market and find promising opportunities. With time, they expanded and by now there is hardly a place where they are not active, including behind the "iron" and "bamboo curtains." Just the nine *sogo shosha* already have nearly a thousand offices in over two hundred cities. And they employ over 21,000 personnel in their overseas offices and subsidiaries, 15,000 of them locals.

The shipping companies were also among the pioneers of Japanese investment simply to have the necessary facilities in the places where their ships docked. As Japanese trade grew, and especially while they prospered in the 1960s, they opened more offices and acquired more operations. To handle this trade, insurance companies covering the related risks opened offices abroad. By the late 1970s, 14 non-life insurance companies were doing business in 26 countries. It was only later that life insurance companies made their appearance. For, this time, they could only succeed by gaining local customers in addition to the Japanese community. Their first real breakthrough came when Tokyo Marine & Fire, Japan's largest, acquired three subsidiaries from Equitable in 1980.

Some of the larger banks set up branches or representative offices abroad from the earliest days. They were gradually followed by smaller ones. By 1983, they had over 160 branches and 95 subsidiaries in dozens of countries and the network was growing rapidly. Gradually, while servicing their predominantly Japanese clientele, they made greater efforts to attract local customers. This was done by accepting deposits and granting loans, so as to create a real local presence. It also took a more vigorous form as Japanese banks bought into, or bought up, local banks. The trend started when Sumitomo Bank acquired some branches of the Bank of California and built up substantially when the Bank of Tokyo took a major share in the California First Bank.

While much less expansive, securities companies have also increasingly sold Japanese stocks and bonds to locals and launched Japanese issues abroad in addition to buying foreign securities for their customers back home. Some even entered the local stock exchange while many Japanese companies were listed abroad. With this, the Big Four—Nomura, Nikko, Daiwa, and Yamaichi—have created a very solid presence in Asia, America and Europe.

During the early period, most of the manufacturers left the bulk of the work, and the commissions, to the trading companies. This may have been because the actual sales were not adequate to warrant overseas offices or because they thought the trading companies were efficient and cheap enough. When sales in a given market rose sufficiently, the manufacturer might send some staff to get a feel for the market and have closer dealings with the customers, while leaving many of the formalities and services to the trading companies. However, beyond a certain point, some manufacturers felt that they could handle things as well themselves and proceeded to do so.

This arose particularly for certain types of companies. Obviously, the larger the company and the larger its sales, the easier it was to make the changeover. But this was more urgent for those companies whose products required considerable after-sales care to maintain their quality and keep the customers happy. Thus, producers of watches, cameras, sewing machines, etc. would have to set up repair shops in order to service their products and make the warranty meaningful. For motorcycles and automobiles, it was desirable to set up one's own chain of dealers as well as garages and service shops. Just how big an establishment could be is shown by the fact that the Japanese automakers had over 3,000 dealers in the United States alone by 1980.

Obviously, as soon as they had offices and staff for one purpose, there was a tendency to take over many of the other tasks. Gradually, major manufacturers established their own separate presence and looked after nearly all their own needs. They took care of shipping, warehousing, distribution and the like. They dealt with customers and studied the market to determine how best to shape their product line. They also kept an eye on the advertising and publicity. Although they were primarily manufacturers, sales were no less vital and thus much of the overseas activities were more commercial in nature than industrial.

While the trading companies and manufacturers quickly organized to sell their products, it was only late in the day that the major Japanese retailers have done the same. This includes some large department stores as well as chain stores. Names like Daimaru, Mitsukoshi, Isetan, Seibu, Tokyu and others quickly became known as places to shop for Japanese goods, and ultimately just about any product, in a growing number of countries. The first efforts were offshore in Asia, cities like Hong Kong and Singapore, where many customers were actually Japanese tourists. More recently, they reached such far distant shores as New York, London or Paris. While promoting Japanese exports, they have also begun selecting potential local products for sale back in Japan.

Meanwhile, there has been a growth in the services normally related to tourism. JAL, the national airline, and also ANA and TDA, the domestic airlines, have increased the number of their offices abroad. So have the travel agencies, first and foremost Japan Travel Bureau, as well as many second-line and eventually lesser ones. To cater to the Japanese tourists, hotel chains have not hesitated to put up huge hotels in leading destinations like Hawaii, Los Angeles, San Francisco, Paris and Amsterdam. Among the sponsors are the Prince, Okura, New Ohtani and sometimes JAL itself. More numerous, and proliferating rapidly, are the Japanese restaurants, whether of the traditional type or fast food places like the Yoshinoya "beef bowl" chain.

These various operations gradually added up. Cumulative commercial investment reached $8,482 million by 1982, investment in finance and insurance another $3,802 million, services hit $2,717 million and shipping $1,649 million, while real estate and the cost of establishing branch offices amounted to $2,163 million. All in all, this represented about 33% of Japan's total investment.[1] Nor should it be forgotten that much of the money included under manufacturing investment was actually intended for commercial purposes as opposed to actual production. Not surprisingly, the distribution of this investment geographically runs quite parallel to the share of the regions in Japan's trade, with the United States way out front.

Manufacturing For Money

From this it should be crystal clear that the primary thrust of the Japanese companies is to produce goods at home and subsequently export them. They do not hesitate to make whatever investments are necessary to facilitate the transfer of goods to the overseas markets, to improve the local distribution system, and to advertise and promote them on the spot. This already gives them a rather noticeable presence and a stake in the domestic economy. But there is no reason to assume that they wish to go any further in the direction of local production.

YKK Plant In Swaziland
Credit: Yoshida Kogyo

Manufacturing abroad is quite a different matter. It involves operations that are not just a continuation or an extension of what they have been doing in the past but a big leap into what for many Japanese is nothingness. Most would usually prefer increasing their market share gradually, selling more or different kinds of products, and growing with the economy (or a bit faster). Terribly few are actively seeking a new site for production.

Nevertheless, there are some advantages to shifting the production site elsewhere. Most of them arise out of normal economic motives. The most obvious is to save on transport. No matter how much the Japanese may cut costs, it is still much cheaper to move goods from a local factory than to ship them across the ocean and then land them in the foreign market before even feeding them into the distribution network. The amounts saved can be quite substantial for many products and especially those that are bulky, fragile, or perishable.

In just about every country there are a number of basic inputs that are cheaper than in Japan. Given the crowded and mountainous nature of the homeland, it is cheaper to acquire industrial land almost anywhere else in the world. It is also cheaper to obtain things like water, which can be required in large quantities by such industries as pulp and paper or metals. Frequently, the essential utilities, gas and electricity, are cheaper. Telephone and mail may also be so.

Crucial raw materials for processing or manufacturing are frequently cheaper as well. Thus, in the case of plastics and petrochemicals, there might be access to cheaper naphtha or associated natural gas. Since this also provides a base for synthetic fibers, cheaper textile goods could also be produced. In a similar manner, steelmakers could obtain cheaper coal and iron ore and aluminum smelters cheaper bauxite. Producers of processed foods might benefit from cheaper meats, vegetables and fruits. More specifically, soy sauce makers could get cheaper soybean and saké makers cheaper rice. Nearly all manufacturers would profit from cheaper energy.

In some of the countries, these cheaper inputs could be combined with cheaper labor. In the developing nations, basic wages are considerably lower than those in Japan and, even if workers show somewhat less diligence or lower productivity, the gap might remain. This labor would be ideal for garments, footwear or electronics. Even in the more advanced countries, the drawback of higher wages might be compensated for by greater education or specialized training. It would thus be possible to produce—or do basic research on—highly sophisticated pharmaceuticals or computer software.

Although not usually considered among the standard reasons for making investments, the question of exchange risks connot be neglected for Japanese companies. Over the past decade or so, the yen has kept on rising in value against most other currencies and, each time it rises, Japanese goods become more expensive. To sell abroad, the companies often have to cut costs and pare down their margins. More seriously, when prices are quoted in U. S. dollars, which frequently happens, the amount of money they receive after conversion into yen can be considerably less than what had been expected some months earlier when the deal was concluded.

To avoid making losses, and as a hedge against the often erratic fluctuations in exchange rates, it would be safer to produce locally. Production costs would then be in the same currency as the goods are sold for and more rational cost benefit estimates could be made. Moreover, since the trend has consistently been toward an appreciation of the yen, all of the cost advantages already mentioned would tend to increase with time. The higher the value of the yen, the relatively cheaper the raw materials, labor, energy, and so on. Thus, over the years, many Japanese companies kept reviewing the situation from time to time. Even if the cost advantages were not sufficient the first time they made the calculation, they might well turn out to be so some five or ten years later.

Aside from the advantages related to cost, there can be gains arising purely from the fact of a local presence. In some trades it is essential to follow the situation very closely and that can hardly be done from Tokyo or Osaka. Of course, a local agent might be able to inform the head office. But, where fashions or trends change rapidly, it can be better to do a degree of manufacturing locally and adapt some of it to specific needs. This is most evident for garments, where last year's designs are worthless. Makers of fabrics or accessories like zippers also have to know what is in the offing so as to come up with the right colors or qualities in time. Even producers of ball bearings find it necessary to know exactly what types are becoming popular.

In earlier days, the Japanese often found it advantageous to adopt protective coloration and make themselves more a part of the local scene so as not to appear too alien. That happened because Japanese products were then held in low esteem. Now that they are admired, and feared, it does not hurt either to become a "local" company quite simply by buying into another firm or setting up your own. One could hardly guess that Motor Iberica is largely owned by Nissan or that America Telecommunications is none other than Fujitsu. The customers of the California First Bank think of it as a neighborhood bank and not an emanation of the Bank of Tokyo. Going a step further, Fujitec, a leading maker of elevators, tried to Americanize by moving its headquarters from Osaka to New York City.

Finally, some companies have found that a local operation can also serve as a precious listening post or intelligence center. It can be used to monitor what is going on in competing firms and, on occasion, pick up key employees of such firms whose experience would be most useful. This has resulted in an "our man in Silicon Valley" syndrome, where Japanese companies recruit particularly talented engineers and research workers, paying them a considerably better wage, yet getting the accumulated knowledge they possess much cheaper than by going through the whole R & D process themselves. In a somewhat different vein, top Japanese designers have found it almost indispensable to move their headquarters to Paris, even if the bulk of the manufacturing and sales are done at home.

Despite all this, it was very far from certain that the natural advantages of local production would be sufficient. The drawbacks could be just as numerous and perhaps more telling. The biggest problem was quite simply the sheer size of the cost. An electronics factory could run into millions of dollars, a textile mill, tens of million, and an automobile plant, hundreds of millions. It was not every company which had that sort of money and Japanese companies were less able to finance such investment out of their own resources than most foreign firms. For, they were usually in debt to their banks and would have to pay substantial interest on whatever they borrowed to float a project.

Aside from purely cost matters, Japanese managers tended to shy away from manufacturing anywhere else than at home because that was the only economy they really understood well. Most of them had very little familiarity with how business was done in other countries and few enough even spoke a foreign language. It is not an easy thing to go through the investment formalities, establish a company, open offices and factories, recruit personnel, and finally—a few years later—market the mass of products coming on stream.

One particular worry was the quality of labor. This is even more important than the cost of labor since the Japanese management system is rather particular and its methods are unlike those applied in most other countries. Japanese managers did not really know how to handle labor whose customs and traditions were different. And they had trouble dealing with trade unions which were not also company unions.

Another specifically Japanese concern was the existence

of an adequate suppliers network such as they had built up with considerable patience back home. More than other manufacturers, the Japanese leave a considerable portion of the work to subcontractors and suppliers which provide as much as 50% to 70% of the parts while the lead company is engaged largely in assembly. Here, it is not only a question of getting parts of acceptable price and quality. Major Japanese companies also impose the tasks of quality control, on-time delivery, prior warehousing, etc. on their suppliers. If they were to have endless headaches in getting good suppliers, they would rather not go.

The final reason that argues against moving into local production is the painful fact that this will immediately decrease the exports of the home plants. The obvious purpose of import-substitution projects is to cut off foreign goods and the very companies that accept to produce locally will in this way be hurting themselves. It is conceivable that after some time this will be more than compensated by bigger sales in the local market. But, even if this actually does happen, it will be preceded by a period when exports simply slump and the advantages of local production are still outweighed by the drawbacks.

Impressed Into Manufacturing

No matter what the result of their calculation might be, Japanese companies were not always allowed the privilege of making their investment decisions purely on the basis of commercial considerations. Political pressure might be applied, directly or indirectly, and it could strongly influence the decision. This could take the form of "persuasion" which, as everyone knows, consists of fine moral arguments plus a latent threat. Or it could take the form of trade barriers such as tariffs and quotas. By raising the cost of imports, it would alter the selling price on the market (if they got in at all) in such a way that local production would suddenly become more attractive than before.

The Japanese have been faced with two waves of such maneuvers. The first came as early as the 1960s from the developing countries. The second was unleashed more recently by the advanced countries. Neither wave has completely rolled past and Japanese investors are still very conscious of the pressing appeals made to them to invest . . . or else.

The 1960s was the time when most of the former colonies obtained their independence and became acutely aware of the need for more rapid development. Development to them usually meant taking great strides toward industrialization. They were tired of being largely agricultural economies and annoyed by living off the sales of raw materials. They, too, wanted to produce their own manufactured goods rather than just import foreign articles. To this end, they put up tariff barriers or imposed quotas to protect "infant industries," whether or not they actually existed. They also offered incentives to companies that would manufacture their products locally rather than export them.

During the 1970s, the Japanese economy approached the peak of its power and began threatening even the older industrialized nations. Some of its exports overran their markets and destroyed national production. This started with textiles and garments, then moved onto televisions and cameras, and ultimately proceeded to such vital sectors as steel, shipbuilding and automobiles. In order to protect these industries, and the labor force employed in them, many advanced countries began putting up their own protective barriers. Due to a residual respect for free trade and various agreements that had been reached, the moves came either as an exception (temporary, in theory) to the GATT regulations or in the form of restraint by Japan itself.[2]

Whatever the method adopted, the Japanese were faced with a very constraining "invitation" to take up local production or accept that the market might be closed to them. For a company which had worked very hard to build up a clientele, and hopefully imagined that it could be expanded with time, this was a very painful choice. Certainly, it did not want to lose the sales. But it had definite doubts about local production and, although tariffs would make imported goods more expensive, the qualms were obviously not all overcome. If it felt optimistic about the country, it might take a chance. If it saw its competitors (especially other Japanese firms) starting local production, this would encourage it further. Yet, it was not under such conditions that it really wished to take this big step.

These "tariff-induced investments," that is the technical term for them, left the Japanese with a simple either-or decision, either produce locally or get out. In some cases, they were not really left much of an "or." Political pressure might be brought to bear to make them invest if they wanted to maintain proper relations with any partners they were tied to. They might have to invest for the sake of many other products they sold there or expect harassment and a worsening image. Or, in return for supplies of raw materials, they might have to install processing plants and manufacturing facilities to show that they were not just benefiting from natural resources but took a long-term view of the country's development.

Thus, one way or the other, a producer that would have been perfectly content to continue sending exports was "invited" to go over to manufacturing or processing. This could turn out to be a very good thing; it could also be a disaster. It all depended on the underlying economic factors which were always obscured and distorted in such cases. At any rate, rather than getting a foothold in the market, as the phrase so nicely goes, the investor actually got his finger caught and was pulled in further than desired.

When the foreign exporter is "persuaded" to set up a manufacturing facility, it usually tries to limit costs and go just a little bit of the way. This is possible in nearly every industry, albeit in different ways. For radios, TVs or cars, this can imply assembly of imported components or even assembly of prepared kits on a knock-down basis where the assembly work is really minor. For chemical or pharmaceutical firms, it is usually sufficient to make the gesture of producing a few articles in a vast range of products, and this perhaps from preweighed and presorted ingredients. For textiles, it may mean just weaving.

This is usually enough to keep the host country happy for some while. Then, it discovers that there is more to manufacturing than that and insists on taking another step. This may mean more complete assembly work or production of more articles in the range. Or it may be necessary to raise the "domestic content" of the product. In textiles, it may imply spinning as well as weaving. For electronics, it may become necessary to produce some of the components locally, and then some more. During the early phase, it was at least possible to continue importing the necessary base materials, parts and components, and intermediate goods. Now, most of these are restricted.

Alas, this passage is hardly gradual or painless. In many industries, when one integrates additional operations, each step can be more capital-intensive and therefore costly than the other. It also involves production which, if it is to be economical, must be in larger quantities, so large that it may not be justified by the market. It almost always entails greater skills among the work force although they may not have adjusted to simpler ones yet. Thus, if the investor tries to avoid or evade this, it is not necessarily due to ill will.

Radio or television assembly involves taking components, cheaply mass produced by or for the parent company, putting them on a stand and inserting that in a casing. It can be done easily and in rather small quantities. Components have to be produced in much larger quantities. Yet, even as rudimentary a product as a radio uses dozens of components, and a television set, hundreds. The actual production of all these components requires very substantial facilities. To be justified, a lot of radios or TVs must be sold. The technology is not simple. And quality control is crucial. More serious, faulty production of just one of the components could mean that the whole thing would not work and is unsalable. Why then should one be surprised if a foreign electronics firm dreads the thought of having to move from assembly to full production?

The textile sector offers a more interesting case. Often the first thing a developing country does is to restrict the import of fabrics, since it assumes such ordinary operations as weaving and dyeing should be handled locally. Once this has been accomplished, it may feel that spinning is also feasible, and persuade those who invested in the first phase to open a spinning plant as well. Then it pushes for further integration, insisting that the fiber making side be added. Just in case, it clamps down on fiber imports. While this is a logical progression, it must be remembered that weaving and dyeing are relatively simple processes compared to spinning and fiber making. Moreover, the equipment required is relatively cheap and can produce efficiently even for smaller quantities. Fiber plants are very sophisticated, extremely expensive, and only economical with a huge output. Passing from the first, to the second, to the third phase therefore requires more highly skilled labor, a larger market, and greater capital investment that escalates in a proportion of 1, to 5, to 24.[3]

These concerns are generally valid for all investors. For the Japanese, there is an additional complication arising from the fact that most assemblers are not also the producers of basic parts and components. The widespread practice of subcontracting means that a major company does not necessarily possess the essential expertise. It can, of course, work with local suppliers. But that would be a terrible blow to the suppliers back home which depend on it for their livelihood. And the Japanese government might object. The other alternative is to convince them to take up

YKK Plant In Holland

Credit: Yoshida Kogyo

production abroad as well. Yet, many of them are rather small companies and such a move could exceed their financial and managerial capabilities. In the end, only some are likely to come.

Despite the cost, effort, and risks involved, many host governments, especially in developing countries, have kept pushing their captive investors further. They have rarely listened to, or cared to believe, the explanations and protests. Sometimes they have lost, sometimes they have won... in the sense of getting the investor to go further. Whether they have won in any other sense will be dealt with later.

At each step, since the ante is raised considerably, the investor has to decide whether to insist and stay where he is, to put up more money, or to pull out. Withdrawing is easier said than done, since normally this means selling out and trying to get something for his original investment. But, in most developing countries, there are few likely buyers and he cannot get much. So, that alternative is often discarded unless things are really bad. Not moving ahead means attracting the enmity of the host government. It also means giving the competitors a vital chance. They may take over the budding market without a fight. And, if they are making the components or base materials, the investor may be forced to buy from his keenest rivals. So, that alternative is not good either unless the economic situation is seriously clouded. The remaining alternative of moving ahead may not be a welcome one... but it sometimes is the only real possibility given the circumstances.

In such ways, after letting them grab his finger, then the hand, and next the arm, before he knows it the investor is pulled in completely.

Export Or Exit

The Japanese companies, which had only wanted to sell their goods locally, then were obliged to commence production and gradually expand in quantity and degree, were frequently urged to take one more step. After progressing, on the local scene, from an importer to a producer, they were expected to become an exporter. This grew out of the gradual switch in development policies from import-substitution to export-promotion. It was by no means an unwise choice for countries which had already exhausted the more obvious possibilities of replacing imports or wanted a more dynamic industrial sector.

The logic to introducing exports was compelling. The industries concerned could expand production, increase specialization, and attain greater economies of scale. This would bring down the costs not only of exports but what was produced for the domestic market and thus combat inflation. For resource-poor countries like Korea or Taiwan, it was essential to boost exports merely to earn enough to buy the crucial imports to countinue their development. There was no need to explain this to Japan. It had gone over to exporting a long time ago for these very reasons.

Unfortunately, there were other less valid reasons pushing the developing (and some developed) countries in this direction. Many of them had become financially strapped due to the large amount of imports they accepted, whether capital goods for development or less essential consumer goods. Some had also contracted too many loans. Increasing exports was a good way of earning foreign exchange to pay for necessary inputs or reimburse loans. But they occasionally seemed to regard exports as intrinsically good, a proof that they had come of age (as once just having a factory was a sign of economic maturity). An automobile or ship exported was looked upon as being of greater worth than one sold locally, even when they had to subsidize exports and made less money out of it. This meant that a policy which did have merit could be distorted or pushed through in a way which emptied it of much of its value and created serious problems.

Moreover, no matter how logical and potentially beneficial this change in emphasis could be for the host country, there was absolutely no reason to assume that it was also attractive and convenient for the foreign investors. After all, they had predicated their original investment on the assumption of sales exclusively on the local market in most cases. This meant that they had chosen articles that were popular there, which could easily be produced using local labor and inputs, and which would be turned out in quantities implying a given size factory and suitable technologies. None of these aspects might be appropriate to the production of goods for export. Thus, the switch might require substantial changes and probably new injections of capital and technology.

In addition, many of the investments had not been made out of purely commercial considerations but to evade tariffs or other trade barriers. The original step was taken to get inside of the walls, not just to be able to sell but also because they protected any manufacturers in the country, local or foreign. Only because of them could operations which were less efficient and more costly than those at home be justified. In some cases, the protective walls were so high that they permitted a comfortable existence for all the manufacturers whether they were efficient or not. So, the goods were not very likely to be competitive as exports.

The swing toward exports therefore introduced many unexpected and unwanted factors in the equation. Among the imponderables, probably the most significant was where one could find markets. Since so many countries

were intent on industrialization, and since more protectionism had arisen for certain products, a lot of potential
markets were relatively closed. In addition, goods produced in more backward countries were sometimes not of
quite the same quality as those made in Japan and therefore
could only be sold at lower prices and with more difficulty.
Finally, for overseas operations that produced in small
quantities, the actual cost price might be too high to make
exporting profitable.

Over against this, there were obviously some reasons
that militated for exports. Among other things, it might be
possible to get a better price by selling on other markets.
This applied especially to the more affluent ones. By
increasing exports, it would be possible to attain greater
economies of scale or, more important to companies which
had misjudged local demand, to finally produce at closer to
capacity. Or, it would be possible to get around strict
currency regulations and channel some money back home,
particularly if the goods were sold to Japan or a country
with a convertible currency. Finally, there was also pressure from the trading companies, sometimes a partner or
at least an interested observer, whose main purpose was
commerce not manufacturing and which would be pleased
to handle exports.

These reasons were not usually enough to convince the
Japanese investors and turn the scales in favor of voluntary
compliance. (And some of the reasons were not truly in the
interest of the host country, either.) But it did not really
matter much what the outsiders thought once a determined
government had made up its mind. Thus, the greatest
annoyance was not even the change in policies but the way
they were imposed. Companies were rarely asked what they
wanted, or allowed to act in their own best interest, but told
what the authorities had decided was in everybody's best
interest.

The first indications of this policy shift arose in the provisions for making investments. Increasingly companies were only allowed in if they expected to export a given share of their output. This was written into the investment codes and sometimes the specific arrangements. Gradually, the required share of exports increased. In earlier days, many companies expected to do all their business locally, then they were urged to export at least a quarter, and sometimes more. Meanwhile, it was made harder to invest in the country itself and relatively easier to locate in the export processing zones where usually 100% had to be exported.

Elsewhere in the economy, subsidiaries or joint ventures that were operating like other local companies were subjected to the same general rules which placed emphasis on exports. They would be informed, like the others, that it was desirable—or obligatory—to sell 10% of their output abroad. Then the figure might be raised to 20%, 30%, or more. The incentives to do so varied. There was a good deal of moral persuasion and political pressure. Those which refused to obey might face administrative harassment or difficulty in obtaining import permits or bank loans. In certain countries, like Korea or Taiwan, there were also positive incentives such as special loans, favorable exchange rates, or subsidies, which made it much easier not only to comply but to succeed in exporting.

In some ways, by their very nature, multinational companies were the ideal vehicles for promoting exports. More than national companies, they had rather good contacts abroad. The larger MNCs had offices around the world and could check on any opportunities. They also had a head office in Japan which might be interested in some of the products. If they had, as they increasingly did, an international strategy, it would be possible to arrange sales between various subsidiaries and with the parent company.

They might actually develop an integrated production plan making use of various facilities. Even the smaller ventures were useful. Most had their own marketing setup back home. And many were actually subcontractors of larger companies they could supply.

But in other ways the foreign investors were bound to be more reluctant. After all, they often had not really wanted to produce abroad because this would cut into the exports from back home. Naturally, they were even less happy when they were informed that henceforth they had to export from their overseas plants. This meant that they would now be competing against the produce of the Japanese plants on third markets. If worst came to worst, they would also be competing against them on the home market.

Several different types of outlets were eventually found for these exports. One approach was to use offshore centers to export to their traditional markets. Japanese companies which were no longer competitive for labor or other reasons would shift production overseas and then sell to the same old markets in the United States or Europe. This tendency was reinforced as Japan became restricted by quotas, tariffs, and voluntary restraint. In order to get around these measures, its manufacturers set up bases in other countries. This path was known as following a "circular export strategy." Somewhat different were the triangular operations of the trading companies which bought goods in one foreign country for sale in another.

Another route was worked out within the large multinationals which tried to coordinate production in their various subsidiaries. If they had an overall strategy, this could be planned from the outset to the greater advantage of the company. Thus, an electronics firm might have different products made in different countries and sell them to one another. Or they could have different components made in different places and exchange them for assenbly in any or all of the sites. Big textile firms built their synthetic fiber plants and spinning mills large enough to supply the whole region. In some cases, this cross-hauling was purposeful both for the multinationals and the host countries. In others, it was merely a way of showing that they did export . . . although they may have imported as much or more in return.

What was surprising, however, was that so few of the Japanese investors thought of channelling their goods toward Japan itself. Obviously, if these same products could readily be sold in advanced countries of Europe and America, the quality must have been acceptable. The differences in costs of inputs such as labor or raw materials were roughly as great so the goods should have been price competitive. But there was definitely enough resistance within the Japanese companies and doubtlessly also the Japanese government to block this seemingly normal and direct path.

However, it did not take long for the developing and developed countries to notice the anomaly. It was highlighted by the increasing trade imbalances with Japan. They all purchased tremendous amounts of goods from Japan, the advanced countries largely consumer goods, the developing ones both consumer and capital goods. Yet, if they did not supply raw materials in return, they were constantly running a deficit. To cover this gap, they naturally called for more imports by Japan, and particularly imports of manufactured goods. The result was eventually to grant special tariff preferences to the developing countries within the Generalized System of Preferences and some minor consideration for the others.

Gradually, exports of these goods did rise. But the growth was nowhere near as rapid as hoped. And most of the manufactured products came from plants owned and operated by Japanese firms. Still, even those plants found it easier to export to third countries than to the one which had invested in them. For example, in Korea's Masan export processing zone, whereas the Japanese provided the bulk of the investment the bulk of the shipments went to the United States and Europe.

The World Factory Expands

One way or the other, Japanese manufacturers decided— or were persuaded—to make increasing amounts of investment in other countries. While industrial investment tended to lag behind commercial or raw material-related investment in the earlier period, it began catching up once much of Japan's own industrial plant was in place by the 1960s. By now, it outstrips both of them with some $16,952 million in all which represents about a third of total investment.

This investment is spread over a broad range of sectors, from light to heavy industry. But there are a number of headings which are particularly prominent. Among them are textiles with 11% of total manufacturing investment, electrical machinery and electronics with 14%, and transportation equipment (motorcycles, automobiles, trucks) with 11%. These items, however, are exceeded by two groups in heavy industry. Chemicals (mainly petrochemicals) account for 19% and iron and steel and nonferrous metals account for another 21%. Aside from that, there are lesser items like foodstuffs, timber and pulp, and machinery.

While the amounts of investment give us some idea of the priorities, quite another order arises when one looks at the number of individual investments. Then some of the items are reversed. Despite their huge value, chemical projects are much less numerous than those for textiles, at 1,015, while iron and steel are just a bit ahead. Electrical and electronics projects come at the top of the list with 1,375. The discrepancy arises because the average amount of investment per project varies so much from one sector to the next. It starts with a low of $0.9 million for foodstuffs, rises to $1.7 million for electrical and electronics and $1.8 million for textiles, peaking at $3.1 million for chemicals and then $5.7 million for transportation.[4]

These investments are rather broadly spread. But there is no doubt that Asia is well ahead for both the number of projects and the value, 4,943 and $5,800 million. Even the second and third largest sites, North America and Latin America, only run into three-quarters and half that amount. The others follow behind. It is, however, interesting to note that some regions are more, or less, represented than one might initially expect. Latin America long exceeded North America, a far more industrialized region, partly due to investment in several major projects. But North America recently moved ahead. Europe was rather neglected until lately and it can also be expected to rise in position. The Middle East has obtained substantial investment, but very few projects, because of the emphasis on petrochemicals.

One rather striking thing about Japanese investment in manufacturing has been the relative willingness of the investors to accept only partial ownership and to permit, or actually seek out, joint ventures. This is unusual when judged by the practices of American or European multinationals with their emphasis on 100% control. But it even stands out when compared to Japanese investment in other sectors. Whereas the average ratio of Japanese equity for manufacturing is only 61%, it is several percent higher for mining or agriculture and an average of 85% for commerce. Among the industrial sectors, the ratio is somewhat higher for general, electrical, and precision machinery and somewhat lower for textiles, chemicals and iron and steel.

There are two basic reasons for this. One is that some Japanese firms are quite happy to enter a joint venture either because they lack the industrial expertise or don't have the marketing connections. Trading companies are in the former category; small Japanese manufacturers in the latter. There is also a general tendency among those which are new to investment to feel more comfortable with a local partner. Old-timers, however, usually prefer to go it alone or maintain at least 51% control, including companies like Bridgestone, Sony, Honda or YKK. The other reason is much simpler. By the time many Japanese companies launched their projects, there were already stipulations in the investment code and laws in the book which prohibited full or even majority ownership and it was obligatory to have partners.

The requirement of accepting local participation also goes far toward explaining some other seemingly strange practices. While it is understandable that the host government should want Japanese investors to take on local partners, this rule sometimes ignored the prevailing circumstances. Often, especially in developing countries, there were not very many qualified entrepreneurs who had any expertise in what was either a new sector or at least a more sophisticated operation in a known one. And very few of them possessed the sort of money a partner should provide. So, to comply with the law, the Japanese tended to turn former agents or distributors into partners or bring in some prominent, well-placed citizen. In other cases, they tied up with a semi-governmental agency or state bank. But they still had to make up for any failings in these partners by handling more than their share of the commercial functions or actually lending money to the joint venture and sometimes the partner as well.

This kind of requirement is much less frequent in

Ishibras Shipyard In Brazil
Credit: IHI

advanced countries. But there is another anomaly, as far as most students of investment are concerned, in that the Japanese have a very strong preference for setting up their own companies rather than acquiring going concerns. This can best be explained on psychological, rather than economic, grounds. Japanese managers usually want to instill deep loyalty in their personnel and create a specific type of worker. They also wish to have their orders applied pretty much like they are back home. And, they often have rather little respect for the quality and productivity of whatever companies they find locally. It is therefore best, they feel, to turn a new page and hire workers fresh off. Then they can run things the way they want with less fear that the old way of doing things will intrude.

Increasingly, however, they have come to realize the value of acquisition. While most Japanese electronics companies made fresh ventures in the United States, others acquired existing companies as for Matsushita which absorbed Motorola's television division, NEC which picked up Electronic Arrays in Silicon Valley, and Bridgestone which took over a factory from Firestone. More of this sort of thing can be expected in the future. For, the new company may thereby appear as an old established one and enjoy the advantages of a local reputation. It will also start off with a working factory, a trained staff, experienced suppliers and an effective distribution network. As for the nasty old habits, the new owner can always change the machinery, replace the personnel, or alter the marketing channels if it wishes.

Straightforward investment has also given way to some novel methods of late. For example, some Japanese companies have been going into co-production rather than their own operation or a joint venture. This is almost inevitable in dealing with the People's Republic of China, whose low-cost labor force is very tempting. Through compensatory trade, Japanese firms have provided Chinese companies with machinery and materials and received the finished products in return, a certain quantity of labor or goods being regarded as compensation for the inputs. For example, in one case the trading company Itoman exchanged sewing machines for pajamas.[5] Even more intriguing variations arose, this time in the West, when Japanese automakers allowed nominally foreign competitors to manufacture vehicles designed by them, as for Honda and British Leyland or Toyota and General Motors. This was much more than mere licensing and far less than actual production, the two usual alternatives.

These methods have their advantages and drawbacks. For the investor, there is no need to provide capital, although he certainly transfers assets worth money to others, such as machinery, raw materials, parts, designs and knowhow. It is also possible to avoid direct involvement in running the production facilities, recruiting, training and supervising the workers, marketing the goods, and so on. Thus, the risk is much smaller than in a normal investment. But, so are the possibilities of control and chances of exceptional gains.

Although it is not investment by any means, it is still necessary to consider a process that has been growing over the years because it frequently replaces investment. It also accomplishes some of the same goals sought by host countries and implies some similar cooperation from the outside partner. That is the trend toward purchasing turnkey factories and even larger projects in many developing countries or advanced ones. This arises especially where the country has adequate funds, or can borrow them, and does not want an extended foreign presence. Major sites for this are the Middle East and some particularly dynamic developing countries.

The scope of such activities can be judged from the vast increase in sales of plant, equipment and technology which have been growing by 20% and 30% a year, faster than most other exports. By 1982, the value of such plant and equipment hit $13.4 billion, only a small portion of which was delivered within the framework of Japanese investment. The bulk was provided to customers which wished to go it alone.

Producing Almost Everything

While the overall figures for investment can give a general idea of where projects are located and what sectors are most popular, they shed little light on more important matters like how projects were chosen and why. This takes some extrapolation and also a closer look at the actual ventures. Those dealt with here do not include pulp and paper, petrochemicals or aluminum smelting which, although manufacturing sectors, are conceptually more closely related to the processing of raw materials.

Among the first industries to attract investment were textiles. This occurred for several reasons, the most salient being the advantages of using low-cost labor in certain branches and the strong desire of many developing countries to initiate their industrialization there. This resulted in a combination of incentives for Japanese companies that would cooperate, some of them economic, others more political, since the only way they could maintain a presence was to go along with the host government's policy. During the late 1960s, many textile companies set up subsidiaries to handle their flourishing trade and, when tariffs or quotas seemed likely to wipe that out, they often agreed to go over to actual production.

The first major step was to establish weaving operations, still using imported yarn. But this phase did not last long as the host government urged that spinning mills be established and some local entrepreneurs were already entering that branch. In response to this, Toyobo, Unitaka, Kanebo, Chori and others launched dozens of ventures in a broad range of countries, most of them developing. But it was not long before the host government became fascinated with the possibility of synthetic fiber production and pushed for such plants as well. Again, these and other companies responded, but with some initial hesitation since the capital outlay was very high and they were not certain if the market was large enough to sustain them. The result was fewer units somewhat more strategically placed by such leading makers as Toray and Teijin.[6]

Much of this investment took place during the 1970s, passing through several distinct phases, and moods, in this short period. There was a sharp rise in investment during the early part, when the world economy was expanding and textile manufacturers felt optimistic about making their

new subsidiaries a success. The level of investment remained high right after the oil crisis, although the basic
economics of the fiber industry were progressively undermined by rising raw material costs. The encroaching
worldwide recession, and intense competition among too
many textile producing nations with too much domestic
capacity, also brought hard times to many ventures. By the
end of the decade there was little eagerness to expand
overseas operations and the weaker ones were being
rationalized or liquidated.

The next major industry to see a proliferation of overseas
ventures was electronics. Given the diversity of products in
this field, however, there have been even more phases and
greater variety in the techniques applied. The first, and still
ongoing shift, was to move labor-intensive operations to
the many "cheap labor" countries near Japan. Most prominent were Taiwan, Korea, Hong Kong and Singapore.
They were later joined by the Philippines, Thailand and
Malaysia. One side of this has been to produce a vast array
of parts and components for one article or another since
often the quantities needed were relatively small and did
not justify production in more advanced factories back
home, which became largely assembly plants. Many of the
parts suppliers abroad were thus subsidiaries of leading
suppliers or assemblers in Japan, although increasingly
local ones sprang up. The other side, once manufacturing
such articles ceased being much of a secret, was to have
assembly done abroad. This was partly to benefit from
lower labor costs again, but even more to get around the
tariffs and quotas aimed specifically at Japan. Gradually,
these latter motives have lost some of their validity as trade
barriers were erected against the newly industrialized
countries as well and their own labor costs kept rising.[7]

Most of this production was limited to consumer goods
including televisions (monochrome and color), record

players, stereo and other audio equipment, radios and radio-cassettes. For such items, Japanese investment provided a major impetus and, along with American and other investment, accounted for the bulk of production and an even larger share of exports of certain East Asian countries. At the same time, offshore production rose to the point that, by 1980, nearly a fifth of the total output of Japan's consumer electronics makers was actually accomplished abroad.

Japan's preferred tactic of exporting and, when forced by trade barriers, switching to offshore production, only worked so long. By the early 1970s, the United States was complaining about a mounting tide of television imports with foreign TVs gradually exceeding domestic production. To save its makers, the American government finally imposed quotas on Japan, then Korea and Taiwan. With this, another tactic was tried. It originated already in 1972, when Sony opened its television factory in San Diego. By the end of the decade, all the leading Japanese makers were producing locally, Matsushita in premises bought from Motorola and Sanyo in a former Warwick factory, and Mitsubishi, Toshiba, Sharp and Hitachi in brand-new plants of their own.

While the flood of television imports receded, the American makers found local competition from the Japanese even tougher. They had better quality products, better production techniques, and incorporated more cheap imported components, giving them a definite edge. Thus, the Japanese makers reinvigorated the industry while squeezing the Americans out. Altogether, Japanese "made-in-America" TV sets won about a third of the market, with another third going to imports and the rest held by American makers. Meanwhile, they began repeating the same exploit in Europe, starting with Great Britain and then moving into Germany, France and other markets.[8]

Trade friction was also at the root of later waves of investment in the advanced countries. To avoid tariffs or quotas, and perhaps outright prohibitions, one consumer product after another was introduced by makers such as Sharp, Matsushita, Sanyo and Toshiba, which opened factories to produce microwave ovens and other articles. When Japanese companies launched sales of video tape recorders, the reaction was exceptionally hostile and the only way to defuse complaints was to take up domestic production. Within a matter of years dozens of joint ventures, tie-ups and licensing agreements were reached in the United States and most Europeran countries. Among the major advances were factories by Sanyo, JVC and Mitsubishi in Britain and Sony, Hitachi, JVC and Matsushita (with Bosch) in Germany.

The computer industry, and related semiconductor production, proved even more sensitive. To avoid provoking another trade war, the top semiconductor makers started production in the United States in the late 1970s. The move was taken by NEC, Hitachi, Fujitsu and Toshiba, among others, either by acquiring a local company or creating their own operation. But these makers were not only interested in the American market. They were strongly attracted by the excellent engineers and scientists they could recruit and who proved useful for R & D and even more vital to create suitable software. Thus, research centers and design offices were opened by NEC, Toshiba, Fujitsu, Oki, Omron, Sony, Ricoh and many others.

For some of the same reasons, Japanese machine tool manufacturers began expanding overseas production. Some of the most advanced took the lead. Yamazaki Machinery Works, known for its "flexible manufacturing system," set up factories in the United States and Britain and decided to establish its most modern facility for making NC machine tools in Kentucky. Fanuc, a top maker of numerical control systems, agreed to build the world's most automated factory (run by only three people) in Luxembourg. Meanwhile, Makino Milling entered the market by acquiring Le Brond Machine Tool of Cincinnati and Toyoda formed a tie-up with Bendix. Robot manufacturers also decided it was wiser to go into joint ventures although no specific conflicts had yet arisen. The pathbreaking agreement was between Fujitsu Fanuc and General Motors.

While ball bearing makers had to worry about trade friction, a more significant cause of investment was to be near their customers. Only in that way could they follow the trends and adapt quickly to needs. The step, however, was greatly facilitated by clever production techniques which allowed them to set up very small, yet efficient, facilities. Among those most prominent in this sector were Koyo Seiko, Nippon Miniature Bearing and Nachi-Fujikoshi.

Investments were made in various other branches of light industry. Camera makers invested largely in overseas sales outlets but also had some production facilities, largely in East Asia and for the purpose of using qualified but cheaper labor. Manufacturers of sewing machines, like Janome amd Maruzen, had a few ventures in Asia for similar reasons or to skirt European tariffs. But the most impressive investor was somewhat unexpected, Yoshida Kogyo (YKK). Japan's largest zipper maker, with 90% of the domestic market already, naturally had no place to expand but abroad. Its primary advantages, like the bearing makers, were highly sophisticated manufacturing techniques and the ability to establish a manufacturing unit of nearly any size, from small to large, that could meet the needs of a given market. Even more than the bearing makers, YKK found it necessary to keep abreast of rapidly changing fashions.[9]

Yet less expected, but exemplary in some ways, were several ventures in processed foods. Ajinomoto, a top producer, runs a dozen factories abroad to make mono-sodium glutamate seasoning. It also makes fats and oils, amino acids, and instant noodles. Nissin Food is another producer of instant noodles in America, Europe, Singapore and Brazil. Ozeki, a small saké company, tied up with San Benito in California to make this alien brew. And Kik-koman, the leading maker of soy sauce, opened its plant in Wisconsin in 1972. A major purpose of some ventures was to use cheaper local raw materials such as wheat or soybean, which was essential to bring prices down. But, to sell more than modest quantities, they had to make a tremendous effort at cultivating a taste among the local population, an effort which would seem to have succeeded.

There are few industries in which overseas investment makes as little sense as transportation machinery. Auto-mobiles, trucks and even motorcycles incorporate an incredible number of parts, all of which must be strong and flawless not only for the vehicle to work but to avoid serious accidents. The assembly operations then require a very large scale to be efficient and profitable. For auto-mobiles, 100,000 units is often regarded as the minimum efficient output. This means that there are exceptionally few places where Japanese companies could hope to create successful ventures. In the developing countries, there are insufficient parts suppliers, and those that exist may be of insufficient quality. Few new nations have a large enough market either since, even when they have a huge pop-ulation, the purchasing power is too small to make many people potential buyers. In the advanced countries, where suppliers and customers do exist, there are already established competitors vying for the business. The Japanese much preferred expanding their own factories to produce additional units for export.

But free and unhampered trade turned out to be a vanishing alternative. More and more, governments around the world imposed barriers or regulations that forced the Japanese to invest. The first round of projects was launched in the Third World where, after trying industrialization with simpler products like textiles or televisions, many countries became more ambitious. They also objected to the drain on their limited foreign exchange caused by vehicle imports. While most admitted that they could not make a car or truck, they did feel that motorcycles were more in their reach and Honda, Suzuki and Yamaha were induced to assemble some units locally. Automobile assembly later became a growing fad. To meet this demand, Toyota, Nissan, Honda and the others opened literally dozens of small plants to put together knock-down kits that had been specially prepared at the home factory. Even while sales of finished vehicles stagnated, KD sales rose. Most of these operations were in Asia, but they also existed in Latin America and Africa. Only in Korea and Taiwan were the local industries ready to tackle full production. In Korea, Hyundai brought Mitsubishi in as a junior partner. In Taiwan, Toyota beat Nissan in a tight contest to be selected as the partner in a joint venture with state-run China Steel that would ultimately produce some 300,000 compact cars a year.

By the late 1970s, many Western countries found that Japan was too strong a competitor and imported motorcycles and automobiles swamped the market, weakening and sometimes destroying the local manufacturers. They too urged the Japanese to invest locally. But they did not even offer the basic advantage of developing countries, namely cheaper labor. And most governments were not willing to provide special loans or protection during the initial phase. Worse, what was expected of the Japanese was not merely assembly but full-scale production with the bulk of the parts procured from local suppliers. Here, there were problems of cost and quality. Thus, most of the Japanese makers resisted as long as they could. Only Honda, a smaller and more outward-oriented company, took up the challenge on its own, voluntarily building an automobile plant near its existing motorcyle facility in Ohio. Nissan decided to make pickup trucks in Tennessee after a 25% duty was levied on cab chassis. Toyota, despite considerable pressure to invest, held out even longer. It adamantly refused to be pressed into automobile production in a country where, in addition to the various cost factors, it was suspicious of the labor force.

Nevertheless, the 1980s were bound to witness many more ventures of one sort or another. For motorcyles, there was a sudden burst of tie-ups, Honda and Peugeot and Yamaha and Motobecane in France, Suzuki and Puch in Austria, Yamaha and Acermex in Mexico, and more overseas assembly than ever. For automobiles, Honda led the way again, through its tie-up with British Leyland. Nissan finally agreed to build a small assembly plant in Britain. And it was cooperating with Alfa Romeo in Italy and Motor Iberica in Spain. Even Suzuki formed a joint venture in India and Pakistan. Finally realizing that it was going against the current, Toyota entered negotiations with Ford and, when they failed, General Motors. The result was a tie-up in which they would produce one of its models for the American market.

It is not hard to imagine why the Japanese makers hesitated. The sheer cost of a major facility was enough to faze all but the hardiest. Honda's automobile plant in Ohio was expected to cost $250 million, Nissan's truck plant in

Tennessee, $660 million, and Toyota expected to put up about $250 million as its share in the Taiwan joint venture while the whole project, including investment in necessary satellite industries, could amount to well over $1,000 million for all concerned. That will explain why so much imagination was shown in seeking compromise solutions. Thus, Honda simply licensed a first model to BL before agreeing to jointly develop and manufacture the next. And Toyota preferred a joint venture with GM to opening its own plant. In such cases, the Japanese company provided designs, various parts and components, and technical assistance and advice. But the basic responsibility for running the factory, hiring and supervising workers, and selling the completed vehicles remained largely with the foreign partner.

Another cause for concern among Japanese investors was the quality of local parts, this more even than cost. Realizing that the domestically produced vehicles would not sell well if there were too many defects, and that would hurt the image of their exports as well, they were worried about the suppliers they would find. Meanwhile their customary suppliers in Japan realized that these overseas ventures would deprive them of work which might just be compensated for by launching their own overseas operations. Thus, the vendors began migrating in the wake of the major assemblers. Among them were Sankei Giken (mufflers), Tokyo Seat, and Stanley (electrical parts), related to Honda, Atsugi (motor parts), Nihon Radiator and Kinugawa Rubber, related to Nissan, Akebono Break and Daikin (clutches). Bridgestone, the top tire manufacturer, also joined the move with plants in Taiwan, Thailand, Indonesia, Australia, Iran and, finally making a big leap, the United States. Soon, the Japanese would be able to rely on their own "families" of suppliers abroad as well.

There was considerably less investment in the shipbuilding sector, although Japan quickly rose to the top position. Most of the shipyards were too interested in expansion at home during the boom, and short of funds when the bust came, to think of overseas ventures. The sole exception was Ishikawajima-Harima Heavy Industries (IHI) which is the second largest and seemed eager to expand its capacity in this way. As early as 1959, it established Ishikawajima do Brasil (Ishibras) in which it held 95%, the rest going to the Brazilian government. Much later, in 1977, it bought into a ship repair company, also in Rio de Janeiro. Meanwhile, in 1963, IHI became involved in the Jurong Shipyard, a project with strong backing from Lee Kuan Yew, in which it took 51% equity while the Singapore government financed the rest. Since then, the bulk of the ownership was transferred to the government and local interests. The size of these operations can be imagined by noting that Ishibras employs some 7,000 personnel while Jurong has about 2,400.

Few sectors attracted quite as much investment as iron and steel. Yet, given the vast size and cost of most installations, the efforts were concentrated on just a few major projects. The first came at an amazingly early date, making it one of Japan's earliest experiments in construction of overseas plants, transfer of advanced technologies, and also economic cooperation with a foreign government. It is perhaps for that reason, namely to show that it could be done, that the venture actually got started. The idea of using the massive iron ore resources of Minas Gerais state seems to have impressed the Japanese steelmakers as much as the Brazilian government when it was mooted in 1956. Only a year later, the Japanese cabinet agreed to provide governmental assistance and a group of 6 steelmakers, 25 machinery and electric equipment makers, 6 trading companies, and 12 city banks formed Nippon

Usiminas Co., providing 62% of the ¥30 billion capital while the Overseas Economic Cooperation Fund put up the rest.

This company then went into a joint venture with the Brazilians, particularly the Banco Nacional de Desenvolvimento Economico and the state steel corporation, Siderbras. The firm was named Usinas Siderurgicas de Minas Gerais (Usiminas) and capitalized at 7.7 billion cruzeiros. Nippon Usiminas initially held 40% of the capital but this was gradually reduced to about 20%. Total investment in the project has amounted to some $2.2 billion. For this, the Japanese cooperated financially to the extent of ¥175.7 billion, with ¥34.2 billion invested by Nippon Usiminas and ¥141.5 billion in suppliers' and buyers' credits. Part of this was put into the purchase of equipment or payment of engineering work provided by the suppliers and contractors, led by Nippon Steel and Nippon Kokan.

The original steel mill, whose construction began in 1958, was reasonably modest with a capacity of 500,000 tons of crude steel a year. It was finished in 1962. But, in 1965, it was decided to create an integrated steel-production system. Then it went through a three-stage expansion as of 1974 bringing it to a total capacity of 3.5 million tons. This made it the country's largest and capable of handling over 20% of Brazil's total needs. During the earlier period, the steel mill was not really profitable. However, as the economy expanded and the second and third blast furnaces were added, it was able to do reasonably well and there was even talk of another expansion to double existing capacity.

Despite the fact that Japan had invested so much in this huge showcase project, it was gradually drawn into a second major steelmaking venture. This was clearly the work of Kawasaki Steel and its trading company, Maru-

beni, which were only allotted a very small role in the
Usiminas project. In 1973, they sent a team to Brazil to
look for partners for a modest steelworks but met with little
success at first. However, even then the Brazilian government was thinking of another huge steel project, one that
might eventually be nearly twice the size of Usiminas.
When it first came on stream, the steel mill would have an
already impressive capacity of 3 million tons of crude steel
a year. During a second stage, this would be raised to 6.8
million tons, making it one of the largest in the world. It
would be located in Tubarao, Espirito Santo state.

The Brazilian government was delighted to find such
eager investors and quickly reached an agreement with
Kawasaki, a shipbuilding company and 12 trading firms. It
also brought in Finsider an Italian steel and financing
corporation and, on the Brazilian side, Siderbras. Together, they formed the Companhia Siderurgica de Tubarao (CST), in which Brazil held 51% of the equity and the
foreign partners 24.5% each. The financial arrangements
worked out at that time seemed reasonable. Then the oil
crisis struck and the costs of plant and equipment shot up.
A project estimated at $900 million was revised to $2,000
million and then pegged at a total cost of $3,047 million
(although it might eventually hit $3,400 million). Of this,
the Japanese side was expected to provide $761 million,
including a $167 million investment in CST, $90 million in
loans and $504 million in suppliers' credits. Meanwhile, the
Japanese government was persuaded to extend a $100
million loan to build the nearby port.[10]

While this massive cost overrun would probably have
halted a purely commercial undertaking, there was little
doubt that the Tubarao project would proceed given the
strong political backing. In September 1976, during his
visit to Tokyo, President Ernesto Geisel obtained the full
support of the Japanese cabinet. Moreover, the Brazilian

government promised to supply the essential infrastructure and offered various fiscal incentives and other benefits. Still, there was some hesitation on the Japanese side while new studies were made. Although they apparently showed that the potential was great enough to justify the effort, it was only decided to go ahead with the project two years later. And the actual construction did not begin until June 1980. Although scheduled for completion by December 1982, this proved impossible as new problems cropped up including Brazil's failure to build the port on time, Italy's delay in delivering some equipment, and especially Siderbras' difficulty in obtaining financing. Worse, it turned out that domestic steel demand had not increased as much as anticipated making it unnecessary to hasten construction of the first stage and even more dubious that the second would be launched very soon.

Building the Tubarao Steel Complex

Credit: Kawasaki Steel

Given the tremendous cost of these projects, and the unpleasant complications that could arise, the Japanese government has become considerably more reluctant to take up new offers. The steelmakers have also tried to avoid actual investment, much preferring to provide equipment or knowhow and get paid for that. Thus, there was little interest in a further extension of Usiminas. When pressed by Argentina to invest $200 million in the Somisa project, this was whittled down to $50 million, and then dropped after the Falkland war. But Prime Minister Ohira could not really turn down a potential oil supplier like Mexico when it asked for participation in a plan to develop its steel industry. Still, while Japan was willing to offer about $1 billion in aid, the steelmakers involved only provided some of the installations and kept their exposure low. For the Philippines industrialization project of a $1.9 billion integrated steel plant in Mindanao, the Japanese were eager to sell equipment but not to invest in what was hardly regarded as a profitable venture.

If anything, they showed more interest in cooperation with an industrialized nation like the United States. They entered a series of tie-ups and technical agreements with leading steelmakers such as those between Nippon Steel and Armco or Kawasaki and Bethlehem. Then they became hardier, trying to buy equity in existing companies. Negotiations between Nippon Kokan and Kaiser, Kobe Steel and Wheeling-Pittsburgh and, later, McLouth, fell through. When Nippon Kokan tried to obtain a major interest in Rouge Steel, this was blocked by the trade unions. Finally, in 1984, Nippon Kokan bought 50% of National Steel for $322 million. This tie-up between Japan's second largest and America's seventh largest steelmaker was also the biggest overseas acquisition ever. But it would not be the last since other Japanese companies were eager to penetrate the American market from within.

While the various projects outlined above are typical or symbolic of Japan's overseas investment in manufacturing, they are naturally only a small portion of the whole effort. And even all the investments put together are over-shadowed by the mass of projects in which the sponsors only buy Japanese plant, equipment or technology. Actually, in some of the major investments mentioned, the profits from such sales seem to have motivated the partners as much as any conceivable long-term gains. Thus, Japanese steelmakers were equally pleased to help Korea establish its steel industry by equipping the Pohang works and they delivered many of the installations for China's huge complex at Baoshan. The same companies that cooperated in the Iranian or Saudi Arabian petrochemical projects had no hesitation to install similar facilities in Kuwait or Algeria for cash. In fact, with little concern as to the consequences, the Japanese have continued selling plants of all kinds, electronics, textiles, plastics, cement . . . the more the better.

NOTES

1. Ministry of Finance, *Japan's Direct Overseas Investment*, 1983.
2. See Jon Woronoff, *World Trade War*.
3. Yoichi Konishi, *The Japanese Textile Industry*, September 1979, pp. 28–9.
4. Ministry of Finance, *op. cit.*
5. JETRO, *China, A Business Guide*, pp. 156–62.
6. For more on textiles, see Kunio Yoshihara, *Japanese Investment in Southeast Asia*, pp. 91–132.
7. For more on electronics, see Yoshihara, *op. cit.*, pp. 133–78.
8. See Woronoff, *op. cit.*, pp. 115–22.
9. See Woronoff, *Inside Japan, Inc.*, pp. 96–103.
10. *Marubeni Business Bulletin*, "How The Tubarao Project Was Won," August 1979, pp. 6–9.

6
Enrolling Foreign Labor

More Hands Needed

One thing the Japanese certainly did not think they would
ever need was additional labor. As long as people could
remember, Japan had always been a tight and crowded
country. Since much of the land was mountainous, the
population was heavily concentrated in a few coastal
plains. This created a human reservoir that could be used
in various ways. First, it fueled the economy and ran the
factories when industrialization began; later, it filled the
ranks of the army and flowed into the conquered ter-
ritories.

After the war, Japan still had a teeming population
living on the congested islands and it was further inflated
by millions of returning soldiers and settlers. With more
millions released from the wartime industries or who
otherwise lost their jobs, one of the primary challenges
was to avoid massive unemployment. This was done, not
very satisfactorily, by allowing many to engage in petty
trades or services while others returned to the farms.
Unemployment or underemployment remained a major
problem well into the 1950s. Then, as the economy got
back in swing, most of the labor force was absorbed in
proper jobs and companies had to bid against one another
for workers.

With this, wages also began rising slowly, and then

more swiftly as the country passed through one boom after the other and launched the so-called "economic miracle." Indeed, wages were soon rising by double-digit rates from year to year, pretty much at the same pace as the economy and earnings actually spurted ahead just at the time of the oil crisis, although they were brought under control later in the decade. This change domestically was compounded by a sharp rise in the value of the yen, which made Japanese wages look yet more impressive on an international basis.

As Japan caught up with, and sometimes passed, the West in its mad dash toward prosperity, its wage scale also began catching up, somewhat more hesitantly, but no less implacably. Whereas Japanese workers were only earning about a tenth as much as Americans in 1950, it was closer to a fifth in 1960 and a quarter in 1970. By the end of the decade, they were only earning about a quarter less than the Americans. But this was already about a quarter more than British or Italian workers received.

This placed many Japanese companies in a rather nasty bind: there was a shortage of labor and what labor did exist was dreadfully expensive. Some of the companies, especially larger ones and those in sectors which offered considerable scope for rationalization and automation, were able to replace people with machines. But there remained a fair number of industries in which that could not be done or where, even if it could, the proprietors simply did not have enough capital to make the change-over. In general, this included many of the older crafts and simpler branches that required considerable manual labor and thus remained highly labor-intensive.

These companies and sectors were frequently in the lower range of Japan's dual economy, meaning that they were not only smaller and less capitalized but also often served as suppliers or subcontractors for the larger companies. As such, they had a somewhat different labor force to draw on than the "average" worker. For years, they managed to benefit from cheaper than average labor by recruiting less educated youths and especially unskilled workers fresh from the countryside. In Japan, almost as a matter of course, younger and less educated employees earn less.

However, along with the other changes wrought by growing affluence, there was a rapid increase in the number of young people going on to higher education. This promptly shrank the pool of middle school and high school graduates the smaller companies had been drawing from. Whereas the share of middle school graduates seeking employment was 27% in 1965, only a decade later it was a mere 6%. During the same period, the share of high school graduates who took a job rather than going on to college dropped from 60% to 45%. As the number of these potential workers fell, the demand for them rose markedly. By 1975, there were six job offers for every middle school graduate and about three for each high school graduate.

Obviously, as demand rose so did the wages for this category, since they could only be coaxed into the work force rather than studying further by more attractive pay. At the same time, since there was still a widespread need for young workers, the wages for beginners rose as a whole despite the seniority system. This meant that although the categories usually taken on for comparatively lowly work were still earning less than the average, their wages had risen proportionately more than anyone else's. In spite of the economic slowdown and some unemployment, this group is still very popular and only available on terms some companies cannot quite afford.

As if that were not enough, prosperity and higher levels of education brought about a general distaste in the working population for anything that resembled dirty, unpleasant or menial tasks. People wanted to enter sectors that carried more prestige, not only heavy industry as opposed to light, but preferably trading companies, or banks, or the civil service, rather than manufacturing. In general, job seekers also preferred large companies to small ones.

So, those running companies in any relatively backward sector that required much manual labor or entailed offensive conditions or environment, the suppliers and subcontractors, and more generally any small company, were faced with a combination of unbearably high wages and a shortage of labor. Even if they could get over these hurdles, by raising wages, improving conditions, and offering better prospects, they still faced the ultimate barrier—young people simply did not want that kind of a job for reasons of taste or snobbism. Gradually, as it became ever harder to recruit young workers, their staffs dwindled and aged.[1]

Already by the late 1960s for some, and then during the 1970s and increasingly 1980s for others, the alternative was to find other sources of labor . . . or close down.

This was far from the first time that a country, due to its unusual growth and dynamism, should find itself relatively short of labor, and particularly of those willing to perform the less remunerative and prestigious chores. In the United States, such problems had been solved by receiving untold millions of immigrants. In Europe's northern tier after the war, it was done by bringing in "guest workers" from the south and even further afield. During the war, the Japanese had forced Koreans and Chinese to toil in their mines and factories.

But, in a modern and enlightened Japan, this sort of thing was out of the question. The country was already packed and there was little room physically in its cities and towns to accept more. There were also many cultural barriers that made it hard to assimilate outsiders. Even the Koreans and Chinese who stayed on remained partly unassimilated. If large numbers of foreigners were allowed to come there would be all sorts of undesirable economic and social consequences as well as a risk of their becoming a resented and resentful subproletariat.

On the other hand, all about Japan there were countries which had large populations living at considerably lower levels of affluence. Potentially at least, they offered workers earning much lower wages and whose energy could be harnassed to Japan's economic machine. Although they could not be brought to work in Japan, the alternative existed of taking the work to them. "Offshore" production was perfectly conceivable. If new plants had to be built, they could just as well be located in one country as another. Japanese managers could be sent to supervise them. And raw materials, most of which had to be shipped to Japan anyway, could just as well be sent there directly. The important thing was the wage gap. If it were large enough, the method would be viable.

For the system to function, there were two basic prerequisites. One was a sufficiently large and competent work force. This was not a major problem because the industries thinking of relocating were exactly the ones that were most backward and required the least skills. What was basically needed, for some, were strong arms and backs. For others, especially assembly operations in sectors like garments, electronics, and optics, keen eyes and nimble fingers. This existed widely in Asia and much of it was woefully unemployed or underemployed. Thus, the second essential condition was created, sufficiently low wages.

Even when the idea did not occur to them spontaneously, Japanese managers were soon bombarded with publicity brochures from investment promotion bodies

and export zones which carried a very seductive message.
One of them read as follows:

"The manual dexterity of the Oriental female is famous
the world over. Her hands are small and she works fast
with extreme care. Who, therefore, could be better
qualified by nature and inheritance to contribute to the
efficiency of a bench-assembly production line than the
Oriental girl? . . . Our labor rates are among the lowest
in the region and female factory workers can be hired
for approximately US $1.50 a day."[2]

The Labor Pool

While some manufacturers were being pushed to the point
where they had to think of closing down and disappearing, another alternative arose, that of migrating to countries where labor was cheaper. In the midst of the earlier
economic booms, they hardly noticed how rapidly
Japan's wage level had risen compared to levels in countries quite nearby. Japan was actually the only country
then which boasted a high GNP, impressive growth rates,
and decent salaries. Most of its neighbors were still
relatively stagnant and their wages had hardly risen. Only
somewhat later did a few edge toward development, while
others never really got started.

During the 1960s, when the move began seriously,
Japan's wage level was well above that of other Asian
countries. Its workers, on the whole, earned about six
times as much as Taiwanese workers and ten times as
much as Koreans. For countries further afield, in
Southeast Asia or especially the Indian subcontinent, the
disparity could be as much as fifteen or twenty to one.
Only with the more recent development of some economies, although far from all, has the gap narrowed a bit.
So, even now, the differentials are quite substantial.

And these overall figures only tell part of the story. For the wage figures are only averages, while the actual labor force that is ultimately recruited may be much cheaper. The reason is that so many of the employees working in these older sectors and the assembly industries in general are females. In many export zones, female workers represent three-quarters or more of the total, and their wages are only about half that of the men, which brings the actual wages for this segment of the labor force well below the national average. In addition, in these countries social overhead costs tend to be much lower, there is little if any social security, and fringe benefits like travel, uniform and meal allowances are meager. Finally, there is scant labor legislation to impose costly infrastructure and safety devices, while the average working week is longer and holidays less frequent.

But it was not only a matter of relative wages and conditions that determined where the Japanese would invest. At that time, not so long after the war, it was still a question of who would allow them to use their labor force. Even countries urgently seeking investment did not necessarily approve of projects that were geared primarily to sources of cheap labor as opposed to more sophisticated sectors. Actually, it was only with the introduction of export zones that much could be accomplished in this line. Then, the doors opened. By the late 1960s, there was no lack of alternative sites.

The Japanese investors also had their desiderata. The managers who ultimately took the decisions had their own ideas as to what constituted a valid labor force and they were attracted in differing degrees to different regions. At first, many of these ideas were just stale stereotypes developed by those who had done most of their travelling with the military or inculcated by glossy images projected by the public relations men of the host countries. But they

Matsushita's Television Factory In Indonesia

Credit: Matsushita

gradually got to know the workers more closely through the early experiments and, in a closed society like Japan's business world, the news spread very quickly as to which were best. Doubtlessly, proximity played some role. The closer they were, the cheaper transport and travel would be. Yet, in the final analysis, it was the cultural distance that counted most.

The quest for labor spread in successive waves flowing outward from the Japanese islands. Taiwan, a long time colony, where many people spoke Japanese and knew how to get along with them, was the favorite site as long as the investors were not overly worried that this would jeopardize later relations with the People's Republic. Then South Korea began to attract large numbers of investors and, given its size and dynamism, it got a big chunk. Hong Kong and Singapore, more distant and much smaller, received lesser numbers. All of these countries belong to what has been called the "neo-Confucian" realm which purportedly lays great stress on work ethic and discipline. Although still quite different, the social and cultural background are closest to Japan's.

The next group of countries consists of Thailand, Indonesia, the Philippines and increasingly Malaysia. They were a bit more remote and unfamiliar. The tropics conjured up images of friendly, if not particularly hard-working people. The cultural and linguistic gaps were more complete. The only exception was that all these countries had a large Chinese minority, usually prominent in business, with whom many of the Japanese felt a greater affinity. This tendency to prefer dealing with the Chinese, however, ran contrary to national policy and could create friction. But few of the indigenous groups, at least in the beginning, could serve as proper partners or associates and they were unknown quantities as workers.

Sources further afield, although sometimes mooted, were less attractive for various reasons. The distance to either Latin America or the Indian subcontinent was considerable. Few Japanese had much familiarity with them. Although Brazil quickly occurred to mind, and second generation Japanese could be recruited, the mass of the labor force turned out to be illiterate and unaccustomed to industrial work. Nor did the Japanese really know how to deal with the Indians or Pakistanis and others of an entirely different culture and customs. Even if the workers were cheap, and apparently diligent, a pettifogging bureaucracy constantly got in their way.

Just as most readily accessible labor had been tapped, late in the 1970s, the biggest pool of what looked like highly desirable workers opened up on mainland China. The most populous country in the world, very near at hand, with workers concentrated in huge industrial cities, seemed an ideal site. The labor force had a reasonable level of education, although not always the best for those who grew up during the Cultural Revolution. The government was eager for them to learn new skills and a potential employer did not have to worry about labor unrest or unions. But, neither the Japanese investors nor the pragmatic new leadership in Beijing realized how strongly some of the indoctrination and what had become standard practice in many factories could undermine the work will and zeal of the labor force.

Finally, by the 1980s, a new and highly unexpected source of labor appeared on the horizon. While Japan's economy had been expanding rapidly, the progress among other industrialized countries had been much slower. From year to year, the wage gap narrowed and, by the 1970s, Japanese workers were earning more than those in some parts of Europe. This included not only the peripheral nations like Spain, Portugal or Ireland, but even Great Britain and eventually Italy. If the same trends continued, it could be assumed that one day perhaps German and American labor might be cheaper. The differentials were certainly not as great as with the truly low cost labor suppliers in Asia, running about 25% for most and exceptionally 50% lower. So it made no sense to introduce very labor-intensive production. However, in reasonably capital or knowledge-intensive sectors, where it was necessary to have trained and skilled personnel, certain countries offered them in profusion and at good rates.

Moreover, the mere fact that labor was getting relatively cheaper in Europe and America would encourage Japanese companies to initiate other types of projects to take advantage of their often promising markets. Labor costs were always a factor in any investment decision and many manufacturers which might have liked to produce locally for various reasons failed to do so as long as costs were so high that exporting seemed a preferable policy. As the situation changed, gradually decisions were made to go over to production or at least assembly with a local labor force whose wages were no longer as great a disincentive.

In this group of countries, the Japanese also had very definite preferences. Some priority was given to cost factors, and countries with a cheaper labor force and favorable investment policies, like Ireland or Spain, benefited. But their markets were small and thus Great Britain became the favorite site, or nearly, due to comparatively low labor costs, a large domestic market, and access to the European Community. However, the Japanese were greatly taken aback by the actions of the trade unions, whose strike record was particuarly bad and which could not even prevent walkouts by dissenting members. Italy, and France to a lesser extent, appeared even more unreliable to stolid Japanese businessmen. Thus, despite higher costs, there was a tendency to congregate in Germany and enter into joint ventures there or especially to establish commercial offices to cover the whole continent.

Japanese companies also avoided Canada and Australia as sites for manufacturing investment, when this could be done, and turned to them mainly for natural resources. The markets there were not terribly big and the labor force was unruly. In the United States, things looked somewhat better, if not as concerned labor, then certainly with regard to the market. Moreover, in an attempt to solve the labor problem, the investors picked a number of regions where they felt the climate was best. This consisted especially of California, where a fair-sized *nisei* population lived, parts of the Mid-West and more recently the "Old South," centering around Atlanta which became a popular headquarters. But the real industrial heartland around the Great Lakes, and especially near Detroit, did not appeal to them at all.

For the Japanese, labor sourcing is a very serious matter. No one is more particular about the quality of workers than they. And, from start to finish, Asia, and principally East Asia, remained the place of predilection for companies that had to relocate. It is not surprising that the Japanese should take such a decision. However, almost to confirm their wisdom, this also turned out to be a very attractive site for American companies although they had the run of the world, with cheap Latin American labor nearby. Even the Europeans began subcontracting their work to much the same countries. In many ways, Taiwan, Korea, Hong Kong and Singapore did become a vast factory for the world . . . although some regarded them more as a huge "sweat shop."

Labor-Intensive Employers

It is naturally a bit difficult to know exactly why a given investment was made. Such decisions are never taken for just one reason but rather a generally satisfactory mix in which one factor or another may have more weight. For many Japanese investors, labor was a significant factor in almost every case even when it was not the primary one. And, even if it were the primary cause, they would rarely be so frank as to admit they went to a specific location just to benefit from cheap labor. Nevertheless, MITI's surveys on direct investment show that a reasonably priced labor supply is high on the list of priorities.

Tracing the types of companies which stress labor, and especially labor costs, and analyzing the behavior of various companies, it is possible to attempt an approximate description of labor-oriented investment. At first sight, however, the results are a bit confusing. Among the companies involved are both small and large ones, some in rather backward sectors and others with very advanced products and sophisticated technologies. Some only have investment in countries offering cheap labor while others are operating around the world. To get any clear understanding, it is wiser to break them down into several categories.

The first is obviously companies in declining or ailing industries, those which have existed in Japan for a long time but were gradually losing their competitiveness. Although frequently described as "obsolete," this does not mean that their products are less desirable or even that their plant and techniques are hopelessly outmoded. What it really implies in practice more than anything is that they tend to be rather labor-intensive in a country where the trend is toward more capital-intensive operations.

The sectors which come under this heading are already numerous and the list is still growing. They arrive in waves that coincide with the pressure of labor costs in Japan as well as the progression of its own industrialization. Among the earliest were traditional handicrafts and simple cottage industries like pottery, metal objects and furniture. Garments and basic textiles followed soon after. Then came toys, plastics and footwear. Eventually, it ran into more modern sectors, if still rather rudimentary products, like still cameras, transistor radios, or black-and-white television.

The companies in these sectors had to migrate because they needed both a cheap and a none too fastidious labor force since the type of work was often heavy and unpleasant or perhaps repetitious and monotonous. This was not much of a compliment to the host country. But it tied in well with the labor structure it then possessed, consisting largely of unskilled and semi-skilled workers, many of them fresh from the countryside and sometimes with limited education. Another advantage, although grudgingly admitted at best, was that these rather old-fashioned industries used relatively simple techniques that could be learned readily enough by the labor force and employed comparatively primitive machinery that was cheap enough to buy or was simply dismantled in Japan and shipped over.

Most of the companies which invested in such overseas ventures were quite small since they tended to inhabit highly fragmented sectors and the prevailing stagnation hardly encouraged growth. This smallness, as already explained, implied greater difficulties in obtaining good personnel, and especially younger workers, and thus they were eager to move to other places where the supply was more plentiful. Among the small companies, some were independent operations which made products that were sold directly to the consumers. Others, however, were little more than suppliers for far larger companies. They, too, suffered from labor problems, partly due to their size but much more because the leading assemblers purposely dumped the more labor-intensive operations on their subcontractors.

This helps to explain what was long regarded as a peculiarity of Japanese investors. In most other countries, especially the United States and also in Europe, the companies which invested abroad tend to be among the biggest that exist. They usually possess exceptional knowhow or proprietary rights over technologies and products that are rather unique. Often they also boast a brandname that is widely known. This is what one usually thinks of when hearing of multinational corporations, and certainly not the bits and snatches of backward and sometimes vanishing industries that spawned so many of Japan's overseas investors.

Of course, smallness and backwardness as characteristics of Japanese MNCs only appear as anomalies to academic "experts" or big-time managers. The situation was much clearer—and more pressing—to the investors who did not know much about economic theory but felt some harsh realities. If labor was becoming expensive in Japan, and they needed more than others, they had to seek it elsewhere. They were motivated much less by possible gains than imminent losses if they did not take the step.

But, in a fair number of cases, they were only able to do so because they did not have to act alone. Sometimes the smaller firms were aided by their trading company which helped find them a new site (often in an export processing zone), perhaps a local partner as well, and then kept on marketing their products. Others followed in the wake of the much larger companies they subcontracted for, convinced that they could make good on the basis of their traditional links and products. In this way, even quite small operations had a bit more substance and what they could not do for themselves others might provide.

Numerous big companies also migrated to cheap labor countries. This included some of the most prestigious names in Japan, what one usually thinks of as an MNC. Prestigious or not, they had their own ways of benefiting from potential savings. Basically, most of them are assemblers and, more than in any other economy, they tend to have a large share of the parts and components made by other firms. This quite commonly runs into two-thirds and three-quarters of the total and can rise even higher. They only make certain essential components which they do not want to farm out or which can be greatly mechanized and automated, and then put all the parts together. Many of these parts can be produced more cheaply abroad.

Moreover, assembly itself is a very labor-intensive operation which is hard to automate and, in order to remain competitive, they can take advantage of cheaper labor costs for this as well. While they may not wish to have special products completed anywhere but in their own premises, they would not hesitate to have smaller parts, peripheral elements, or lesser subassemblies handled overseas. To some extent, this would normally be a job for local subcontractors, and for a rather long time large Japanese companies were urged by the government (and their own suppliers) not to take the work away from them. Yet, with the years, they have given some of the new items and overflow, and then also the basic work, to their own subsidiaries abroad.

This is often done in very advanced sectors and involves highly sophisticated articles, which explains why the range of investors and products is so great. However, a lot of this is just an illusion. True, the investments are made in such modern sectors as optics, electronics, even computers. In practice, as a Max Planck Institute report pointed out: "What appears in the statistics as manufacturing of a highly sophisticated technical product consists in reality in the performance of a few routine operations, mainly soldering and assembling under a microscope by semi-skilled cheap labor."[3]

Having noted some of the characteristics of companies that are eager to obtain cheaper labor, it is somewhat easier to estimate how many there might be, although it is out of the question to come up with more than a rough guess.

One approach is to consider the fact that these are frequently rather small manufacturing companies. Quite naturally, they would be setting up shop in host countries that offer low cost labor, and this limits the geographic spread basically to East and Southeast Asia. Thus, one can note, as Ozawa did: "By the end of 1975 nearly half of the total number of Japan's overseas investments were made by small- and medium-size enterprises. The ratio of manufacturing investment made by these small firms to the total number of manufacturing investments is as high as 41.8% on the whole. The ratio becomes even higher in some Asian countries; it is 58.6% in Taiwan and as high as 70.0% in South Korea. In fact, Asia is clearly the place of predilection for these companies. Taiwan and South Korea alone host 56.6% of Japan's manufacturing ventures made by small and medium-sized enterprises. 82.3% of them are concentrated in Asia."[4]

Another approach is to consider that much of the labor-oriented investment is being made for offshore production either to service existing markets or to send parts back to, or do assembly for, the Japanese parent companies. Thus, it is instructive to look at the export processing zones, since any investment there *must* be to benefit from cheap labor since they offer few other advantages and are cut off from the domestic market. It is not possible to get the exact figures, but, as noted, most of Korea's, a large part of Taiwan's, and lesser parts of other zones are occupied by the Japanese.

However, the rapid growth of local personnel employed by Japanese companies, no matter where they may be, is an interesting phenomenon to consider in its own right. Here we will see, on the basis of a sample survey by MITI, that the vast majority of employees were engaged in the manufacturing sector, some 84% against a mere 16% in commerce. And the majority of that, namely 61%, were located in Asia. Roughly 620,000 people were working for the firms surveyed and nearly a million would probably be working for all Japanese manufacturers abroad. This gives us more than an inkling of just how big Japan's "world factory" has become.[5]

"Quality Of Labor"

If the Japanese were going to establish factories in other

countries largely to benefit from foreign labor, or had to use such labor anyhow, naturally they were going to be very picky about just which employees they hired. Although most industrial inputs are relatively homogeneous and can be easily graded, that is impossible for the human element. Admittedly, it is possible to calculate the cost of labor per hour or some such indicator. Knowledge and skills can be roughly evaluated. But more abstract human characteristics like diligence, discipline or dedication are extremely hard to measure. Yet, this is what Japanese businessmen appreciate more highly than anything else.

This task has led to serious concern with what, for them, usually looms as the biggest problem . . . the "quality of labor." That this is just a euphemism should become clear shortly. For, when they reject a given worker or labor force, it is most often for the sort of reason one finds it hard to speak about openly nowadays, like unruliness, laziness or disloyalty. Alas, it is not often that they find a labor force that offers the quality they seek.

When moving to a developing country with a more backward population, there may be any number of drawbacks that can counter, and sometimes more than cancel, the advantages of low cost. In basically agricultural societies, the workers are usually drawn from among subsistence farmers and have no familiarity with industrial work. They may not accept the regularity and meticulousness imposed by the processes. They may even find it hard to keep to the schedule. Complaints are frequently made that the workers come late, take too many breaks or just goof off, or there is considerable absenteeism. In addition, the job may not be seen as an end but simply as a means of earning a certain amount of money. This can result in a high turnover rate.

In most developing countries, the educational system is so inadequate that there are still many people who are poorly educated or actually illiterate. This means that it is hard to train them for anything but the simplest tasks and not likely that they will improve themselves through self-study. Feeling ill at ease, they may also be either stubborn or hopelessly apathetic. Meanwhile, their more educated countrymen may assume that a diploma, any diploma, automatically qualifies them for a better, preferably white-collar job, and that they are above getting their hands dirty.

Managerial skills are far more difficult to transmit even than production skills. Anyone can be taught to repeat a few simple motions on an assembly line, and many can learn to operate a lathe, but it is the rare person who knows how to direct others. Yet, the Japanese must eventually find replacements for their own managers among the personnel available on the labor market and put them in a position to help run the company itself. It is not certain that those they come by will be good at other things than giving orders, a talent most people find almost inherent. Knowing which orders to give—and how—is quite another matter. Even then, it takes a long time to work them into the team. And there is no guarantee that they will not quit soon and sell their skills to another employer at a higher price or set up their own company.

Thus, it is anything but easy to recruit a work force that avoids the extremes, namely one that has a sufficient level of education to do the job and shows some loyalty to the company. These are the basics. But the Japanese usually want much more. Their success is traced not only to comparatively inexpensive products but ones showing the highest quality and reliability. This implies more than just strict inspection and rejection of defective products, it requires a motivation to make the very best. While the Japanese supervisors are bound to urge such attitudes on their subordinates, quality control will not succeed unless it is supported voluntarily. Despite the recent wave of popularity, there is no sign that QC is taking root strongly even in Japanese overseas ventures.

Far more important for the Japanese, as mentioned, are such abstract characteristics as dedication and loyalty. They are not interested only in getting a person to do a job but rather to become part of a broader team and actually almost a permanent fixture in the company. Even in times of relatively high unemployment, there is little likelihood that the average employee will stay as long as is usual in Japan. And, even if he stays, it is far from certain that he will give his primary allegience to the company as opposed to his own country, his family or... himself.

In the developing countries, the Japanese have not often been entirely satisfied with what they found. In some places, skilled workers and talented managers were avail-

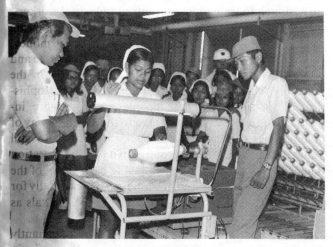

Training Indonesian Textile Workers

Credit: Toray

able, and could be attracted, but that was far from the general case. More often than not, the workers had to be trained and the managers painfully taught the ropes. Then, when they really knew what they were doing and could contribute properly to the company, many left. Some employees actually joined Japanese companies just to find out how they worked and then apply that knowledge to their own advantage. Still, balancing the pluses against the minuses, a rough order of preference was established. Among the more underdeveloped countries, only Sri Lanka was very popular. Filipino and Indonesian workers got much lower grades. Thanks to their own work ethic—and despite their tendency toward job hopping—workers in East Asia remained at the top.

Oddly enough, the most serious problems do not seem to arise with the developing countries. It is apparently easy enough to train most peasants as industrial workers. Harsh conditions, long hours, monotonous and tiring work are nothing new to them. And they need the money. It is harder to get city folks to reach the required pace and intensity. Thus, the Japanese face more trouble in the relatively "advanced" countries with their more "sophisticated" population. These people are also more individualistic and do not really take to the Japanese way of doing things, although most backward countries still retain the various forms of group activity and cooperation that exist traditionally. Finally, having been ahead of the Japanese economically and presumably also culturally for so long, it is hard for Westerners to accept Orientals as their teacher.

So far, the Japanese have formed a predominantly negative opinion of workers in most advanced countries in general, aside from Germany until recently, when it also seemed to succumb to what is usually referred to as the "advanced country disease." Once the only variety known was the "British disease," which the Japanese were prone to criticize until they detected new strains in a growing series of countries. One aspect is a lassitude, a loss of work will, a disconcern for others, that has admittedly spread there and aggrieves not only Japanese investors but domestic companies which do not know how to cope with their own labor force. Still, it is rather crude and inelegant to speak of such vices in public, and the Japanese have resorted to complaints about the "quality of labor."

A recent survey of Japanese companies established in the United States made by Nikko Research Center gives some insight into the problem. About 47% of these companies felt that the labor quality was rather poor, and 18% that it was very poor, while only 29% thought it was as good as in Japan. Serious weaknesses were indicated for ability, reliability and morale. For education, it was mentioned that part of the labor force were Latin Americans, who didn't even speak English, while the average level was pretty low for native Americans due to disruption of the public school system. The result was such a high turnover rate that it was hard to train or improve workers or even to suitably transfer new technology.[6]

The other aspect, which is even harder to express openly, is annoyance with the trade unions which few Japanese companies know how to handle. In Japan, relations with the unions are close, perhaps too close; abroad, the unions more openly and aggressively defend the interests of the workers as they see it. This makes things tough for Japanese managers, who are not really used to acknowledging union leaders as equals or allowing union members to determine, or even influence, company policy. And they often find the demands regarding wages and working conditions to be excessive.

An allergy to the unions has made the Japanese very wary about setting up factories in Great Britain, Canada or

Australia. And it has led to a rather bizarre pattern of investment in the United States. Most of this has been done in California, the Mid-West or the South. Often the actual site was patiently sought for years until the Japanese found just the place they wanted. More than coincidentally, it might well be in a non-union or "right to work" state. Even then, the personnel was carefully screened to avoid former union members or potential organizers and other "troublemakers." And the management sometimes announced when hiring workers that there was no union then nor any intention of having one later.

This sort of thing is very widespread. Many Japanese factories are located in small towns with no other major industry, where people seem to preserve that good old work ethic and are beholden to the company for providing employment. In such a context, rather than extreme, Nissan's truck plant is almost a typical case. It set up shop in Smyrna, a minor suburb in the outskirts of Nashville, Tennessee. It could afford to be highly selective in recruiting for 2,650 jobs from among more than 60,000 applicants. Yet, rather than take skilled and experienced workers, it apparently preferred people who had never worked in an automobile factory before. It sent 425 of them off to Japan to see how things were done there and invested $62 million in training, part of this an introduction to Japanese-style management with much stress on the company as a "family" and the need for teamwork between management and labor. It promised lifetime employment and wanted loyalty in return, this often implying a dislike for union interference.[7]

So, in practice, "quality of labor" usually refers less to skills than attitude. Otherwise, how else can one explain why so many Japanese companies have located factories in developing countries and accepted quite uneducated and unskilled labor while avoiding countries whose labor force is already highly skilled and much more experienced? How can one explain the great eagerness of Toyota and Nissan to produce cars in Taiwan and their notable reluctance to do so in America and Britain? It is not only a question of cost. Rather, there is the idea that it is far easier to teach skills to someone with the right attitude than to change the attitude of someone no matter what skills he may possess.

This sort of approach leads many observers to conclude that the Japanese companies are anti-union or do not want to grant their workers any rights. This is not strictly true. The degree of unionization in Japan is as high as elsewhere, although the nature of the unions is quite different. More than anything, the Japanese managers want to solve problems in relation to the specific company or plant and not the broader level of workers' demands let alone an ideological concept of what labor deserves. In fact, to keep their own workers out of the union, they are usually willing to grant more than average wages and greater fringe benefits and welfare. This doubtlessly also helps keep their workers under control and "loyal" in a way.

More important than the material questions, however, there is the inability of Japanese managers to negotiate directly or simply to deal with often abrasive union leaders who insist on being treated as equals or at least taken seriously. Nor would they find it easy to maintain proper relations with a work force that would resort to strikes even if they knew it would hurt the company. The adversary relationship which is typical of so many other places is largely alien to Japanese managers and, as such, they do not know how to cope. Thus, rather than reach an agreement with the unions, they try to steer clear of them or keep them out, even by methods that are not very acceptable nowadays.

Some critics, especially those to the left, take the argument further and insist that the Japanese prefer investing in countries under an authoritarian regime whose dictators allow them to exploit the people with impunity. This they see as part of an insidious plot to impose capitalism and exploit a labor force which is kept in an impoverished state by its rulers. One of the hidden advantages of the export processing zones, they insist, is that special efforts are made to keep workers from organizing or creating trouble. "The foreign capital investor," it is said, "can almost certainly count on the host country restraining any form of industrial or political activity on the part of his work force, and he will have little or no labor legislation to bother about."[8]

Doubtlessly, there is a tendency to invest in developing countries which are not models politically. But it would be hard to do anything else. In the Third World at present, among the countries whose labor force is sufficiently cheap to attract investors, the vast majority are run by strong men of one sort of another and the democracies are few and far between. Under such conditions, it is patently absurd to ask the Japanese to invest only in democratic developing countries. On the other hand, they have not shown any tendency to seek out the most ruthless regimes which, by the way, are not always capitalist.

Instead, they have set upon countries which, either despite or sometimes because of their strong central control, have made a serious effort at economic development. This includes Korea under Park and Chun, Koumintang Taiwan, Singapore under Lee Kwan Yew or Marcos' Philippines and Suharto's Indonesia. In each one of these countries, especially the former, there was not only an opening for investors but also a broader policy of economic development that offered some hope for the rest of the population. And, although they naturally cooperated with the regime, by setting up projects there the Japanese often provided a stronger base for a nascent business community and middle class which demanded at least greater freedom of decision in economic matters and could help broaden the power structure.

If Japanese investors can be related to the ruling class, they cannot quite be assimilated with it in the specific case of labor-oriented investments. For, as repeatedly mentioned, much of this came from relatively small enterprises in rather backward sectors in Japan which had to shift operations quickly or collapse. They did not have much political clout in Japan and certainly none to speak of in the host country. And even the major groups and *keiretsu*, the successors of the more powerful and notorious *zaibatsu*, were merely the supporters of established regimes but certainly not their creators or sponsors. With its present lack of military might, Japan could at most bestow gifts on countries which cooperated; it was in no position to engage in nefarious schemes to manipulate them.

Thus, the worst fault of the Japanese investors was to equate a certain kind of regime with a more or less propitious investment "climate," especially as concerns the sort of labor force they were likely to encounter. If it turned out that one or two companies went and found it easy to work in a given country or export zone, this news would gradually spread and more investors would come. Naturally, these investors would have to curry favor or seek good relations with the powers-that-be. This was essential simply to obtain approval and run their projects efficiently. And they did not like it if the workers became overly demanding or defiant. But they were much too small and insignificant a group, despite their higher profile, to set the general tone.

That is not to say that Japanese investors do not like a tame and docile labor force. They most definitely do, even if they are not necessarily in a position to create one. That is shown most clearly by the tendency to hire substantially more women than men in their operations. True, the women's nimble fingers are particularly adept in handling the work involved in assembly operations for garments, electronics, and other sectors most often developed. Women are also considerably cheaper and they have a relatively short career, leaving to get married after only a few years's work. So, they are much easier to direct and control and tend to raise rather few demands. But they are even nimbler at leaving an employer they do not like or going to one who offers more.

In any analysis of Japanese investment, it is most unwise to ignore the underlying reasons for acting one way or the other. It must be perfectly obvious to anyone, Japanese or not, that any project stands a better chance of success if the employees are disciplined, loyal and hardworking. Seeking such a work force is therefore a justifiable goal. At home, Japanese managers have their own ways of obtaining such staff. When they go abroad, they also want the closest to this they can get. But they are hardly in a position to impose it. However, what they can do is to consider the many sites available and pick the best. That is not unusual or unfair, anyone else would do the same.

As for the workers, who many see as crushed and ground between harsh rulers and Japanese capitalists, they also have some degree of choice. No matter how strong the ruler, and how weak they are individually, collectively they still are partially responsible for how their country is run. If they cannot do anything to change the regime, they can at least decide whether or not to work for Japanese companies. No matter how much they may be criticized by academics, students or ideologists, it is surprising to find how often these companies are singled out by the workers as potential employers. Japanese companies have always been able to hire the workers they want and this is usually by offering better terms than others. If ever this changes, they could more appropriately be accused of exploitation.

Japanese-Style Management

Running a company is not just a question of making people work hard but rather of making them work wisely, efficiently, and well. Without suitable organization and direction, no group of workers, not even the cheapest, will produce very much of value. And, if they can be convinced that they are not only working for the company but for themselves or in their own interest as well, the operation should run that much more smoothly. For such reasons, every society has created management systems and philosophies, even if they were not always recognized as such or given a clear definition.

Since their system is in many ways distinctive, there has been much talk about the Japanese management system and whether or not it can be introduced in overseas ventures. This ties up with the question of whether it is better or worse in general and, more particularly, how it will work in some other context. No matter what view specific Japanese managers may take, they are so accustomed to the system and their attitudes and behaviors are shaped so much by it that it is almost impossible for them not to want to apply it wherever they go. Those who are convinced that the Japanese system is inherently superior, or just works better, will naturally try to propagate it more assiduously.

But this is not easy. The reason the system is so different from, say, Western-style management, is that Japanese culture itself is very different and shaped business practices in ways that do not exist or may not make sense elsewhere. It can be argued that many Asian cultures, and many developing societies in general, are much closer in their customary patterns to the Japanese system than those of the West. This frequently is true. But it does not help when part of the thrust of modernization is to throw off these old concepts and methods and adopt more rational and efficient ones. Since the Japanese are outsiders, no less than Americans or Europeans, the idea of borrowing from them is not always tempting unless one believes that they really offer something better.

Until recently, many regarded Japanese practices as old-fashioned, inefficient and unproductive. Of late, however, the success of the Japanese economy—and the failure of many others—has led to a drastic revision which makes it almost fashionable to talk of "learning from Japan."[9] This fad is unlikely to succeed very well in those countries where the foundations are poorest, due to the cult of individualism, although it may sink deeper roots in parts of Asia. The most propitious conditions exist in other so-called "neo-Confucian" societies, like Singapore, Korea and Taiwan. Yet, even there, what has arisen is still just a pale reflection at most.

Under the Japanese system, new employees are only recruited once a year, when young people graduate from schools and colleges and quickly enter a company. They plan to stay with this company throughout a career and, in return, the company offers them "lifetime employment." Recruitment into a company is usually based much more on attitude and personality than actual knowhow or skills and the company will lavish time and effort on training its own staff. Gradually, from year to year, the employees will rise through the ranks, their wages will increase, and periodically they will be appointed to higher posts. To draw them into the team, employees will be rotated from job to job and division to division and gradually participate in the amorphous decision-making process. This makes them an integral part of the broader "company family." That, at any rate, is the theory of it.[10]

No matter how fine this may appear, and no matter how much Japanese managers or some Asian governments may wish to introduce it abroad, difficulties immediately arise. The first, one which is so petty that few bother thinking of it, quickly throws the whole scheme out of kilter. In just about every country in the world, the educational system is geared to training students for specific types of work, giving them certificates and diplomas that show they are qualified to do certain things, perhaps adding their proficiency at it. Thus, when people look for work they want a specific job which offers certain benefits and status. They are not merely asking to enter a company which can do with them as it wishes.

Thus, in their overseas ventures, Japanese companies have no choice but to do like everyone else, namely to indicate which jobs they have open and to seek candidates on the labor market. Even if they wished to recruit students straight from school and train them in-house, they could not do so. For it would take twenty or thirty years to fill all the posts in that manner when, in practice, they usually only have a few months or years, at most, to round out the whole staff. In recruiting personnel by their skills, they lose any leverage for imposing their control over the person since he can sell the same skills elsewhere. And it is impossible to install seniority since most employees insist on being paid by their skills and not as a function of how many years they work.

When working with employees who owe everything to their skills, rather than everything to the company, it becomes harder to introduce even quite unexceptionable and useful aspects of the Japanese system. One of them is in-house training. The Japanese are perfectly right that an employee can always learn more and will be worth more to the company. And it is a worthwhile investment to teach them new skills whenever possible. But this becomes an endless and thankless task if the employees then take their newly acquired skills and ask for higher wages which make it hard to cover the costs of the teaching effort or, what is worse, simply quit and look for another employer who will pay them more.

This raises even greater havoc with the concept of quality control as practiced in Japan. The idea is that it is far better to prevent defects than to correct them and the personnel is encouraged to work more intelligently, make helpful suggestions and join quality control circles that will solve any problems that crop up. In Japan, for workers who expect to spend most of their career with the company, this is bound to pay off over time since their company will prosper and be able to grant higher wages. Someone just doing his job, and not very certain of being around long, will not make many voluntary efforts nor give of himself unduly. At best, he will engage in quality control activities if paid, and even then without much enthusiasm.

With so many of the crucial elements of the Japanese system lacking, or ineffectual, it is interesting to note that one of the most popular and successful is an element that hardly exists in Japan. Many foreigners have latched on to the idea of group discussion, collective decisions, and supposed "bottom-up" management as a way of democratizing work practices and they try to take it much further. In Japan, however, such techniques function within a very hierarchical structure in which those further down would not dream of contradicting those further up. That is why it is tolerated, and partly successful.

In other countries, however, the Japanese may be dismayed to find how many initiatives their staff takes or, in countries where lower level staff are accustomed to taking no initiative at all, they may be put off by the expectations vested in them. Also, whereas the junior staff may be pleased to have a chance to participate, their local superiors may be none too happy about such activities. And, even the junior managers, who are delighted to make their thoughts known, may be annoyed by hints that they should mix with those beneath them, especially workers on the shop floor, and make sincere efforts to keep them contented.

Many Westerners, used to concepts such as "time means money," will also be troubled by the fact that Japanese decision-making methods are extremely slow and vague. Even if they do not enjoy quick decisions tossed at them by a Western-style boss, and which everyone must hop to, they will feel uncomfortable under a Japanese boss who is painfully unclear about what company policy actually is and just asks them to do what they think is necessary. They also find it hard to do a job, which is their basic task, when the rules are so loose and the very definition of their job may be hazy. Moreover, having been hired for a specific job, they tend to reject attempts by Japanese managers to have them do some other job, a request that would hardly disturb a Japanese employee who is hired simply to work for a company at whatever it wants.

But the most alarming effect of the attitudes that prevail just about everywhere aside from Japan is the lack of loyalty to the company. That can hardly be avoided since people who sell their skills rather than themselves will always have something to offer another employer. And the cults of individualism and freedom only make loyalty look more like regimentation while the endless talk about what one owes the company sounds like rhetoric or indoctrination. Foreigners simply do not feel they owe the company that much or that they have to strive as hard for it.

So, in order to encourage loyalty, Japanese companies are forced to increase the material incentives which are more convincing than the moral ones. They may provide somewhat better facilities in the factory, offer housing to single workers or subsidize it for married couples. They will set up a sports ground and perhaps organize clubs and excursions. But the frills are considerably less interesting to most employees than the essentials, namely somewhat better wages than can be obtained from their counterparts (and potential employers). To promote seniority and loyalty, they may also reshape the wage structure somewhat so that those with longer years service are paid a bit more and they may tend to promote more officers from within the organization.[11]

Still, there is a limit to how far they can go. After all, labor costs are a major element in total expenditures and, especially if they came for cheap labor, the Japanese are not willing to exaggerate. Higher wages and benefits are carefully balanced against what is gained by having a more reliable and experienced work force. Usually, they would not really bind anyone who had strong reasons for leaving or even someone who simply wanted to fill out his career, do something more challenging, or get away from the old routine. Indeed, the danger might be that such incentives would only tie down those who were least dynamic and imaginative while the better elements left.

In Japan, loyalty does have benefits for both sides, but it has been so constructed that the company certainly gains more than the average employee. And that is why it is praised so highly. If it becomes a setup where the workers who want stability and job security can find it without reciprocating, even the Japanese would not wish to impose it. Nor would they stand for it being one-way. They do want to hold on to their staff, and make them loyal, but if too many still quit when they want to little is gained. In such cases, the Japanese can probably do just as well with a Western-style management where they can also hire and fire as they want.

These incompatibilities between the different management systems, and the sort of circumstances they constantly encounter abroad, have made it quite impossible to run a pure or even a largely adulterated Japanese-style management. Much of the talk about this is rather theoretical and even those companies praised—or condemned—for supposedly having introduced the system, have at most adopted some few aspects. As often as not, it is the frills and not the essentials which are there. And it often boils down to little more than a bit of exoticism, somewhat better conditions, and more friendliness. People are asked their opinions, they are treated as well as possible, but the crucial decisions are still taken by the Japanese executives.

This conclusion may not be very satisfying to those who want to know how Japanese companies can still outperform American, European or Asian ones while using the same staff. Part of the answer resides in the slightly different and marginally superior use of the local personnel they do find. But much more of it can be traced to the introduction of new machinery, various improvements in layout, and especially the adoption of production methods that were pioneered back home. This is combined with excellent products whose reputation is already solid. The result is a Japanese subsidiary that is more efficient and productive than its competitors and, feeling that they are on a winning team, this gives a tremendous boost to the morale of the foreign employees as well.

Labor Troubles

Despite all the precautions they take and the often painstaking selection of a site for labor supplies, things do not always run smoothly or well for Japanese overseas operations. There has been a number of serious clashes and crises. But these were often not as telling as the wearing grind of settling into a new society, understanding the labor force, responding to changing circumstances and solving the normal, petty problems that crop up anywhere. Thus, the switch from costly Japanese to cheaper foreign labor proved to be anything but a cure-all.

Perhaps realizing that they did not know much about the local labor force or prevailing customs and practices, many of the investors actually preferred going into a joint venture in which a primary task of the local partner was to select and look after local staff. When they did not do so, they quickly promoted locals within their own organization to handle this function. Nevertheless, it was impossible—and undesirable—to shift all the responsibility for labor relations to others and such companies were still regarded as Japanese in the eyes of the public and the employees no matter what happened.

Contrary to expectations, less of the trouble arose at the lower level, among the rank-and-file workers, or in the developing countries. Most of these people were new to industrial life. They had pitifully few skills to offer, and most of those learned from the company. Wages in other companies were not any better and life on the farm was harsh and unrewarding. So, the slightest show of kindness or attention by Japanese managers was often enough to win their support. Some aspects of the Japanese system were almost ideal for them. The method of training based

less on book-learning than working side-by-side with
instructors, the fact that even supervisors and foremen
wore the same uniform and were reasonably helpful, and
especially the existence of canteens, lodging, and other
welfare frills.

The philosophy of familism, that the company was a
family with the managers looking after the lesser members, was founded in a rather backward Japan not unlike
the society encountered in many developing countries,
especially those of Asia. It was thus not too hard for
ordinary workers to think of the company as their family,
especially when they were uprooted from the countryside
and still felt uncomfortable in the city. But, much to
everyone's surprise, this also struck a sympathetic chord
in the hearts of many Westerners, certainly more sophisticated, but who were tired of the distance that existed
between managers and workers in their own companies. It
was not hard for wandering journalists to pick up comments like the following: "They talk about the Sony
family and all that. Listen, I believe in the Sony family."[12]

Unfortunately, that comment from an Alabama machine operator was less likely to come from the lips of lower
and middle-level managers in Japanese ventures. In fact,
the attitude was likely to be completely different. Within
all too many Japanese subsidiaries, there was a notable
gulf between "them" and "us," between the Japanese who
monopolized the top posts and the locals who had little
hope of rising much further. Reasons were given for this,
such as the need to know how the company operated, or
the need to maintain proper relations with the head office,
or simply the need to speak Japanese. Or the onus was
shifted to the local staff, that they had not been there long
enough, that they might leave their job later, that their
primary interest still lay with themselves and not the

company. But no explanations could hide the existence of friction at the interface where two sets of managers came together.

It was also at this level that the difference in treatment of men and women became more shocking. In most developing countries, especially Oriental ones, women were used to being treated as inferiors and most girls actually only wanted a job that would earn them some pocket money or a dowry. If Japanese companies paid as well as others, and the factory was bright and modern, they were more than happy. In the West, women expected to be given the same career opportunities as men and, when they clearly were not, they revolted. In the trading company offices of major cities, women might complain by refusing to serve tea to visitors, insisting they were not hired for that. More angry or audacious ones would bring suits against unequal treatment. Here, too, it took a good deal more than smiles and friendliness to win support.

How these conflicts were resolved varies. Sometimes the Japanese managers realized that the society was so different that they had to adapt their practices to the new context. Others took the opposite tack, they made an all-out attempt to convince their staff that the Japanese management system was better for everyone. If they did not succeed, which often happened, they would be more anxious than ever about what might happen if they transferred more of the control and responsibility to locals (as the first group had done) and they would try to keep things in order by retaining as many Japanese nationals on the staff as possible.

Either because of such reactions, or because most Japanese companies tend to have excessive personnel at higher levels, it quickly became noticeable that Japanese ventures in most countries included a higher proportion of expatriates than most other multinationals. American,

Toyota Assembly Plant In Kenya

Credit: Toyota

British or French companies made the transition much faster and this increased the visibility of Japanese companies in a negative way. That sort of thing was disapproved of not only by their staff, who wanted the jobs, but the host government, which wanted as much of the work as possible to be done by locals, and also the general population, which regarded this as an affront to the national honor.

Gradually, policies were adopted officially or informally requiring a localization or indigenization of staff. This could be entirely voluntary, in theory at least, or through guidelines that indicated how many expatriates given companies could keep. If they were not amenable, visas might simply be refused or cancelled by the immigration authorities. In some places, this was coupled with a much more complex and delicate policy of shifting jobs to a specific segment of the population. In Malaysia, it was the Malay majority referred to as *bumiputra* or "children of the soil" and, in Indonesia, the *pribumi*. On the other side of the Pacific, it was the minorities and women who were promoted by equal opportunity clauses in American labor legislation.[13]

For the Japanese, who had enough difficulty in dealing with foreigners in general, it was particularly hard to know how to juggle different categories of workers. This was hardest for them in Southeast Asia where, for traditional reasons, they tended to deal more with the Overseas Chinese. Nor did they like having to favor specific ethnic groups which they found to be less educated and less familiar with a modern economy. That these same people not only had to be hired as workers, but gradually promoted into managerial positions and ultimately even made partners in some places, was rather hard to take. But there was not much alternative as long as they wanted to do business in those countries.

Although Japanese companies tended to set up shop in places where there was relative labor peace, sometimes actually legislated into law, otherwise imposed by strong leaders or authoritarian parties, they could not always enjoy the expected fruit. There could easily be a change at the top. In fact, investments are usually a much longer term proposition than political regimes and it is almost certain that a company would have to work under many, sometimes radically different, governments. Thus, abuse of their workers under one regime could be repaid in kind under the next. Moreover, while the police could put down riots and strikes, it was not able to turn lazy or intractable workers into busy and obedient employees.

Japanese companies have been repeatedly accused of pushing their staffs harder and paying them less than is proper. That is most unlikely, for they tended to follow the going rate where they were located and sometimes gave a bit more. If they had done anything else, they would have lost their employees. But the argument can and is being made in many poorer countries that, as major enterprises and outsiders, often parts of a multinational group, they should be even more generous than the rest. When such campaigns build up, most Japanese companies eventually do give in and offer a sop to their work force simply to maintain peace.

But it is not always peace that they get. Instead, by showing that they will knuckle under rather than face a confrontation, they end up attracting more trouble than otherwise. This was shown in Thailand during 1979, at a time when the military regime had imposed martial law and enacted legislation that supposedly banned all labor actions. Despite this, there were repeated work boycotts and even hunger strikes by the workers directed against Japanese firms in the Bangkok industrial zone. Japanese managers were subjected to threats, blackmail, and attacks by gangsters. Making concessions well beyond those of Thai companies accomplished nothing. The disturbances only ceased after Thai Bridgestone, a subsidiary of the leading Japanese tire maker, decided to get tough and hold the line. And this, it might be noted, was only possible because it received strong backing from the local managers.[14]

In other Asian countries, at various times, Japanese companies have also been disrupted by similar unrest and faced strikes or other action by the workers. If things did not go that far, the alternative might be a very strained atmosphere and some degree of uncooperativeness. This occurred even when such measures were forbidden by the law, and although similar phenomena did not arise in many national companies. Thus, if anything, the Japanese were used as a test case rather than enjoying a more protected status. Still, if they managed to meet some of the demands and maintain more attractive wages and conditions, they could ride out the storm.

This does not mean, by any stretch of the imagination, that the workers in these factories were particularly fortunate. Many were delighted to be out on their own and earning some money. But their life was hardly a bed of roses. Nelia, a typical worker in a Philippine zone, barely earned enough to get by and any raises were quickly eaten up by inflation. She worked an eight hour day, six day week, with plenty of overtime. Her accomodations, food and transport were mediocre. And she might have to look for a new job if her employer lost clients. Yet, no matter how her biographer dramatizes the case, she was obviously one of the lucky girls to even get work. And, as long as developing countries are plagued by unemployment, instability and inflation, their workers will be forced to lead this kind of a life whether employed by multinationals or not.[15]

In the West, and especially the United States, the basic situation was different. For, the Japanese companies were facing strongly organized unions that were backed up by solid legislation and public opinion. Naturally, the Japanese were aided in their efforts to remain free of such unions by areas and groups that disliked unionism for one reason or another. Yet, it is not certain that by keeping the unions out the Japanese were following the wisest policy. This immediately made them a target for unionization and the object of very energetic drives that could disrupt their operations far more than working out a peaceful arrangement. Sony, Honda, Nissan and others quickly discovered this. Moreover, eventually they might be unionized anyway.

Japanese managers involved in such conflicts frequently claim, and sometimes rightly so, that most of the grievances do not really come from the workers but outside agitators who push them toward unionization or use the workers for political purposes. Given their visibility, it is not surprising that these companies, especially the larger ones, should also become targets for various opponents of the existing regime which is regarded as being buttressed by Japanese investors. They have thus faced boycotts of Japanese goods organized by radical students, occasional damage to their property through arson and bomb attacks, and broader anti-Japanese campaigns as well, like those organized during tours of Japanese leaders to Southeast Asia. In Central America and elsewhere, Japanese managers have been kidnapped, and even killed, as punishment for "siding" with the government.

Although this sort of action is anything but typical, it should be perfectly clear that using foreign labor, let alone "squeezing" it, is easier said than done. As long as things run smoothly, the investors are satisfied. However, once trouble erupts, they are basically in a no-win situation. Their reaction is only exceptionally to try to impose their will or brazen it out. Much more often, they avoid problems and overcome resistance by offering a bit more than local competitors or giving in when reasonable demands are made.

At the same time, they consider two alternatives. Each of them involves placing less reliance on the workers they have supposedly come for. When there is doubt about the work will or ability of the local personnel, they compensate by introducing much more machinery than otherwise. In Southeast Asia, for example, despite the low cost of labor, "plant engineers tended to rely heavily on semi-automatic and continuous processes rather than risk possible production breakdowns and deterioration of product quality by using unskilled workers," according to Professor Tsurumi.[16] Then, each time there is labor unrest, they think of rationalization, not to increase efficiency but to replace more workers with machines. In the United States, where the automakers had strong qualms about the "quality of labor," this could only be overcome by setting up the most highly automated and robotized factories they were capable of.

The other solution is simply to withdraw. When they face too much unpleasantness and too many complaints from the local workers, the Japanese tend to lose interest in them. If they are engaged in major, capital-intensive projects, and they cannot afford to leave the machinery behind, they may stay until it wears out. But, for most labor-intensive operations, the machinery and equipment are quite minimal. They can be taken down and shipped to another site or, if worst comes to worst, just written off and left behind. Then the company will resume operations in another country where the quality of labor is better and relations with the workers are more congenial.

This is hardly the behavior of people who want to "exploit" labor at all costs but rather of managers who want employees they can rely on and cooperate with. To this end, they are willing to make some changes in their own way of doing things, and they are willing to make material sacrifices, but if they do not ultimately get a work force they can use well they would rather leave than fight for it.

Moving On

There is no doubt that the various difficulties referred to earlier led Japanese companies to choose one host country or another or, more exactly, to avoid certain particularly bothersome ones. If, after they were established, the labor situation should take a turn for the worse or the investment climate should degrade, they might be forced to pull out. But their biggest problem was of a very different nature... and one that was hardly expected. Some of the "cheap labor" countries started getting expensive.

Economic growth had been so rapid, and had gone on so long, that wages in Korea, Taiwan, Singapore and Hong Kong kept climbing steadily. Their very success in selling labor, combined with the emergence of indigenous producers, created a situation of rather continual and relatively full employment. Even though the unions were not strong, and the workers could not readily impose their conditions, the demand for labor was so great that employers had to offer more. The usual process was for newcomers to the sector to tempt away workers through better remuneration, which older units had no choice but to match.

The result was a pretty constant rise in wages, somewhere in the range of 10% or more a year, over most of the 1960s and into the 1970s, only tapering off somewhat after the oil crisis. This was the regular undercurrent. However, a sudden change in circumstances could make the wage level swing up sharply. This happened when labor unrest suddenly broke out, and had to be satisfied before subsiding or being brought under control, as during the period after Park's assassination in Korea. Or it might result from a spurt of inflation. In Singapore, the cause was a conscious decision of the government to discourage labor-intensive industry by increasing wages by 20% two years in a row.

Although this had not been anticipated by the investors, and the foes of neocolonialism claimed that it was impossible, the wage gap between Japan and some of the host countries was narrowing. And this occurred despite the fact that the yen was gradually appreciating while other currencies slipped gently or were occasionally devaluated more drastically. By the 1980s, workers in the newly industrializing countries of Asia were earning closer to a quarter, sometimes even half, of what Japanese earned. To outsiders, this may not have seemed like much. To local workers, it certainly made a difference.

In fact, it made the same difference that such improvement had made in Japan a generation earlier. With jobs somewhat more plentiful, with more youngsters going to school and staying on longer, with some funds to fall back on, there was a trend away from older, unpleasant sectors and toward the services and higher technologies. Fewer men, or women, wanted to work in factories and more hoped to sit in air-conditioned offices and fill white-collar or executive positions. Naturally, they also wanted to earn a bit more for doing a bit less. Thus, these countries were no longer quite the ideal site for labor-intensive operations they used to be.

This became a serious problem for the favored four. Just like Japan before them, they did not relish the idea of losing companies. Even if they were a bit behind the times, or had archaic machinery, they did employ a large number of workers. Too rapid a movement, too many leaving at the same time, could result in a bout of unemployment. More significantly, it would look like a sign of distrust in the economy and might perhaps shake the confidence of other investors. Yet, at the same time, by trying to move up-market they were exerting greater pressure on certain industries. Only capital-intensive sectors could keep up and this of itself raised wages for the remaining labor force. Even when they did not push out old investors, more recent changes in their investment codes made it perfectly clear that investors in less advanced branches were not really welcome.

The only way to induce higher wages, to make the economy more sophisticated *and* to keep most of the existing investors happy was to upgrade the quality of the labor force at the same time. If the workers could provide more for the additional money they were paid, that might compensate. Thus, Singapore in particular initiated special training courses and opened more schools. It even launched a "learn from Japan" campaign. The others also provided better vocational and technical training. Quality control circles and productivity activities were introduced. But this only helped the companies that also had the capital to upgrade and could use this more specialized and skilled work force. If they were unable to improve their machinery and techniques, or did not care to, better staff with greater skills were of no use to them.

The outcome was not always positive. Some investors actually went bankrupt and others earned so little they decided to withdraw. As in Japan, there was a tendency in the more backward and labor-intensive sectors to think of moving elsewhere while those that could adapt might hang on. Even if this did not lead to an abrupt departure of old investors, it did cause many of them to stop any planned expansion and sometimes to cut back on existing operations. The more decisive reaction was only noticeable from Japan. After checking their calculations, potential investors concluded that it did not make much sense to move there only to fall into the same trap. By increasing automation and robotization they could make do with less labor. Of, if they really needed access to cheap labor, they would have to go further afield.

For, what happened in the "gang of four," as they were sometimes called, was far from a generalized phenomenon. There were still plenty of countries which had only improved slightly and some that were actually worse off than at independence. In those countries, wages were dreadfully low, even as compared to what had been cheap labor countries a decade or two earlier. By the 1980s, wages in places like Taiwan and Korea were twice as high, and sometimes more, than in Southeast or West Asia and the gap with the People's Republic of China was even greater.

This gap, although not as large as what once existed between Japan and East Asia, was crucial after the oil crisis when the competition in certain sectors became increasingly fierce. For labor-intensive articles like garments or footwear and for the labor-intensive aspects of electronics production or assembly, it was enough to win or lose the decisive edge over a growing pack of contestants. To keep ahead of their opponents back home, Japanese companies had to find the cheapest sources of capable labor and, in so doing, they sometimes entered into competition with their older factories in East Asia. They also were immersed in rivalry from upstart companies in Korea, Taiwan and Hong Kong which tried to outdo them locally and internationally and also began moving some of their own operations offshore.

Such a transfer of activities was quite difficult in more sophisticated or highly capitalized sectors of the economy. One could not just close down a spinning mill and automobile assembly lines were pretty much fixed. But other operations were very "footloose" and did not hesitate to shift from place to place in keeping with the opportunities and wage levels. The most conspicuous ones were garments and footwear, electronic components and assembly, audio and optical goods, sporting gear and toys. They did not require very much machinery, could be set up quickly in nearly any site and with particular ease in an industrial estate.

Thus, the step was greatly facilitated by the proliferation of more export processing zones in the Asian region, in countries which felt that offering cheap labor as an inducement for investment was a good proposition or just the only quick solution. Since this met the needs of growing numbers of manufacturers, the migration became even broader and swifter than the move toward the first generation of zones. By the 1970s, the new frontiers appeared in the Philippines, Indonesia, Malaysia and Thailand. A decade later, they had been pushed as far back as India, Pakistan and Sri Lanka. Other sites might eventually arise further off, or quite nearby, if China opened up for real.

Meanwhile, the seesaw between Japan and the West, within the group of supposedly advanced nations, continued tottering toward the east. Japanese wages kept swelling rapidly while those abroad were slimmed by inflation and unemployment. For all their lack of clout, Japanese workers soon earned more than many of their European counterparts or people in depressed parts of the United States. This obviously pleased the Japanese workers. Not so their employers. Even while paying tribute to the nation's work ethic, they began calculating how much could be saved on cheaper labor abroad.

NOTES

1. See Woronoff, *Japan's Wasted Workers*, pp. 192–212.
2. *Far Eastern Economic Review*, May 18, 1979, p. 76.
3. *Ibid*, p. 78.
4. Terutomo Ozawa, *Multinationalism, Japanese Style*, p. 26.
5. Ministry of Finance, *Japan's Direct Overseas Investment*, 1983.
6. *Japan Times*, June 6, 1981.
7. *Japan Times*, August 4, 1982.
8. Halliday and McCormack, *Japanese Imperialism Today*, p. 72.
9. See, if you have time to waste, William Ouchi, *Theory Z*, Richard Tanner Pascale and Anthony Athos, *The Art of Japanese Management*, and especially Ezra Vogel, *Japan as No. 1*.
10. For a less naive view, see Woronoff, *Japan: The Coming Economic Crisis* and *Japan's Wasted Workers*.
11. See Mitsuhiko Yamada, "Japanese-Style Management in America: Merits and Difficulties," in *Japanese Economic Studies*, Fall 1981.
12. *New York Daily News*, September 25, 1980.

13. Among the companies which got into trouble were Sumitomo Shoji America, sued for discriminating against women and Americans by some of its local female secretaries, and Hitachi, fined for not hiring enough black and Hispanic workers.

14. *Japan Economic Journal*, September 11, 1979.

15. Robert T. Snow, "Multinational Corporations in Asia, The Labor-Intensive Factory," *Bulletin of Concerned Asian Scholars*, October-December 1979, pp. 26–9.

16. Tsurumi, *The Japanese Are Coming*, p. 183.

7
Neocolonies. . .

Loser Scenario

It is said that the aboriginal tribes in New Guinea were amazed to sight a strange bird flying overhead, one far larger than any they had ever seen and obviously different because it moved straight ahead and advanced without flapping its wings. On occasion this bird suddenly dropped from the sky and they found bits of metal around the spot where it had fallen. Such objects were collected and worshipped. Eventually, some tribesmen gazed down on civilization from hiding and saw this great bird land on a long tarmac strip where wonderful things were taken from inside. Wishing to capture the bird, they could think of no better idea than to clear an area in the midst of the jungle and lay out a rather crude but hopefully inviting landing place to attract it.

Many developing, and some advanced, countries seem to be doing much the same thing with foreign investors. Although they have little infrastructure or supporting industries, they have become enamored of steel mills and petrochemical plants or, if they are more modest, television and motocycle assembly units. To obtain them, when they cannot afford the costs or lack the knowhow, they have simply cleared a landing place for others who possess those assets in the hope that they may come and roost.

A cozy nest has been provided in the form of highly encouraging and generous investment codes complete with a battery of incentives. Going a step further, there has been a trend to build industrial parks and export processing zones which provide all the necessary infrastructure and facilities for any investor just to land and start operations. But many of the zones are in the middle of nowhere with scant contact with the rest of the economy and even the best projects are rarely inserted in an overall plan or concept.

It is only much later that people begin to realize that attracting investment is the easiest part. It is still necessary for the investment to yield its true value and contribute to broader development. Thus, knowing how to treat investors, and also choosing the right ones, is crucial. If this is not done properly there is no guarantee that a country will be any better off than before. In fact, despite their "success" in attracting investors, many countries noticed some years later that there had been relatively little improvement. Indeed, things had often gotten worse in certain ways. And people looked on investment as a false god or delusive idol.

In countries which are not suitably prepared, or where the investors or hosts have made some fundamental mistakes, there are now the remains of ill-fated projects which are pointed out to visitors as proof of how investment can go wrong. They are the many "white elephants" that seem to proliferate especially in warm, tropical countries of three continents. But relics like this can be encountered elsewhere as well.

It occasionally happens that mines are opened before any road or railway has been constructed to bring the ore to the nearest port or distribution center. Or the road exists but the port hasn't been completed. And this does not exclude the possibility that the port and road have been built but the mine is not ready, or the ore is not high enough grade and therefore hardly worth mining. These seemingly incredible mishaps, where just one aspect of the project goes wrong, are quite adequate for the whole project to fail. And they pale in comparison to the many once successful operations that cease working because the price the ore fetches on international markets has fallen.

What happens in mining occurs in different ways for major cash crop projects in agriculture. The new miracle grains require more fertilizer and irrigation, which means higher costs. The payoff can be excellent. But if it does not come quickly the farmers may sink under the burden of debt. And, if the population is too poor to buy, there may be no market. Meanwhile, more extensive farming replaces the old family farm and peasants are torn away from the land.

Industry, however, offers the broadest variety of mishaps. In fact, it is extremely difficult to design a successful manufacturing project because so many different aspects must be considered. Thus, we find factories that are operating poorly because the necessary raw materials were not delivered adequately, or on time, or of proper quality. Basic inputs and components that should be produced locally are not and have to be imported instead. Inside the factory, there may be problems because not enough skilled labor is available or the labor force does not work hard or rejects the essential discipline. Even if the factory runs well, it may produce goods that, due to some oversight, are not really appropriate for the local population or do not meet local needs, no matter how popular they may be elsewhere. Or, due to more than an oversight, the economy has not grown as much as hoped and people simply cannot afford to buy them.

Of course, such extremes are not often attained and entirely worthless projects are few. Many more are those which are simply a bit less efficient or a bit more costly than expected. Because of inexperienced local suppliers, less than ideal parts are procured and result in less than ideal products. Or the more vital parts are imported, which adds to cost. If the workers are incompetent or lazy, the products will be of poorer quality and higher price. More frequently, the plant simply does not run at an optimum scale. Either it was built smaller, and has to be less efficient, or it was built to an ambitious scale which was not reached and leaves much excess capacity.

All this leads to inefficient operation and higher costs which must be reflected either by bankruptcies or special support. Sensing they cannot truly prosper, some companies will withdraw only a few years after entry. Others will accept a bad show a bit longer in the hope that something may turn up or to save face. In certain cases, the government, which has promoted investment and is also judged by the success of these projects, may offer subsidies or tax rebates and the like to keep them afloat. As part of a broader development policy, it may erect protective tariffs to keep out imports. Then the ventures can limp along or even flourish, depending on the level of protection. But the products will be that much more costly, and perhaps even more expensive than sticking to imports.

Thus, the cargo cult of investment has sometimes re-sulted in rather grotesque and misplaced ventures or ugly outcroppings of modernism that blend poorly with the surroundings. Even while they are admired, they may be envied and ultimately reviled because they did not fulfill the promises they made, or rather, that others made for them and expectations that were sometimes quite unrealistic to begin with.

This, however, is not the end of the story. As the most visible symbols of modernization and the religion of economic development, they are related to much broader phenomena.

If the projects cost the host country nothing, then a failure might be excused. But, one way or the other, there is usually some burden on the state's finances as well since it has to build suitable industrial parks or export processing zones. It has to provide much of the needed infrastructure. And it is expected to run a reasonable educational and health system so that skilled workers are available and foreigners can live there safely. In return, the investors seem to offer little other than the supposed benefits of their projects. It is known that they often enjoy tax rebates for a considerable time, import many goods duty-free, benefit from certain subsidies, and then repatriate profits and the original capital.

This makes them look more like freeloaders than benefactors to some, especially when it is forgotten that valid projects should bring long-term advantages to the economy while the special incentives are more short-lived. So, foreign investment is regarded as more of a drain on the nation's wealth than a contribution. It is not really noticed how small a drain it is proportionately, since far more is spent on general requisites like education and health, infrastructure needed for the whole country and occasionally some rather pointless frills like fancy public buildings, an inordinately large bureaucracy or military establishment, and some otherwise useless monuments to the regime.

In countries which are sinking deeper into debt, it is rarely the costs deriving from overseas investment that make the difference. It is the many loans taken out on hard or soft terms, but certainly more than the country can really afford, which lead to a real hemorrhage of currency. It is also the many imports, some of them far from essential, some actually sheer luxuries, which have to be paid for and keep the trade balance consistently negative. It is also the occasional flight of capital to safer places, expedited by locals who should be investing in their own economy but leave that to outsiders. Yet, even if they are not the major cause, foreign investors are certainly the most visible presence and take the rap.

In relatively backward countries, even a project that is not terribly viable or successful will stand out as an oasis of prosperity in the rather desolate surroundings. The factories and farms of foreign investors are most usually larger, more efficient, and more prominent. They are run better and enjoy more support. While others suffer, they appear to do relatively well. Their managers are paid more, their workers are paid more, and the expatriates enjoy a comfortable standard of living that may appear absolutely scandalous.

These enclaves become targets of envy and scorn for those who fare less well, especially if there is no hope of rising to that level. Morever, the cities where modern industry is concentrated and the wealthy foreign investors tend to congregate, become a strong pole attracting those who live in the poorer, more hopeless backwaters. Whether drawn by the bright lights and beckoning opportunities, or simply dispossessed of their land, the peasants and their families may join a growing rural exodus. But, what they find in the cities is rarely what they dreamed of. They flow into the dismal slums and shantytowns which may be worse than what they had before.

Certainly, industry will offer promising jobs at higher rates of pay. But it takes a tremendous amount of industrialization to absorb the numbers of people who leave the countryside in much of the Third World. So, work is provided for the few while the many remain unemployed or underemployed, eking out a living as best they can. Yet, their very existence as a massive reservoir of employable people makes it unnecessary for managers to offer very high salaries. The level may indeed be so low that some speak of "starvation wages," although the average farm worker earns much less and the unemployed would give their soul for a job.

This sort of situation naturally creates political pressures that are very hard to contain. Trade unions may arise which make "excessive" demands in the eyes of the foreign—and local—capitalists and which the government may reject to protect industry, or investment, or because the farmers are so much worse off that urban workers look like an elite. Stymied in their demands, the workers may turn to socialism, while the intellectuals dabble in Marxism. Strikes can break out giving the country a bad name among investors and encouraging some to leave. Then the campaign is taken up by militant students.

Rather than risk continuing social unrest and the political implications this can have, some governments have conceded that perhaps foreign investment was not always the best thing and singled out specific cases that were reprehensible or at least given their tacit support to more spontaneous grassroots action. Others have actually jumped on the bandwagon. They realized that part of the complaints levelled at the foreign investors were actually meant for them, but were deflected toward foreigners because that was safer. To keep the movement from turning against them and leading to a political reverse, they do not hesitate to make the regime more radical, verbally at least.

So, the investors can end up as scapegoats for both sides. They are cursed by those who expected more results, or who do not share the advantages, and regard investment as far less necessary or essentially exploitative. They are associated too closely with the government, which approved their projects and sometimes supported their efforts. If it is a venal and corrupt one to boot, they may have become a major source of illicit funds. Yet, there are very few regimes that would stand up for the investors' rights if they felt endangered. Attacked by one side or the other, and sometimes caught in the middle, foreign investment has to work veritable miracles to reap much praise.

Investment Backlash

When it happened that the great benefits expected from foreign investment did not accrue, or did not seem adequate, many countries began to backpedal. They amended their investment codes, making them less favorable. They took away some of the incentives or watered them down considerably. This might mean less cheap land or facilities, shorter or no tax holidays, restrictions on repatriation of profits and capital, and so on. It often applied not only to newcomers who arrived at a later date but also to the investors who had been there for years and expected to continue using the advantages promised them.

Investors being what they are, the measures they liked least were those which deprived them of the fruits of their labor. This could be done by raising the taxation rates radically. In almost all investment codes designed to attract fresh capital there were provisions for tax rebates to be followed by normal taxation later on. The investors somewhat naively hoped that normal taxation meant the levels prevailing at the time of making the investment. But taxes have a tendency to rise and thus it was rather natural they should be somewhat higher. However, some governments, feeling they had been too generous at first or acting under pressure from the opposition, jacked up the rates tremendously and when the company had to pay taxes they were very high indeed.

More seriously, the rules on transfer of capital and profits as well as distribution of dividends were usually assumed to last indefinitely. However, if the country had gotten into a balance of payments squeeze, it might have to restrict the outflow of currency. Since many countries tended to borrow too much at the time they were building up the economy, it could well happen that they would not want the investors to take back their money. The more decent might encourage them to reinvest or put the funds to other uses. But even then there was a limited need for local currency. So some companies were stuck with lots of unusable money or had to exchange it at unfavorable rates.

But it was not only the specific measures that annoyed the investors. It was the very idea that the rules could be changed so readily. Investment is a very long-term proposition and it is essential to have stability in the conditions. So, what was most bothersome was not even the new rules, in many cases, but the mere fact that rules were not relatively fixed and could be changed at the whim of the government. Thus, some investors felt betrayed and sought their own ways of getting around any changes or solving the problems that arose in an expedient, if not necessarily proper, manner. Others decided to withdraw. But the most noticeable reaction was usually a sharp decline in fresh investment. If it were too precipitous, the country might be worried and improve the code again.

What happened in Thailand, for example, was rather typical of many developing countries. In 1962, it adopted an "Industrial Investment Promotion Law," one of the first countries to do so. This offered special advantages and incentives that led to considerable investment from Japan, the United States and Europe and also quickly boosted Thailand's growth rate. But the effort was too great and the development was lopsided while balance of payments difficulties loomed. So, in 1972, it adopted the "Foreign Corporation Restriction Law." This, plus the oil crisis, plus some nationalist agitation, certainly accomplished that goal. The value of direct investment slumped markedly. As a result, the Thai economy slowed down and a recession set in. One way out was seen to be stronger measures to promote foreign capital inflows culminating in a new "Investment Promotion Law" in 1977. This was not quite as generous as the original law, but more lenient than the restrictive one.

Such fluctuations arose not only in the developing or "soft" countries. More advanced nations, like Britain, Australia, or France, were not much better. Aside from a strong zenephobic streak, and fear of Japanese investment, there was also the continual tug-of-war between the pro-business and pro-labor forces. When the Conservatives were in power, they would issue calls for foreign investment to get the economy going. Then, when Labour or the Socialists took over, they would make threatening noises and adopt some discouraging strictures. When the Conservatives got back in, and called for more investment, the investors were less than forthcoming since they never knew when the situation would be reversed again.

Although foreign investors were unhappy about losing the various fiscal and financial incentives, there was something that irked them even more, namely tampering with the rules regarding ownership. The original legislation in many countries permitted 100% ownership by foreign investors, although some asked for a larger share of local ownership running up to 49%. With this, the foreign investor still had a majority. At 50–50 he at least had an equal say. And investment codes with such provisions were far more successful in attracting investors, almost as a function of the share of ownership left to outsiders. The Philippines, which rarely granted more than 30% foreign ownership, was never quite as successful as Thailand, Singapore or others with higher ratios.

Unfortunately, for various reasons, some economic, far more political or even psychological, certain countries gradually began squeezing out the investors. Each new law regulating investment allowed a lesser share of foreign control, not only for new investors but the old ones as well. Thus, the Japanese companies found their holdings were steadily being diminished. If they grumbled when the first percentage points were withdrawn, they became very annoyed and increasingly nervous as they were pushed into a minority position.

These policies of continually nibbling away at the ownership and rights of investors arose in a rather large number of places as parts of various policies of "indigenization." This could be Malaysianization, Indonesianization, or assorted breeds of Africanization. The policies went to differing lengths in different countries and

Sintering Plant In The Philippines

Credit: Kawasaki Steel

also were achieved by different methods. Usually, it was quite simply an order to sell a given share of the company to locals and often also to have a given number of locals in management and on the board. In Malaysia, it took a more imaginative form of having the companies sell their stock to the public, and then buying them up.

If the foreign investors ended up in a position where they only had a small share of ownership, say 20%, 30%, or even 40%, they could easily be outvoted by the local partners who conceivably had quite different interests. They would also have to put up with suggestions from managers or partners who sometimes knew relatively little about how to run such an enterprise. (If they knew more, they would not have needed the foreign investors in the first place.) This does not mean that the operation could not run smoothly. Often, it did. But, if it didn't, residual ownership was enough to make the original investor feel it was no longer worth the effort and to pull out since he no longer had enough of a vested interest.

Still, if changing the rules was an unpleasant event, certainly it was much worse to simply break the rules. That happened in countries that were most dissatisfied with investment as such or felt that they should make a new start after overthrowing the old regime which had entered into the agreements. Even here, the measures could vary. The government might order the investor to sell out promptly, theoretically allowing him to be reimbursed. However, with a tight deadline and the knowledge it had to leave soon, the company could hardly drive much of a bargain and had to accept what it got. In other cases, the investment project might be allocated to a state corporation which paid what it felt was justified. The payment might, alas, be made in national currency that was hard to exchange or devalued or in bonds of yet more dubious worth. Or the venture could simply be expropriated without compensation, it being argued that the motherland had already been exploited enough by foreign capitalists who deserved to be driven out.

What many host countries did not realize—and some do not realize to this very day—is that it is relatively easy to invite an investor in, and not even that hard to take his project away from him, but it is terribly difficult to make it run. In many cases, all that was obtained was just a piece of productive machinery in the state it then was. If the country was lucky, and had some reasonably competent personnel, it could be operated and continue producing. If the personnel was not as good as hoped, then it might function less well. But, if worst came to worst, it would simply grind to a halt. Such an acquisition was obviously worth nothing.

If a factory was expropriated and the investor was on bad terms with the country, then it would be hard to obtain spare parts and, over the years, the unit would become faulty. Or it would be hard to get the right raw materials, or components, or the essential marketing arm would be lost. But, even when everything ran smoothly enough, the machinery was only as it was when seized. It was in the state of the art not on transfer to its new owners but as it was on arrival many years before. In the intervening time, new technologies and products had been developed, labor and energy-saving devices introduced, and thus the factory could be inefficient and unproductive although it did run.

Even if a captive plant was still run by a captive investor, influencing his action too strongly could force him into decisions that were not economically justifiable. He might have to expand capacity beyond the possibility of sales. He might have to start processes that were poorly handled by the labor force in its present state of competence. He might have to localize and produce parts despite the lack of economies of scale. In such cases, the products would be of poor quality, or too numerous, or unnecessarily costly. . . .

This would then create pressure in two directions. If the company was made to suffer for moves it took under duress, then the director would find it hard to sell such products or he would have to sell at a loss. In the worst eventuality, the company would go bankrupt. Otherwise, it would have to complain vehemently and bring pressure to bear on the authorities. Since a country cannot readily afford bankruptcies that would upset the economy, lead to unemployment and earn the government a bad reputation, it is quite likely that it would support ailing enterprises. This could be done by subsidies or simply by keeping the tariffs so high and quotas so strict that the goods, even if costly and second-rate, could be sold profitably.

None of these solutions is particularly beneficial. Thus, whether a country is in a position to impose them is less important than what the results will be when it does. Countries that have "won" the petty battles of gaining an upper hand over foreign investors and multinationals have all too often ended up losing in their efforts to create a solid economy.

So, since we originally compared luring an investor to trapping a bird, it might be pointed out that nothing is gained by killing the goose that lays the golden egg, or even plucking it, but rather by caring for it, and nurturing it, it will keep on laying golden eggs and perhaps reproduce.

The "Ugly Japanese"

Once investment does not seem to be working, or at least not producing the expected benefits, it does not take long to find a great many things wrong with investment as such. In countries where Japanese investment is prominent, or the Japanese just happen to be conspicuous, any dissatisfaction will be accompanied or punctuated by a series of complaints against Japanese business practices and the Japanese themselves.

Probably the broadest grievance against the Japanese is the self-seeking nature of their investment. They are not setting up projects that are designed for the good of the host country but rather for the narrowly defined good of the investor. More generally, the Japanese are only interested in what they can get and hope to give as little as possible. They are motivated only by profit while ignoring the finer points of the host country and failing to cooperate with the local people. As a Thai professor put it, "Japan is first and foremost a rapacious economic animal, virtually everything it does—or does not do—is linked to its business interests."[1]

There is no doubt that the Japanese were, and still are, very careful about the conditions under which they will enter any country. If the conditions are too exacting or the prospects too dim, they will turn up their nose to one offer or potential host and try another. They will look into the local situation very carefully and only invest if the chances for success are rather good. That is why an amazing amount of investment has come not spontaneously but had to be extorted, as Japanese companies were informed that the only way they could hold on to lucrative markets was by investing more in local production.

Even then, these companies tend to drag their heels and only go as far as is strictly necessary. They keep on extracting raw materials and only process them when put under pressure. The assembly plants they establish usually just put together knocked-down kits without procuring local supplies. They continue importing intermediate goods for years and make as much out of that transaction as possible. Only when new laws gradually raise the amount of local content required does the flow of intermediate goods slacken and any ripple effect become noticeable.

Similar reluctance is shown when it comes to transferring technology. Most host countries regard investment as a form of education in which the local population will gradually learn how to run the factories and mines. The local staff should therefore be made privy to the knowhow and lower level staff should gradually be promoted upward to key positions. The Japanese, on the other hand, assume that their primary, and perhaps sole, task is to teach whoever has to run the operation exactly what he has to do, nothing more nor less. Whether he understands the deeper reasons for what he does is immaterial.

Aside from complaints about a lack of transfer, the Japanese are often accused of not bringing in the finest technologies. After all, given the cost of investment which is so high—in their eyes at least—the hosts want nothing but the latest and the best. Yet, many of the Japanese investors are very small firms in rather old-fashioned and labor-intensive sectors. Such ventures, it is assumed, cannot make much of a contribution either in terms of production or learning experience.

Worse, the masses of smaller ventures quickly appear to be competitors to local companies in the same sectors. In some cases, this is so and, since they are a bit more modern or efficient, the Japanese can be extremely effective competitors. But more often than not the real trouble only comes somewhat later, among local companies that copy them and then compete against them, ultimately seeking political support to make up for any commercial or technical backwardness.

Some of the larger Japanese ventures also rock the boat unnecessarily. Simply due to their size, they have a presence that is immediately felt. Since they are often located in crucial sectors, and many other companies are dependent on them, they tend to make unpleasant waves. If they press their suppliers for lower rates or hike their own prices, the impact is substantial and often judged unfair. If, while expanding their operations they trample some existing firms underfoot, they are accused of cutthroat competition. Much of the actual competition, however, results from the bitter rivalry between Japanese companies which fight one another for market share. Without really noticing it, they manage to expand largely by driving weaker local firms to the wall.

While such behavior is alarming enough when Japanese companies act singly, there is yet greater apprehension when they seem to act collectively. There is little doubt that Japanese subsidiaries tend to help one another, a Japanese bank lending to the affiliate of an old client back home, an automobile assembler or electronics manufacturer procuring parts from the affiliate of a regular supplier. This seems to leave no room for local companies to do business in certain segments of their own market. And the impression is even worse if the Japanese government, broadly disliked for its power and cunning, tries to help its businessmen abroad.

When it comes to their labor relations, it is often felt that such big foreign companies should be treating their employees better than they actually do. There are repeated complaints about the wage levels being too low or the workers being exploited. There are also complaints that not enough of the local employees are being promoted rapidly enough and that too many Japanese personnel remain in key positions many years after the venture is established.

This runs against all the policies of indigenization and a general feeling common to all countries that the locals should be given a chance.

Aside from these more economic aspects, there is a plenitude of grievances about how the Japanese behave socially, a matter which theoretically might be left to them but shocks their hosts' sensibilities and is added to the rest. Much of this is hard to avoid. The Japanese may very well not be of the same religion, and are certainly not of the same race, as the host population. Their customs and practices are different, their manners and behavior are different, and what is more, they don't seem to notice or care. Thus, without thinking, they constantly flaunt native traditions and values.

This has resulted in a view of them as the "ugly Japanese," as earlier there was much ado about the "ugly Americans." Even if the Japanese are not much better or worse, they do have one characterisic that makes it harder to overcome such problems. They tend to stick together, to keep one another's company, and even to live in the same areas. Japanese ghettos have grown up not only in rather backward countries where it is hard to find amenities, and thus common ones are arranged, but in places where it would be perfectly easy to live closer to the rest of the population, such as New York or Dusseldorf.

Part of the problem is language. But that is only part. Another is the ethos of the Japanese company system which implies very close and almost constant relations between the members of the team, with them sharing not only office hours but meals and evening entertainment. There is no room for outsiders in this, not even other Japanese, let alone any locals. This tight, closed and apparently exclusive approach certainly wins them few friends or defenders. Worse, it makes perfectly natural behavior and acts that are hardly inimical to anyone appear like part of a broader conspiracy or a general attitude of arrogance and contempt.

Of course, those who do not like the Japanese to begin with will not find it hard to toss in some obvious misdemeanors. They are seen too often drinking until late at night and then staggering home drunk. When they carouse, their behavior is hardly exemplary. In countries where girls are plentiful, and accessible, they also become known for whoring and are regarded as worse than economic animals, namely sex maniacs. That so many do seem to regard local women as loose and for sale does not help. But it is often forgotten that most of these people are Japanese tourists and not the more stolid businessmen who must sacrifice more pleasures for the sake of the company than the average local would ever accept.

Also, in countries which are rife with corruption, the Japanese appear to play a disproportionately large role. They often enter into ventures with persons who are known to be particularly well connected with the government. In so doing, they create what is called a "comprador" class of middlemen. In other countries, they are tied up closely with the minority Chinese community which is not generally trusted rather than the broader, but less commercially-minded, native communities. They are known to have bribed one customs agent or another and lavishly rewarded those who approve their investment projects. Seen individually, these acts make them liable to a charge of corruption. Seen more broadly, they are regarded as a pillar of the existing regime, which does not always enjoy the unstinting support of the masses, and thus part of the exploiting class or coterie.

When the Japanese presence becomes too visible, partly because of the activities of its investors, all of the various strands seem to come together in a web of intrigue and conspiracy. If the underlying economic and political situation in the host country is already shaky, the frustration and anger that would otherwise dissipate can instead create an explosion. One such explosion was sparked by Prime Minister Tanaka's visit to Thailand, where the following statement was issued by the student movement.

"Japan is the main cause of our present economic problems. The Thai people have never had any disputes with the Japanese, but during the last ten years Japanese businessmen have come to open businesses in Thailand and have used every trick to gain profits. The Japanese government has both directly and indirectly supported these men here. Although the Japanese government is now improving some of its policies that does not mean that the changes will give benefits or economic equality, because in practice both the Japanese businessmen and Japanese government officials will use every trick to gain benefits for themselves. They have several times done this kind of thing, and Thais have come to understand that the Japanese have no sincerity for anyone in this world."[2]

When faced with such a litany of griefs, the Japanese and even neutral observers were dumbfounded. Obviously, the Japanese have their flaws. More specifically, the businessmen stationed in other countries and in charge of making investments or running projects there make mistakes or act improperly on occasion. But they deny that this reveals any concerted attempt to take over or dominate an economy or systematic failings on their part. In addition, some of the charges look a bit overdone while others appear pointless.

Wages and working conditions, for example. The various studies made all agree that Japanese employers are paying at least the going rate for their staff and in many cases are offering more, either in actual remuneration or through bonuses and fringe benefits. They also provide more welfare facilities. It must be obvious to even their most hard-bitten foes that no one would accept to work for a Japanese company for less than he could obtain elsewhere. That the remuneration may seem low by international standards, or compared to what the expatriates are earning, or compared to what the company seems to gain, is immaterial. Wages and conditions are never set by one employer but all of them acting together, and in this it is the mass of local companies and the government which are more decisive.

Moreover, in countries where corruption is rife, it is hard to even function without joining in. Companies which rejected such practices were usually penalized and some had to withdraw. If valid partners are hard to find, but the investment code makes them obligatory, it is not surprising that they should be sought among those with more experience or able to help out in some way. Nor should it be strange that foreign managers work in different ways and are hesitant to be supplanted by locals. Many of the things that have been criticized are not necessarily bad as such but only when the Japanese exaggerate or prove less cooperative than others.

Many of the complaints are also vitiated by another defect that is more general. They somehow assume that foreign companies should be models, that they should behave better than others and pay more than others. When they do not, they are open to criticism. In actual fact, there is absolutely no reason to expect more of a foreign company than a local one and, all rhetoric aside, it would be more normal to expect less.

The local company is there because it can go nowhere else. The foreign investor has a broad range of alternatives. He can invest in that country, or many others, or simply stay at home. He is not going to go through the effort of making an investment and then adjusting to very different circumstances for nothing. Obviously, he wants to make a profit. Obviously, he wants to be a commercial success. To do this, he will make all necessary efforts within the laws or practices in force. To expect him to act like a benefactor is absurd. It is not only absurd, it is counterproductive. For, if his company does not succeed in its own terms, then it will simply collapse or withdraw.

Naturally, this sort of reasoning does not appeal to those who are systematically opposed to foreign investment or have found the Japanese to be the worst practitioners of neocolonialism. People like that would tend to agree with the assessment of the radical historian and educator Renato Constantino. "The growing Japanese presence in the Philippine economy should be a cause for concern for the Filipino people. We should see it as a threat to our inalienable right to benefit from our own resources and enjoy the fruits of our own labor. We should be aware of the long-term implications of increasing Japanese econ-omic penetration—the specter of Japanese militarism which may spearhead another invasion if Japanese in-terests in this part of the world are threatened."[3]

The Odds Against Success

If not very much can be expected from foreign investors when it comes to the general well-being of the nation, at least they can usually be counted upon to make every effort for their own projects to be a success. This they will do less for high and noble reasons than that they have put up a lot of money, attached their prestige and reputation to the project, and they want it to prosper. There are very few investors anywhere who would go to the trouble of creating a venture just so it could vegetate and ultimately crumble.

It is entirely possible that foreign investors would be much more interested in making any venture work for themselves more than for their partners or the host country. But they would not normally risk letting it collapse just because they could not attain all of their goals and had to sacrifice some or because they could not reap as much profit as they originally anticipated. Thus, if dealt with wisely and fairly, there is no reason that the host country or their partners should not be able to realign policy in such a way that the project is mutually beneficial.

Unfortunately, in countries which have come to regret investment, or even regard it as pernicious and just another form of exploitation, it is not only one or two projects which have failed but a great many. Moreover, it is not only the foreign-invested ones but national ventures, whether in the private or public sector, which have suffered. This shows that the causes are usually much more pervasive and widespread and the responsibility may not necessarily lie with the outside investors.

Most countries have a general economic policy which may, or may not, be congenial to investment. The developing countries and socialist nations often have specific plans for longer periods which go into very great detail. And there are usually investment codes to determine exactly what foreign investors can and cannot do. This is the framework for most projects, one which can hardly be neglected. And if this framework is the wrong one, then the chances of cultivating successful investments are much diminished.

The countries in which foreign investment has failed most seem to be at the extremes, either giving too much freedom and leeway to outsiders in deciding on their ventures or binding them so tightly they can hardly move. Neither approach would seem ideal. The outside investor usually does not know the basic concerns of the host country, and perhaps simply does not care, so it would be quite normal for his investment not to take them into consideration. On the other hand, the host country usually does not know exactly how his investment can be most fruitful, and ignoring the investor's wishes could be equally dangerous.

In countries with very little central direction, where there is no real framework for economic development, the investor may have considerable flexibility in choice. But he will not really know how the rest of the economy is going to evolve. This means that he will have a tremendous number of imponderables in making crucial decisions for his own operations. He will not know how much parts or raw materials he can obtain locally and thus opt for much more coming from the home factory. He will not know whether or not he will face other competitors in the sector since the host may well let more investors in or firms may spring up locally. And he will not know what the potential demand is since there is not much notion of what the country will look like in another few years.

A mistake anywhere along the line could be disastrous for the venture. Yet, even the most glaring vices of misplanning proliferate. Earlier, mention was made of basic inputs not being available or roads not being built. They were not just theoretical examples. This sort of thing happens all the time. For example, Thailand built a major industrial estate, to which factories were moved, while forgetting to connect it to the rest of the country with a proper road. Many sawmills were built in parts of Southeast Asia at a time the timber supply was running out. Even in a supposedly coordinated operation, like the Cenibra and Flonibra projects in Brazil, the two units were not linked. Pulp production started before the wood chip side was ready, and now this basic source of inputs may never be realized.

If one would expect everything to be just right anywhere, it should be with the carefully nurtured export processing zones. Nevertheless, the Bataan Export Processing Zone is not fully usable after a decade in operation. Electricity and water supply are inadequate, there are not enough telephone lines, and security is lax. There is much pilfering of imported goods and difficulty in sending out exports. The deep water port has not been built and other shipping facilities are insufficient so goods have to be hauled by truck. Not only is this more expensive, the road is poor and dangerous so that trucks have to travel in convoy to avoid hijacking. This may explain why the Bataan zone is only 60% full and some investors have withdrawn. Yet, rather than improve things there, the Philippine government is eagerly proceeding with the creation of a dozen more.

What happens on a smaller scale can also occur on the larger scale of a whole industry. There are countries which select potential growth sectors and then forget to do the spade work. For example, they decide to establish automobile plants and electronics factories while forgetting that these products need literally thousands of parts and components. They are then upset to find that, in fact, the investors are just importing knock-down kits and putting them together. They keep up the flow of intermediate goods because local suppliers do not meet their demands. The host country may react by legislating local content rules, as when Thailand increased automobile localization from 25% in 1978 to 50% five years later. But, if nothing is done to revamp the supply structure, either the law has to be ignored or the assemblers will be stuck with substandard parts.

Another dimension of integration arises for the processing of raw materials. Naturally, greater value added can be obtained by moving further downstream. But this is easier said than done. While Brazil started with nearby bauxite sources and went on to alumina and aluminum ingots, Inalum first built a huge hydroelectric plant and smelter to process imported alumina, only later processing its own bauxite into alumina. Meanwhile, it apparently forgot to prepare manufacturing industries to use Indonesia's share of the output. Whereas Brazil, and most other countries, started with local or imported iron and coal to make steel, the Philippines strangely enough entered the chain through sintering. It then took many more years to mount the rest of the integrated process in such a way that it left doubts about the possible success of its steel mill.

While a lack of ambition is frequently condemned as a fatal weakness of many developing countries, it turns out that overambition can more perilous. There has been a very disconcerting trend toward giantism in many of the projects, especially those hoisted to the level of "national projects." Indonesia's aluminum complex is already one of the biggest in the world. Yet, Brazil's was even larger. Both of the steel mills in Brazil are unusually large. Iran, Saudi Arabia, and other Middle Eastern countries are taking huge steps toward petrochemical production with installations of unprecedented capacity. Alas, these projects often strain the financial resources of host country and investors alike. Worse, the planned output is more than enough to cover domestic needs which means that they must take up exporting on highly competitive and, in some cases, already woefully congested markets.

Overambition takes another shape in some assembly industries, namely an overcrowding of the rather limited domestic market. When some countries decided to assemble automobiles or electronics goods locally, they opened the door wide to investors and sometimes let too many in. While the more the merrier can apply in some situations, it certainly does not help where economies of scale are crucial. Although a scale of 100,000 units of the same type is commonly regarded as the threshhold for mass production, Thailand had half-a-dozen assemblers for an annual vehicle production of 90,000. The Philippines had nearly as many assemblers for sales of about 60,000. And, for its vehicle production of 200,000, Indonesia had as many as 20 assembly plants, 60 makers and 140 models in the late 1970s. Among the investors, none were more prominent than the Japanese who quickly conquered the bulk of the market. Yet, producing in such small series, even they could hardly regard their operations as efficient or purposeful.

Most of these blunders resulted from excessively loose planning which overlooked economic realities. But it is also possible for governments to be overly strict, either as a matter of principle or in periodic reactions to earlier leniency. This repeatedly happened in the automotive industry. After encouraging too many makers to take up assembly, some governments decided to force most of them to withdraw. Sometimes the selection was left partly to market forces with the stronger units surviving. But it could also be a conscious policy such as Indonesia's "deletion program" which cut the number of makers and models in half at the stroke of a pen. The Japanese were usually among those that remained, although some of them also disappeared from certain countries. It was actually hard to tell which did best. Those that were dropped lost a modest investment and some face; those that stayed gained face but had to invest vast new funds.

While such decisions were intermittent in most "liberal" countries, orders came fast and furious in centrally-planned economies. Hitachi had reason to be upset about what happened to its model joint venture in the People's Republic. Designed for 300,000 television sets a year, it got off to a good start and was soon making a profit. Alas, it was suddenly decided by the government that, rather than selling its sets throughout China, they should be restricted to Fujian Province where they were made. Then came instructions to boost exports to 50%. And yet later, when the priority on consumer goods was lowered, it was told to decrease production to 130,000 sets. It was not easy to run a successful operation with so many vital decisions beyond its control.[4]

In some cases, projects became a clear failure and were withdrawn. In others, they continued operating at a modest level and managed to get by. Yet, on occasion, the investors did extremely well in most conventional terms such as profit or return on investment. It is only on closer inspection that one realized that these "successes" were actually failures in disguise. It is impossible to run a factory efficiently at anything but a reasonable scale. It is also impossible to be profitable when the cost of installations are swollen by repeated overruns or parts and components are excessively costly. Such comments could apply to most "national projects" like the Asahan aluminum smelter, the Brazilian steel mills, or the pulp and paper projects. They would also cover most of the automobile and motorcyle assembly plants, some of the textile facilities and assorted other manufacturing ventures.

The only reason the inherent defects do not become painfully evident is that the host country has taken various measures to subsidize or protect them. By raising tariff barriers as high as 100% and more on imported automobiles, and then adding a quota, it is possible to sell domestically assembled cars no matter how bad or costly. While the consumers will bear the burden to some extent, this policy results in fewer sales. And it cannot help much when an industry is geared for exports. In such cases they, too, may have to be subsidized. For aluminum or steel production, support can take the form of low electricity or raw material costs and cheap loans. Once again, the products can be sold. But this is only because the taxpayers assume another burden. So, beyond a certain point, local production is actually worse than importing.

Most of these examples show that success and failure are relative. Nowhere is this clearer than for raw materials. The problem is rarely that the mine or well is a dud. Admittedly, like everyone else, the Japanese and their partners have hit some dry wells or pockets of oil and gas that were too small for commercial operation. More often, the problem was that the mineral content of ores was below par or the oil had too much sulfur. The product could still be sold, but brought a lower price. This might be combined with higher than expected costs due to extra development work, additional infrastructure, new safety or environmental regulations, cost overruns, rising wages, and inflation. When this happened, the return on investment would shrink because the investors had to put up more than anticipated, as has indeed happened regularly. If the going rate for sales of the raw material sank, an increasingly familiar phenomenon during the recession, some projects which were perfectly viable when initiated could unexpectedly become a losing proposition.

This relativity applies equally to the human element which is the hardest to evaluate. There are many projects which are not functioning as well as they might because the foreign investor was saddled with local partners whose contribution is less than desired. Even if they rarely get in the way, they are still a drain on resources, being paid just to sign official papers or pull strings with the local government. It may also be necessary to hire minority groups in America or majority groups in Asia even if their education, experience, or work will is not as good. It is not often that this seriously handicaps a company, especially if everyone has to do the same thing. But it does result in less efficient operation which hurts productivity and profits. In its own way, job hopping in most of Southeast Asia can prevent efficient operation even if it does not entirely disrupt the manufacturing process. Labor disturbances and agitation, on the other hand, can be considerably more destrucive. Many Japanese companies discovered this in the mid-1970s in Thailand and Honda found that it does not help to produce a superior car if the workers will not man the assembly line in Great Britain.

Naturally, even more acute social conflicts or political upheavals will have a deadly effect on foreign investments (and the whole economy). Thus, many companies found it impossible to continue operations when Iran was engulfed in the Islamic Revolution and subsequently drawn into a bloody war with Iraq. The repeated bombing of the Bandar-Khomeini petrochemical complex obviously prevented its completion. But simply the uncertainties and disruption of wartime blocked other projects. Although somewhat less serious, financial difficulties and lack of foreign exchange could throw things out of kilter, as when Nigeria, Mexico or Brazil prohibited imports, halting the supply of essential parts and raw materials. In cases where the ventures simply cannot operate, it is almost more charitable to put an end to the agony with nationalization.

This listing of the more evident problems that can be encountered by foreign investors should be quite adequate to explain the large number of complete or partial failures. But it overlooks the most frequent and insidious danger. This is the inability of the economy to take off and grow. It is perhaps so obvious that it is rarely considered as a contributing factor, but hardly any commercial or industrial projects would be launched if it were not assumed that the host country would manage to create a more dynamic economy. In its original state, supply and demand are in rough equilibrium and there is little point to making steel, assembling automobiles, or producing

Bandar Khomeini Petrochemical Complex
Credit: Foreign Press Center/Kyodo

textiles if the market will not expand. Modern production techniques, which are increasingly capital-intensive and benefit from considerable economies of scale, require not only a moderate but a substantial growth. If this does not come about, much of the investment is made in vain.

Unfortunately, it has proven more difficult for economies to develop than had been thought. Not more than a few dozen of the hundred-odd developing countries have shown much growth. And most of them only succeeded because they were lucky enough to discover abundant natural resources. So, the bulk of the poorer countries are no better off today than they were two decades ago and any investment made in them would have trouble paying off. Even some of the raw material producers, especially if they had a large population, scarcely increased the purchasing power of their people.

Thus, those who plunged into what they regarded as an "expanding market of 100 million," like Indonesia or Brazil, or the "world's biggest market" in China, were likely to find many fewer buyers for what they produced than the initial market forecasts indicated.

If the hopes of the investors were dashed, so were those of people living in these countries. The urge for growth, rising expectations and misguided policies sometimes left them worse off than ever. Old industries collapsed before new ones were created, peasants left the farms before jobs were found in industry, cities were swollen with unemployed and hungry people, earnings failed to keep up with expenditures, generating anger and frustration. In this context, rather that a boon, investment could be a bane. For it introduced large-scale companies and efficient industries that accelerated the dislocation. Yet, despite their apparent advantages, the investors could not truly prosper as long as the economy remained poor and chaotic.

Losers Take All

If unsuccessful investments were spread evenly among the host countries, the fact that some projects did badly would be much easier to accept. After all, investing has its inherent risks and some ventures just don't work out. But, then, others may be a success and could compensate. It is only when the failures are heavily concentrated in certain places, when some countries are filled with relics of crumbling projects or jostled about by "white elephants" that it becomes unnerving. If there is a pattern to these failures, with certain vices appearing regularly, then it almost looks like a plot.

That failures are not evenly spread can be gathered from the gossip of international businessmen, a look at some of the floundering economies, and even certain statistics. In a number of countries there are more failures than elsewhere and even many of the supposed successes are little more than "disguised" failures. They are only able to get by as long as the government provides special protection or support rather than on their own merits. And, even if they can prosper in that artificial climate, they do not really grow into the kind of venture anyone should really be proud of.

One group of countries which do not offer the most fertile soil for overseas investments may surprise the uninitiated. They are the capitalist-oriented developing countries of the tropical belt. Their governments are all in favor of attracting investment, of building up local business, and creating some sort of affluent society. Frequently their leaders are known to dabble in business themselves and their closest friends and advisors are businessmen. Moreover, some of the regimes are authoritarian, as often as not with a former military man at the head, and thus able to keep rather good control over the population and suppress popular movements and trade unions.

Yet, while the regimes are tough politically, in economic matters they still have to be categorized as "soft" developing countries in the sense that the goals, no matter how dramatically expressed, rarely enjoy consistent or effective implementation. One hitch is that the national policy is not very clearly worked out in detail and tends to change suddenly and rapidly. Another is that, even when a policy is decided upon, the implementing machinery is faulty or lacking and the bureaucrats may be too busy looking after their own interests. To get the wheels moving, they may have to be oiled and bribes may be necessary to obtain things that the investor is legally entitled to. In other cases, implementation may suffer from a lack of expertise, effort or money.

There is no shortage of such "soft" developing countries

and, indeed, they were extremely appealing to foreign investors since the 1960s when it looked as if some of them might launch into sustained economic growth. They possessed abundant natural resources, they had a teeming population, often young and educated, and it was hoped that an affluent market would develop. It was only later that it turned out that progress was difficult. It was not only foreign investments that succumbed, growth in general was lower than expected. Worse, while agriculture was neglected, industrialization progressed too slowly to bring about a take-off.

Among the countries which initially appeared extremely promising and which attracted hordes of Japanese investors, two were particularly prominent, the Philippines and Indonesia. Yet, both countries have only enjoyed modest growth, much of that resulting from the promotion of natural resources, especially oil and gas for the latter. Brazil seemed to be growing more rapidly for a while, and it does have potential, but clumsy economic management has permitted runaway inflation. Thailand is in a somewhat better state, with moderate growth, but certainly less than its natural endowment would lead one to expect. Although now almost forgotten, Iran, once seen as a heaven for investors, suddenly turned into a hell.

It is therefore not surprising to find that some of the projects now facing difficulty are located there. The projects are not only small ones, they also include those which were selected by the host and Japanese governments as "national projects." Others introduced by the private sector, including automobile or motorcycle assembly, textile production, and some electronics, are also doing poorly. Thus, the popularity these countries once enjoyed has slumped and there have been some collapses or withdrawals of Japanese investment.

Nevertheless, such countries are the center of anti-investment movements and a hotbed of criticism of neocolonialism. To read the diatribes one would think that there was a monstrous conspiracy among the Japanese to take them over. This supposedly ties up with active efforts of the government to deliver the people, bound and gagged, to the Japanese capitalists. Such a view was expressed by *Solidaridad II*.

"Among all other semi-colonies this side of the globe, the Philippines under the US-Marcos dictatorship now tops all Southeast Asian countries in terms of its attractiveness for foreign capital. Nowhere else are incentives for foreign capital so generous, energy resources so abundant and cheap, labor so skilled, forcibly kept docile and badly paid. Here too are to be built 15 export processing zones in addition to the three existing ones-making a total of 18 taxless Edens."[5]

A look at the charges of those who criticize investment in general, and Japanese investment in particular, will give a considerably more varied picture.

One sector in which it is most readily assumed that the investors are exploiting the country is natural resources. There is no end to the accusations of "plundering" of natural resources. This is frequently done with no reference whatsoever to the costs entailed for those who wish to procure raw materials and which, as indicated, can run into hundreds of millions of dollars, much of this paid out before the goods are obtained and start reimbursing the investor. The price paid for these raw materials, since they are never given for free, is also brushed over as ludicrously low whatever it may be.

This tends to overlook the actual situation in the sector, in which investors can prospect for or develop raw materials in a broad range of countries and quite naturally choose those that are most favorably disposed. Meanwhile, the producer nations also try to obtain the most favorable rates by picking the right partners. Whereas once the foreign "majors" could control prices, that power has substantially weakened to be replaced by cartels and looser associations of producers. Still, by and large, the price is set primarily through supply and demand on the market and it is hard for any one supplier or any one buyer to be far from that mark for long.

If anything, the Japanese should be thanked for their efforts . . . up to a certain point. If not for their pressing needs, and a desire to circumvent the Western multi-nationals and go directly to the source, some of the natural wealth of countries like Indonesia, Brazil and Australia would have remained in the ground where no one would have profited. In the Philippines, since the conditions were so onerous and the policy so variable, many of the resources are still untapped. The only complaints the more adventuresome hosts might have is that Japan seriously overestimated its needs, bringing some sources onto the market too early. Otherwise, Japan is to be thanked. If it had not been so eager to get at the natural resources, there would be nothing to get nationalistic about!

Another charge by raw material producers is that they are tired of being somebody else's quarry, a source of natural resources which are used by others. Such laments come not only from the developing countries but others that are perfectly well advanced. Yet, no one can prevent any country from making the processing of its own resources a priority goal and using whatever wealth it has, or can borrow, to attain it. This has been done by some developing countries which do not even possess raw materials and others that have moved on to processing with the aid of Japanese investment. If places like the Philippines and India or Australia, Canada and the United States cannot make the effort, it is nobody's fault but their own.

The real problem is that some countries became too

dependent on natural resources as a source of earnings. This applies to places like Indonesia, Australia and Malaysia, as well as the oil producing countries in general. Any loss of sales, or merely a fall in price, was liable to affect them immensely since they could not compensate elsewhere. This was only compounded in cases where they relied more on Japan as a buyer than it counted on them as a supplier. For example, while Japan derived 15% of its oil from Indonesia, this represented 45% of Indonesia's oil exports or, while Japan bought 28% of its copper from the Philippines, this amounted to 77% of the latter's copper sales. And Australia seems to have geared its raw material production to MITI's overoptimistic projections. If Japan stopped buying, these countries were in deep trouble.

With regard to labor, there is still a lot of talk of "exploitation." Much of this is rather vague and little of it can be tagged directly and specifically to Japanese investors. As noted, wages are set largely by supply and demand and, if they are low in a given country, it is usually because the economy has not developed and there is a huge reservoir of unemployed. This, alas, is true of all too many countries and the blame can usually be placed squarely on their own mistaken policies. In such a situation, it does not even take military rule to depress wages. On the other hand, in countries where there is a sustained demand for labor, not even the most ruthless dictator could keep wages down, assuming he should ever set such a goal.

Once again, it has not been borne out in practice that the Japanese investors are particularly desirous of hiring Philippine workers or labor in more relaxed or unruly parts of the world. There are enough countries which have disciplined workers not to seek out those where agitation is rife or employees feel they are being put upon. Thus, for example, the Philippine export processing zones have been largely snubbed, no matter how good the conditions may be on paper. Indonesia and Thailand have not drawn as much industrial investment either. And the promise of educated labor is uninteresting as long as this means law and liberal arts graduates as opposed to technicians and engineers.

But the main reason that more investors have not come, and some are leaving, is that the economy has simply not jelled in parts of Southeast and West Asia. This can be seen from a look at the statistics which place the growth rate at a modest level compared with other nearby countries. This is further reflected by relatively low per capita incomes. So, there is little hope of eventually finding either a large or an expanding market. Yet, even if the Japanese wished to engage themselves more deeply, they would be put off by the chaotic nature of the planning and the haphazardness of the implementation. The best that can be expected is a comfortable life in a protected industry.

It is therefore hard to understand the continuous stream of complaints emanating from many sectors of these societies. Japan's interest in investment in the "losers," for anything but raw materials, tapered off a long time ago. That is why the leaders have to make so many pleas for Japanese companies to come. It explains the apparently generous and subservient conditions that are offered, which actually have to be more attractive than elsewhere to entice the investors. However, despite this effort, a glance at the figures will show that investment is clearly down there although it is rising elsewhere. This makes it very hard to justify the view that the Japanese have decided to exert special pressure on vulnerable countries. A look at cumulative investment per person will show that there is no correlation whatsoever between the actual levels and the attitude of the host population. Places where Japanese investment is highest, like Hong Kong and Singapore, Korea and Taiwan, express much less fear of exploitation. Those which complain most loudly and regard themselves

Relative Weight Of Japanese Investment

Country	Ranking	per Capita Amount ($)
Singapore	1	601
Hong Kong	2	285
Australia	3	179
Malaysia	4	52
United States	5	49
Indonesia	6	47
Great Britain	7	38
Korea	8	32
Brazil	9	27
Taiwan	10	24
Philippines	11	14
Thailand	12	9

Source: MOF statistics for 1981.

as the greatest victims, like Thailand, Indonesia, and the Philippines, have far less.

This shows that some of the grounds for criticizing investment are more imagined than real. Any anger is not based overly much on a rational examination of the economic situation. It is often emotional and psychological more than anything else. Its closest contact with reality is that these are indeed countries where foreign investments have been less successful on the whole. Yet, this is not surprising when one considers that economic development has not been very successful in general either. This makes it hard to place the primary blame on the investors.

Instead, what one might do is ask whether there is not some relationship between bad investments and bad host countries. It is already obvious that overseas ventures are not likely to flourish in a poorly run economy and doubtlessly more failures can be traced to flaws in the country's overall policy than the mistakes of specific investors. But one can also go somewhat further. It is conceivable that the losers actually attract bad investment. In order to get any projects they have to raise their incentives and support high enough to compensate for existing disadvantages. This means that projects which would otherwise not be launched are risked nonetheless on the assumption that something other than their intrinsic merits will save the situation. And, where investment is only possible by passing through intermediaries or giving bribes, it is certainly not the most scrupulous who will apply.

Maybe the best way of putting things in their proper perspective is to take another group of countries, those which have had no investment to speak of. They are countries which were often so worried about neocolonialism and exploitation that they could not enter into any proper relationship with foreign investors. This includes several developing countries such as Burma, Sri Lanka and India, at least when ruled by relatively leftist regimes. It englobes the socialist countries, including those in Indochina, the People's Republic, and the East bloc. And it even includes some more advanced countries when under Socialist or Labour rule.

What is common to them is not only a suspicion of investment but a generally sluggish growth which, in some cases, was more of a gentle decline than anything else. This is certainly more a fault of policy than natural endowment, since some of them are comparatively rich in raw materials, have an active and intelligent population, and sometimes boast a large internal market. Having rejected foreign investment, it is obviously impossible to place the blame there. In fact, a lack of such investment probably contributed more to their backwardness than otherwise.

This hypothesis can be borne out most readily by considering those countries which gradually reversed their stand and opened their borders. Without being phenomenal, Australia's economy at least became somewhat more active when the Labour-inspired restrictions regarding not only investment in but export of natural resources were lifted. Burma's economy is finally coming to life again. Sri Lanka actually attained quite rapid growth through its more open policies. And China is apparently back on the path to development.

Before concluding, it is necessary to say a few words about a further group of countries, those which turned against the investors when they felt investment had been more of a bane than a boon. Two of these included Japanese projects among those which irked them, Ethiopia and Iran. While Ethiopia never achieved very much economic growth under the Emperor, it could hardly be claimed that the revolution ushered in a new era of rapid development, not even in parts of the country no longer troubled by incessant conflicts, repeated purges or periodic droughts. Of all the rulers who attracted investment, and then misused it, few could outshine the Shah of Iran. But years of instability, civil strife and actual warfare have not rectified the situation. Nor has the Islamic regime even come up with a tentative economic policy explaining the new order it wishes to create.

While such political instability makes it hard to evaluate economic progress, there are enough examples to show that foreign investment does not thrive when the investors are treated more as foes than friends. Suspicion of Japanese managers among the new government officials resulted in so many petty hindrances they could hardly do their job. Worse, they could rarely obtain enough essential parts, machinery or raw materials to make the operation run normally. Quarrels with local staff and ordinary workers became part of the daily routine, resulting in strikes, sabotage . . . and demands for higher wages. Taking the venture away from them, and having it run by state agencies, rarely succeeded. Some units kept producing at a moderate level, others were run into the ground, and very few could perform satisfactorily.

Thus, it would seem that if anything is worse than "exploitation" and "neocolonialism" it is to go without investment. This implies a continuation of the status quo economically and technologically, with nothing to provide fresh ideas and conceptual alternatives, good or bad. It culminates in stagnation illustrated by fixed installations, fixed labor patterns, fixed sales channels, old-fashioned methods of production, marketing, publicity and so on. Without the capital investors have to offer, the technologies they can introduce, their drive to succeed at least in their own terms, a country is much worse off. More reprehensible than relative failures, and even absolute failures, is the inability to just give it a try.

NOTES

1. *Asiaweek*, February 22, 1980, p. 35.
2. *Yomiuri Daily*, January 10, 1974.
3. Renato Constantino, *The Second Invasion: Japan and the Philippines*, Manila, 1979.
4. *Japan Economic Journal*, June 22, 1982.
5. *Solidaridad II*, January 1981, p. 6.

8
. . . Or Competitors?

Winner Scenario

In the developing world, in the socialist countries, and even in some advanced market economies, the image of investment—especially when tied up with that of multinational corporations—is not particularly good. There are a large number of countries which have had some investment and yet found themselves little better off than before, and sometimes worse. Rather than check what the causes really were, the inadequacies of foreign investment became a popular excuse. Others feared that, even if the investment projects as such were successful, they would lose more than they gained, or at any rate the investors would get more than they deserved.

This attitude is not surprising. It is far from easy to make a success of investment in general and the odds are much worse in countries which have not managed to achieve much real development on their own. Here, it might be remembered that there are presently more countries whose economy is stagnating or declining than those where it is improving. Countries which are doing so poorly often grasp at straws, and foreign investment is one of those straws. Alas, they usually do not know how to benefit. Thus, from country to country, it is possible to visit model factories, massive mines, and other symbols of cooperation that have ceased functioning as originally planned. The worst specimens are just "white elephants" or the rusting relics of a misguided cargo cult.

But this does not mean that investment has stopped proliferating. Despite the setbacks, despite the failures, there is more of it than ever. The primary difference is that today's projects are less widely spread than before as country after country opts out or is discarded for one reason or another. Instead, the flows of investment are increasingly concentrated in a smaller number of countries which still welcome them and, more important, know how to use them. Thanks to these success stories, the true potential of investment is occasionally glimpsed. Indeed, this may even coax the losers back into the circle as they change governments or their governments change policies.

So, one can describe in very rough terms a winner scenario which is not theoretical by any means. It applies to a reasonable number of countries scattered around the globe, even if they are far from a majority. And, it might be mentioned, these are usually also countries which have shown an ability to grow or upgrade their economy in general so that investment becomes just one more explanation of their success and certainly not the sole key.

There are countries which, a short while back, produced almost no minerals or at any rate not the quantities they now supply. Indeed, they did not even know they possessed such mineral wealth although, like most states, they assumed they must have something to offer. Through prospection, often carried out by the very same companies that later invested in mining, it was possible to discover valuable sources. The necessary infrastructure was provided, frequently by the state alone or with the investors, but sometimes by the investors alone or with their joint venture partners. Gradually, more and more of the crude raw materials were processed locally.

In some of these countries, the influx of imports was

progressively stemmed in the most constructive way, by replacing them with local products. Manufacturing was introduced for import-substitution purposes and the number of factories grew. Admittedly, they were not always very efficient at first and required a bit of protection. But the learning process did begin. The factories provided by the foreign investors were definitely not the only ones, but they were often crucial in creating a model for the others. Either they were more modern, with better equipment and technologies, or they were more efficient due to better management, or they were pioneering a new sector.

Over the years, the intermediate goods that were necessary to feed the factories, and which originally came from abroad, could also be substituted for locally. It was possible to create the necessary supplier plants to produce the essential parts and inputs. Further downstream, the output of certain basic industries could be processed or utilized to produce yet other articles. The plastic base, the textiles, the crude steel were fashioned into a multitude of goods, either by more investors from abroad or by local entrepreneurs.

What is crucial is that these products should become increasingly competitive. In the early days, when the scale of operations was small, the factories still had teething troubles, and the work force was not yet acquainted with the tasks, it may have turned out rather poor quality articles for more than it cost to import them. But the quality was soon upgraded. Then the protection which permitted the infant industries to rise was gradually reduced so that local producers had to become leaner and tougher. Finally, in certain cases, they were actually in a position to switch to exports. This supplemented foreign ventures which had been established primarily for exports and led to a more export-oriented economy.

In countries which had little else to offer than cheap

labor, work was created by investment and more people could be hired than otherwise. In some places, the number of employees in labor-intensive operations, frequently located in export processing zones, became quite considerable. Certainly, these people were pleased to have a job and to earn a living, no matter how meagre. Their governments were freed of one more burden and, rather than offering relief, could take a more constructive approach to labor problems. Where the development process was dynamic enough, the manufacturing sector was actually able to absorb most of the people who left the farms. Meanwhile, the workers—or at least those who made the effort—were able to learn new skills and enhance their value.

While more and better employment was definitely a step in the right direction, the host country would not have gotten much further if it did not also breed its own entrepreneurs. This sort of contribution could hardly be expected from the investors. Still, some of the partners imposed on them or the middlemen who helped them set up shop turned out to be much more than just "compradors." They figured out how a company was established and a factory run, and subsequently decided to do this for themselves. Others, many of them supervisors and managers, a fair number nothing more than technicians or ordinary workers, by closely watching the investors operate learned enough to launch small ventures. Not all of them prospered. And some quickly disappeared. But there were enough who grew and ultimately went into competition with their former masters.

As for the transfer of technology, little of this was gratuitous. Technology is a precious asset and only the most naive would expect it to be passed along voluntarily. But technology can be bought, either outright or through licensing. It can also be borrowed by seeing how things are done in factories and companies established locally or in the investors' home countries. Indeed, it can even be stolen by taking manufactured articles, finding out how they work, and then copying them. But the major source is more accessible than people think, and perfectly legitimate, namely by delving into the vast store of knowledge. Entrepreneurs can follow trade publications, engineers and scientists can read specialized journals and reports, and thousands of young people can be trained, at home or abroad, formally in vocational and technical schools, scientific institutes and universities, or more informally on-the-job. If such efforts are made, all but the most advanced or protected technologies can be acquired.

Through these various processes, investment made a substantial contribution to the host country's economy. It provided more sources of earnings, generated more employment and wages, introduced new skills and technologies. It also produced many articles that were needed and no longer had to be imported. It ultimately offered some exports to generate the foreign exchange needed to pay back the investors. Meanwhile, the state was receiving various taxes, duties, and other revenue to help fill its coffers. Most important, an impetus was provided for general development.

If the more general development was just a pale reflection of what had been done by foreign efforts, then growth would be modest at best. And that is the stage reached by the majority of developing countries and some sluggish advanced ones. But a few others went much further. Their own entrepreneurs or state corporations soon outnumbered the investors and foreign companies and they became competitive enough to conquer a growing share of the market. In so doing, they strived to improve their management techniques and raise the level of their technologies. Many of the national ventures were to meet domestic needs, but others went into exports where they earned money to purchase essential imports. Meanwhile, more workers were employed and, as labor became harder to find, wages began rising. Higher wages enabled people to buy more, further stimulating production. Rather than a vicious circle of economic mismanagement generating poverty, the economy entered a virtuous circle in which rising levels of production led to greater well-being and even some modest affluence.

At the same time, these investments were also generating profits and dividends for the foreigners. They were gradually able to repatriate their original outlay and could happily count the premium that was accruing. Since their operations—the mines, factories, and so on—were running relatively smoothly, there was little hassle with the local labor force or government. In cases where their subsidiaries were expanding and flourishing, they felt that they were onto a good thing. This often encouraged them to stay longer than planned or to do more than initially intended. At any rate, it kept them from regretting the original move and trying to benefit improperly or just pulling out.

There will be some, mainly in the investing country, who regard this as entirely right and proper. After all, there is no reason why investors should not earn a fair return. There will be others who insist that it is grossly unfair, that the investors are getting too much for their modest effort and are exploiting the country. These voices are heard even where investment has been crucial and where the results have been largely positive. But it should not be forgotten that unless the investors get what they regard as a fair return they will cease investing while the host country will not accept more investment or permit old projects to remain unless it gets what it regards as an adequate return. Only when both sides obtain what they want—and not what others think they have a right to—will the process continue.

Techniques Of Success

There is no doubt that foreign investment can contribute to more rapid development and economic growth. But that will only take place if the projects are chosen wisely and implemented efficiently. This can hardly be taken for granted and actually forms a major task for the host country as well as the investors. The distinction between "winners" and "losers" can probably be traced back to how each approached investment more than anything else.

First of all, investment policy cannot be pursued independently from the general economic or development policy. It must be integrated not only in broad principle but in smaller details. Projects cannot be chosen theoretically, out of the air, or as the investors show up, but should rather be inserted in the overall scheme of things. For this, a country must know what sectors will be the major vehicles for growth: agriculture, natural resources, industry, services. Then it can set its priorities and decide how much incentive—or disincentive—it wishes to give projects in these sectors.

But, that is only the start. It must decide which specific aspects of any sector are most important. For raw materials, it is essential to decide which particular type is most promising, or more exactly, will be offering the best return some years hence when it finally gets on the market. It must decide which specific mines or drilling sites offer the best prospects of success. Then, when taking on partners, it must decide just which aspects the foreign investors can handle and which should be reserved for local interests, if any. Sensitivity about overdependence on outsiders is pointless. It is more pertinent to work out a proper contract that gives each side what it wants so the project can go forward.

In manufacturing, the choices are much more numerous, and more difficult. It is necessary to pick the right branches out of a bewildering variety of possibilities. Then, within the branch, it is still necessary to consider the country's basic assets so that it will enter one where it has some inherent comparative advantage and thus a reasonably good chance of becoming competitive. For a more backward country this type of analysis may not be appealing, since it has to include its weaknesses in the balance. There is little sense in entering high technology fields if it has few technicians or applying capital-intensive methods when it is short of ready cash. In addition, if it has substantial unemployment, it must remember that more glamorous industries will not help absorb that excess labor.

But these are still global decisions. Even if it is decided to go into electronics or textiles, there are many points of entry and many different articles that can be produced. Each has its own advantages and drawbacks. Once that decision has been made, the more concrete ones arise. How big should the facility be? Should it be more or less automated, more or less labor-intensive? Where exactly should it be located? How many companies should enter the sector, considering that if there are too few there may not be enough production and if there are too many there can be overcapacity and ruinous competition? Finally, what share of the sector should be left open to foreign investors?

By answering such questions, none of which are simple, an investment strategy can be formulated. It should then be translated into legislation and regulations and summed up in an investment code which lets the investors know what is expected of them and just what they can, and cannot, do.

The first item therein might well be a list of priority sectors where investors are welcome. This list can be graded, showing which sectors have higher or lower priority. And, of course, there should be an indication of the sectors where investors are not welcome and which are being reserved for local capital and talent.

The code can also settle some other crucial matters. One of the most important is the degree of participation. Relatively advanced and liberal economies may accept wholly-owned ventures with little concern because no one investment is likely to be decisive and they have a sufficiently mature economy to absorb it. Other countries, especially those which are backward and fear they cannot adequately defend their interests, may wish to keep a closer watch on the investors. That can be done in various ways.

Many of the successful countries have given very precise indications as to what share of ownership foreign investors may have in each given sector. The rest has to be allocated to local partners, either in the private or public sector. But it soon became apparent that most investors do not like having too small a share of their own venture and, if forced to accept a minority stake, would prefer simply not coming. A 50-50 split often turned out to be the minimal acceptable offer, while 51% was vastly more attractive. However, countries which learned how to live with investment often went further and allowed even 100% foreign ownership.

Another form of control has been to restrict foreign investments to certain geographic areas so that any supervision was much easier and these companies were somewhat more isolated from the general stream of activity. This could be done most smoothly by establishing industrial estates which drew foreign ventures. More strictly, it took the form of export processing zones in which the investors were kept almost entirely out of the local economy but were compensated by special incentives and ready access to necessary resources, especially a steady supply of labor. In other cases, the degree of domestic sales could be negotiated with each new entrant and perhaps related to the degree of local participation.

Part of the concern about leaving foreign investors too much freedom arises from a generalized fear that they were much more efficient and advanced than local companies and could thus outcompete them. This is a reasonable supposition since it is usually the more dynamic and proficient companies which make investments and, when this occurs in developing countries, they are bound to have a definite edge. A somewhat related worry is that if the investors are too small, or in backward sectors, they will compete directly with locals rather than really adding something new. While the latter concern can be met by limiting the minimum size of projects, competition cannot be legislated out of existence. In fact, it is an essential ingredient in the development process. Still, if a specific project is likely to cause more harm than good, it can be rejected.

Finally, rather than worry about being exploited by the investors and drained of resources, the country can keep some control over the outflow of capital by including suitable provisions regarding repatriation. This can be forbidden during an initial period, then restricted to a given percentage of the investment for a further period, and finally opened up. Obviously, the greater freedom the investors are given to repatriate their funds, the more they are attracted. Overly strict conditions will only keep them out.

These various points are centered on the specific project. But it would be unwise to forget the broader context and especially the vital linkages. This is particularly important in developing countries where not all the infrastructure is in place and many supporting industries hardly exist. Thus, when establishing a mining venture, the government should see to it that the necessary transport is there to get the ore from the mines to the port or other distribution center. For factories, it is necessary to check that the basic inputs are all available, if not locally then to be imported. And it is certainly better to coordinate certain projects so that, for example, a steel plant is established at the same time as potential users or an assembly plant at the same time as potential suppliers.

Moreover, it is up to the state or supervisory authority and not the individual investors to consider the overall financial situation. No matter how useful investment may be in the longer run, and forgetting the short-term influx of capital, it must be remembered that there will be an intermediate period when many of the projects are not yet productive. It will be necessary to import plant and machinery, and yet later to keep up supplies of intermediate goods and some raw materials, while it may still be too early to cut off imports of the finished products. All of this can lead to substantial outflows of foreign exchange which may not be balanced yet and can lead to a financial crisis at worst or high interest payments and debt servicing ratios if less grave. This means that too much investment, too fast, can be the most serious problem and the crunch will come during the medium term.

Of course, an investment code and the related legislation is not enough. It is necessary to have machinery that sees to implementation and personnel to administer it. That is where most of the developing (and some advanced) countries go wrong. On the one hand, you can have the finest conditions in the world but no investors will come unless they are well publicized. All too often the investment authority just sits there and waits, leaving things to chance. In more successful countries, either the investment board or more likely the potential partners seek out the foreign investors. This makes it much easier to find the best possible sponsor for any given project and, by chosing the project in advance, it is much easier to only have the right ones initiated to begin with.

On the other hand, it is necessary to avoid the opposite extreme, namely investment authorities which constantly get in the way. The task of the bureaucrats should be to screen the potential investors and accept the right ones, not to generate so much red tape that all the investments get bogged down and hardly any are ever approved. Excessive zeal or nationalism in keeping outsiders out is not very helpful. But at least it is slightly better than having a bureaucracy which can be bought by devious investors so that those giving bribes or pulling strings get in while others cool their heels. Alas, an efficient and honest team is not easy to find.

Once the proper investors have been selected, and do meet the criteria, they should be left relatively alone to do their own thing. There should be enough regulations so that they do not misbehave or engage in unsuitable practices. But placing them under excessive control from a state bureaucracy that checks their every move and limits their frame of action is counterproductive and inimical to the project's success. It is better to let them go ahead, perhaps under some broad and enlightened supervision, and remain able to make their own decisions without needing approval of every last detail. Later on, if they have indeed strayed too far, they can be called back into line.

By creating a proper framework for investment, neither too tight nor too loose, it is possible for developing countries to gain much more or, at least, avoid the worst. That they so rarely think of this is truly amazing. For, there are not more than a dozen which have made serious efforts to incorporate investment policy in broader development policy. The fact that others sport investment codes, distribute glossy brochures and periodically send high-level missions abroad is not proof to the contrary. One need merely think of the speed at which the regulations change and the apparent inability to come up with winners.

On the other hand, a lack of the external trappings in many advanced and some developing countries does not mean that they cannot attract or absorb investment. In liberal economies, where the local entrepreneurs know what they are doing, it is often the individual and not the state who scouts for useful projects or preferably just products and technologies. These can ordinarily enter freely and it is the local business community that lays down the rules. Local companies should prove tough enough to resist competition and wise enough to learn from outsiders. Moreover, whatever investment is induced is normally just a small increment in the economy and its employment, price or foreign exchange effects can more readily be assimilated. Since no special incentives or privileges are granted, there is no reason to assume more investors will come than are justified by the potential market. And it is highly unlikely that an investor would create a venture in a sector that did not offer good returns or in which he was not reasonably proficient. Naturally, things do not always work out the way they should, and there are failures. But that is part of the game and no one has any right to complain.

Taming The Investors

The right techniques in selecting and regulating investors became a hallmark of those countries which have succeeded. But a no less significant characteristic has been the whole approach to investment. If investment is seen more as a potential gain than a possible loss, then the host country will doubtlessly make greater efforts to work out conditions that will meet the needs of the investors even while protecting its own legitimate interests. The result may be a more subtle policy of attracting investment rather than a cruder one of just sorting out the good from the bad prospects.

Similarly, if there is a fundamental desire to cooperate with acceptable investors once they are established in the country, the host government would tend to use the "carrot" much more often than the "stick." Bureaucrats who distrust foreign businessmen, and perhaps all foreigners, will immediately clamp down with negative acts, fines and penalties, for not following the rules. They will create a dense web of prohibitions and controls that accomplish little more than immobilism and frustration. Yet, if they would use their imagination a bit, it would be possible to find a broad array of measures that accomplish the same thing by encouraging the investors to move in the right direction.

The important thing to remember is that there are almost always more ways than one to achieve the same goal. So, in addition to doing the right thing, it is necessary to do it in the right way.

Investment codes in many countries include some incentives because, to be perfectly frank, very few investors would come otherwise. By adjusting these incentives to compensate for existing difficulties or risks and other natural disincentives, it is possible to attract more or less investors or to select those types of investors which are desired most while making it less likely that others will apply. If nothing else, this creates a much friendlier and more relaxed atmosphere and leads to more contented investors. But the host can certainly go much further.

These incentives can, and probably should, be carefully designed *before* the investment code is laid down. As indicated, it is unwise to revise the code too often, since each change will upset those who entered under the earlier rules and may create a generally unfavorable impression of instability. Still, if changes do have to be made, it is certainly preferable to move from stricter to looser, more generous rules. Thus, the incentives might be smaller in the first versions until one knows what the results will be, how much investment will come, and how the investors should be handled. Once this learning process is completed, the conditions can gradually be improved to attract more.

Of course, the older investors should not feel that those who came after are getting a much better deal. This would make them unhappy... although certainly less so than to see the rules tightened up. So, some of the incentives might actually be directed first toward the investors who are already present, and have thereby shown their faith in the host country. They could perhaps be given slightly better terms than newcomers, or allowed to benefit from the new dispensation first, or given priority when new projects are accepted.

One thing incentives can do is to direct investors toward sectors the government wishes to encourage. Naturally, the investment code will indicate the priorities. But this may not be enough to attract the investors. Thus, they can be offered financial benefits such as special tax relief, exemption from import duties and fees, subsidies for constructing factories or necessary infrastructure, and a number of other things. This may be enough to overcome any initial hesitation.

But it may not, especially if the potential investors are manufacturers that already export to the same market. However, it would certainly be an added inducement if the tariffs levied on the product, say automobiles, were raised. This of itself will discourage exporting by making cars more costly and encourage local assembly to get around the barriers. The move from pure assembly to more complete production and greater local content can be promoted by similar incentives and tariffs or quotas.

No matter how much he may grumble while he is outside of the market, the investor is likely to appreciate this support and protection once he takes up local assembly or production. The problem then is to keep the investors (and local producers) from becoming inefficient and lazy because they face little outside competition. Of course, they can be harangued by the authorities and urged on by catchy slogans. But it is bound to be more effective if the incentives are gradually withdrawn and the protection reduced.

In some cases it may be possible to take the investors (as well as the local producers) a step further by introducing subsidies and incentives for exports. Even if that was not their original intention, it can be made worth their while. The added sales would also enable them to boost production and become even more competitive than before. However, once again, the time must come when the government withdraws these advantages so that exporting does not become too easy itself with artificial support replacing true comparative advantage.

Doubtlessly, the investors may complain that they are being manipulated. But there is another way of taming the investors and making them shape up which they cannot complain about, namely fair competition. Thus, in each sector there should be several companies. This may be several foreign operations or joint ventures, with Japanese investors played off against one another or against American and European investors. Or the competitors can be domestic companies. Whatever the case, nothing keeps an entrepreneur on his toes like having to fight for his market share.

There is usually some concern in host countries that the foreign investors are coming simply to make money and get it back home as quickly as possible. That may well be true.

But too blatant attempts at keeping the money in the country, by imposing strict exchange control or limiting repatriation, usually result merely in dishonest means of transferring the currency and a general trend to halt investment which dries up the influx. Here, too, incentives may do the trick. Special advantages can be offered to investors who, rather than repatriating their money, reinvest in the same or other local projects.

Some politicians or union leaders feel that foreign investors are getting local labor too cheaply. The odds are very much against them paying less than the going rate. But, whatever wages they (and most others pay) may still seem too low. Imposing higher wages by fiat would hardly help. However, if serious efforts were made to upgrade the skills of the local workers through more vocational training and the like, then the investors might be willing to pay more for these skills and would upgrade their own operations to match. Still, nothing encourages higher wages like a tight labor market where approaching full employment makes it necessary for every employer, local or foreign, to raise wages to attract the necessary personnel.

Some investors, especially the Japanese, tend to keep too many expatriates rather than promote local personnel. Laying down a numerus clausus, that they must limit foreign staff to a given percentage or increase local staff to a given percentage, is bound to create friction and ill will. Refusing visas to expatriates is not much better. The solution could come in another way. Raising the level of education and competence, so that the company finds more potential managerial candidates, is sometimes quite adequate. After all, expatriate staff is much more expensive in every respect, not only salaries but the cost of travel, home leaves, special housing or other allowances, and so on make it a burden that most investors would gladly reduce.

There are various ways of controlling foreign investors

so that one knows more about what they are doing. One of the most effective is to impose local partners. Many foreign investors do not like this at all, although the Japanese seem to be more willing to enter into tie-ups and joint ventures. Still, if they must have a partner for one reason or another, it is much better for all if this partner becomes a help and not a hindrance.

Quite often in investments that fail, the partner is a state-related agency rather than a private enterprise. This may be because the government trusts it more or because such bodies are filled with political appointees who have to be placated, irate former students who must be calmed with a job, and assorted friends and relatives of the people in power. In other cases, it may be a private company which is not necessarily the best or most dynamic but has very close relations with the government or is led by the president's old cronies or backers who finance the ruling party. In both cases, such a partner is a serious burden for everything but one . . . getting around the rules and paying off the right people.

Most foreign companies do not really want to get on that track. The drawbacks, should there be a change of government, can be worse than the benefits and, anyway, they are a business concern and they want their partners to fulfill some commercial function. If the system does generate capable businessmen and dynamic entrepreneurs, investors will be much more willing to accept them as partners. Indeed, it is sometimes the local man who takes the first step and seeks a foreign partner. In such cases, the investors will obtain help with personnel management, marketing, and perhaps production. If both sides have similar goals and both are competent, the resulting joint venture is far more likely to be a success.

These various techniques and approaches show what can be done to make necessary regulations more palatable or to replace them advantageously. But they all assume, to some extent, a relatively static situation and a need to overcome an initial resistance before the investor will come. The biggest and best incentive, however, is completely different. It is an expanding economy or at least one flexible and dynamic enough to permit the rise of new industries and launching of new products. There is rarely any difficulty in getting even the most finicky investor to enter such a country.

In a buoyant economy, things which once seemed unlikely or impossible suddenly make sense and investors do not have to have their arms twisted to follow the movement. The most noticeable change occurs in the market. The reason many investors hesitate is that they do not think they can sell enough to warrant local production. When the market grows rapidly, they find that sales can be boosted sufficiently to justify the effort. Moreover, factories that once would have been small and inefficient can be increased in scale so that more efficient units are established. This, in turn, lowers the cost price and makes it possible to sell in yet larger quanties.

Once the market has attained a greater size, and more local production is being undertaken, there is bound to be a more abundant growth of smaller enterprises that can serve as suppliers and subcontractors, overcoming another hurdle. The infrastructure will also be growing, adding the essential linkages. It is likely that education will improve and more skilled labor become available, so that more sophisticated technologies can be applied reliably. Meanwhile, as local people learn the ropes, there are likely to be more valid candidates as managers or partners.

In such an economy, it is much easier to raise the finance to sustain growth and permit repatriation of capital. In addition, it may be possible to generate more of the capital domestically to begin with, meaning that foreign investors no longer have to make as great an internal effort and can borrow locally. Most important, rather than worrying about getting their money back as soon as possible, they will feel that it is reasonably safe to let it stay a bit longer. Indeed, if the economy is doing well and their first venture is a success, this will incite them to expand it or to launch other projects. In the final analysis, there is no greater incentive than the possibility of growing with a successful economy.

Making A Go Of It

Among the developing—and advanced—countries, there has been so much economic mismanagement that it is almost startling when someone seems to be doing things right. One way in which certain countries have taken fuller advantage of investment is through an intelligent use of planning. By now, economic planning is so popular that many countries, and not only those of socialist persuasion, have development plans. They lay down the priority sectors, fix some targets, and append an idealistic commentary on their hopes and aspirations. The problem is therefore not so much a lack of planning. The real hitch is a lack of implementation that leaves most of these plans a dead letter.

In some developing countries, however, a plan is considerably more than just a showpiece. There is a planning agency or board which works out the details of the successive programs. There are bodies which actually carry out certain projects while others supervise, or at least keep any eye on, the efforts of the private sector. Among those countries are Korea and Taiwan. In Singapore and Malaysia, while planning is less elaborate, the governments are very keen on getting the job done. Naturally, this helps not only for domestic projects but foreign investment as well.

Korea's Own Steelworks At Pohang

Credit: POSCO

One thing these countries have done is to pick strategic industries and then give them strong backing. But the choice was done intelligently . . . and modestly. A look at the early sectors will show that they were anything but glamorous: spinning and weaving, garment making, plastics, toys and the most rudimentary of electrical and electronics articles. While hardly awe-inspiring, they took advantage of what few assets these countries had, massive sources of labor, still relatively unskilled, but willing to work hard, and just enough ingenuity to set up small indigenous companies.

But this was seen as a step forward. The further steps were increasingly ambitious. They often consisted of a follow-up such as fiber production, mechanical toys and watches, more sophisticated electronics goods in general. Sometimes they went much further, into steelmaking, shipbuilding and even automobile production. Yet, even this was done with some sense of reality. Thus, when ships were first built, only the frame was actually domestic, the other parts, and especially crucial machinery, were imported. Or automobiles were first assembled from knock-down kits. Gradually, the integration proceeded until they were fully made locally.

Greater attention to planning and implementation was essential to carry out major projects effectively. For example, when it was decided to launch an automobile industry, Taiwan and Korea had fewer assemblers than lesser Southeast Asian countries. But they still tried to rationalize, create the necessary suppliers' networks, and reach economical scales. Moreover, automaking came after steel production. This meant a boost for local steel mills, and a savings on imports, which was good for both sectors. A similar relationship existed between steel and shipbuilding. So, the linkages were not forgotten.

For raw materials, as we saw, the planning and implementation were not always flawless in Indonesia and Brazil. It is very likely that the operations will also be less than ideally efficient. But at least they have taken the decisive step toward processing of their own raw materials. A similar effort is being made by many of the oil and gas producers. This means that they, and not others, will benefit from the value added on their own produce rather than leaving that to chance. In some cases, they called on outside investors to get things going, in many others, they went ahead on their own through state agencies of one sort or another.

While this is to the good, it would have been much better if the "softer" countries had achieved a primary goal of what has turned out to be "harder" developing countries. That is to fashion a bureaucracy which is efficient and responsible. This was certainly not easy, nor entirely successful, but Singapore, Korea and Taiwan have managed to keep their civil servants busy at the task and also out of mischieve. This was sometimes done by imposing a martial rigor, as when former generals took over the construction of Korea's Pohang and Taiwan's China Steel works. Or it could be through appeals to civic duty, as in Singapore. But punishment meted out to offenders never hurt. What could happen when this was not done was shown amply by the rise, and precipitate fall, of Pertamina in Indonesia.

This general climate is helpful, but not quite as decisive as the specific policies relating to foreign investment. In these "winners" as well, investment has been accepted as an appropriate development tool and given reasonably high status. Those in charge of promoting investment come directly under one of the top economic ministries, often the planning board or finance or commerce and industry ministry. This makes it easier to process investment applications and obtain the necessary approvals. It also makes it easier to examine the merits of a project and see whether it tallies with the government's own plans.

That means that approved projects are more likely to fit in with both the broader outlines of projected growth and the more detailed aspects of implementation. It helps avoid projects that are bound to fail because of missing linkages. This does not mean that "white elephants" are unknown, and that things are always the way they should be, but at least the chances of muck-ups are fewer. This is both because investors have a better idea of what the government intends to do, and can more readily count on it actually being done, and because the government is more likely to permit investment projects that make a contribution.

In order to promote certain sectors, including those to which investors were invited, Korea, Taiwan and to a lesser extent Singapore, did not hesitate to offer incentives and other support. But this was often extended to all comers, not only foreign firms but also domestic ones. While these advantages were doubtlessly important, there is good reason to believe that investors rated other points higher: a reliable work force, an effectively operating economy, a growing domestic market. So there was no need to be as generous as some other host countries and thereby lose much of what was gained by having investors in the first place.

Of course, the door to investment was always there for whoever would knock. But the basic approach was not to sit and wait. With a broad development plan, there was a much better idea of exactly what products and what technologies were most badly needed. Then efforts were made to obtain them. This was sometimes done by an investment promotion agency, or by sending investment missions to promising investor countries, or by organizing special trips by potential investors to the host country. On occasion, the policy was pursued at the highest levels. When Korean President Chun went on state visits, he was always accompanied by a delegation of top businessmen.

Obviously, investors were more tempted to come if they were well received. This meant a minimum of red tape and some suitable place to start business. An ideal spot in the early days were the export processing zones in Taiwan, Korea and Singapore. These areas are organized rationally, the factory buildings are well-designed and suitably equipped, the various facilities are there and work. The zone itself is located near a port and/or airport. Its administration handles as much of the formalities as possible and provides a broad range of common services. Most important, there is an abundant supply of reasonably cheap labor nearby.

For such reasons, there has been no trouble in keeping

these zones full. By now, total investment in Taiwan's zones amounts to nearly $400 million and about $170 million in Korea's zones. They occupy 80,000 and 40,000 people respectively. For the host countries, there has been a definite pay-off. First of all, the increase in employment. Then the fact that their annual exports reached some $2 billion for Taiwan and $1 billion for Korea. Far more important, it is no longer just a case of assembling imported components. Domestic raw materials and parts are obtained from local suppliers, and other current purchases are also made. So, there has been a spillover.

For all its openness to foreign investment, there were also times when the government decided to go it alone. Even when this was not strictly necessary, it took certain major initiatives on its own or entrusted them to local businessmen. For example, whereas Brazil and Singapore had their shipyards built and run by Ishikawajima-Harima, Korea insisted on creating its own shipbuilding industry with little external assistance aside from special technologies. Brazil's major steel mills are joint ventures with the Japanese. In Korea and Taiwan, the government insisted on using state corporations, although they naturally bought some equipment and technology from Japan. Even for automobile production, Korea's leading company Hyundai steered amazingly clear of foreign participation.[1]

So far, most of the stress has been put on the role of the government. But that is certainly not the whole story. It is only half the story in places where the government did play a prominent role, the other half being the rise of local entrepreneurs. In more liberal countries, however, just about everything was done by the private sector. This includes advanced liberal economies like the United States, Australia, and the European countries. There is also the bastion of laissez-faire economics, Hong Kong. While the workings were certainly less visible, the business community did in many ways select, and reject, and direct foreign investment.[2]

In more dynamic developing countries, it was increasingly the local businessmen who went out and sought investors. They did not wait for the next official mission. They scoured the specialized journals and visited factories, they saw who had a novel product or a promising technology, and they often invited the owner to come and form a joint venture. In the more advanced West, most businessmen were too proud to ask for Japanese aid, at least at first. By upgrading their operations and keeping abreast of technologies, they also showed that there was little sense in intruding in certain sectors. When they fell down on the job, were flooded by imports, and the government had to resort to protectionism, it was patently clear that these were weak sectors in which Japanese investors might do well.

The local entrepreneurs also provided the necessary linkages, with no pressure from the government, as long as there was a chance of gain. They provided the thousand-and-one parts and components needed for most major finished articles, from televisions to automobiles. They supplied the raw materials and sold the finished goods. And they offered the myriad of services that keep an economy moving. It was not at all surprising to find this in the advanced West, but it was also happening in Asia. Untold thousands of small companies were sprouting up, and some became quite large, such as Hong Kong's textile makers or electronics companies like Tatung in Taiwan and Gold Star and Samsung in Korea. The most striking were the Korean *chaebol*, not unlike the Japanese *zaibatsu* of earlier years, with dozens of subsidiaries each.

With the rise of entrepreneurs, small and large, it was possible to benefit more than ever from investors. Some of the companies acted as partners and learned from them.

Others were mere onlookers and learned as well, often without paying the tuition. The transfer of technology was amazingly swift once people simply knew what technologies could do, where they could be found, and what they were worth. While the foreign investors, especially the Japanese, provided a source of emulation for local entrepreneurs, the locals provided the necessary competition to keep the investors in line. With so many other companies springing up in the sector, they could not take things easy or produce poor quality or expensive goods. They had to perform better and better to keep ahead.

Although the foreign-invested firms obviously had a head start, and they also benefited from greater experience, more ready access to funds, and a good reputation, they did not manage to maintain their original prominence in some cases. In Taiwan, the textile industry was orginally dominated by Japanese makers. Yet, while they are still prominent for synthetic fibers, in most other branches they have been surrounded and often overshadowed by domestic producers. The Korean electronics industry owes its early growth to foreign-invested firms and in the late 1960s they produced as much as 50% of total output and supplied 80% of total exports. By the early 1980s, however, their share had fallen to 20% of output and 12% of exports.[3] This shows that enough new entrepreneurs could rise, and some of them could move forward rapidly, so that domestic makers could eventually take over much of the domestic market on their own without any need of government intervention, let alone nationalization.

As things fell into place and the economy finally began to click, the massive unemployment of the early 1960s began drying up in some of these countries. By the late 1970s, it was only a few percent in Hong Kong, Singapore, Taiwan and Korea. This was basically just frictional and most people who wanted work could find it. With the worldwide recession in the early 1980s, things were notably less comfortable. . . but still better than in America and Europe. Exactly how much of the employment was generated by Japanese investment is uncertain. Still, a MITI survey indicated that major Japanese firms employed some 738,000 people around the world in 1982, and the total was probably well over a million. A more detailed study, this time by Columbia University, found that Japanese firms were employing some 81,000 locals in the United States.[4]

Thus, over the whole period there was a trend for wages to rise in the countries where the employment situation had gotten tight. Even in the export processing zones, which were geared to supposedly "cheap labor," the rise of wages was striking (and no slower than outside the zones). In Masan, as we saw, wages rose fast enough to actually drive out some investors. In Hong Kong, Yashica's accounting manager could complain: "When we came here twelve years ago we were paying $40 per month for unskilled labor, now a girl who just graduated from primary school can get $240." The only thing that did not help was to boost wages artificially. When Singapore decided that raising wages sharply would encourage higher value added industry it only managed to discourage investment.

With new entrepreneurs rising, new companies being formed, more people working and earning a living, the economy was obviously expanding at an exceptional rate. This was good for the investors, who took full advantage of their facilities and produced more than ever. But the locals could be equally pleased. After all, they earned higher wages, bought more products, and participated more actively in the economy. In fact, in countries which really knew how to benefit from investment, the economy was growing fast enough for foreign investment to play a diminishing role without driving away any of the investors.

Some Real Winners

Despite all the talk of difficulties and failures in investment, there have been a lot of successes as well. Some were real successes, with countries rising from the ranks of the most backward to become among the most dynamic economies around. This was done not only by absorbing investment but building on it. However, as with the failures, most were just relative successes. They managed to sell some more raw materials, they were able to launch a few industries, the companies and factories they created did moderately well. Certainly, the investment did not hurt. But it did not help much either.

Modest successes are found among the countries which sought foreign assistance to develop their potentially rich natural resources. Without Japanese investment, it is most improbable that some of them would have risen to prominence as rapidly or obtained as large amounts of revenue as they did. Japan was obviously interested in any new supplier of oil or natural gas, but it was even more desirous of finding it closer to home. Indonesia and Malaysia fit the bill. While coal, iron ore, bauxite and so on are more widely spread, Australia was a convenient source due both to proximity and because many of the mines could be worked at huge scale.

Naturally, the host countries gained from this. They did not possess the financial resources to launch as many projects on their own. They were also pleased to have a stable market. But they were only relatively successful for various reasons. One is related to their approach to the problem. Rather than regarding sales of raw materials like those of any other good, they saw it in terms of despoliation. Indonesia and Australia, as opposed to Malaysia, went through acute phases of resource nationalism which accomplished little more than leaving the wealth untapped. When they cooperated, this was not as smoothly as hoped. In Indonesia, part of the problem was the sheer inefficiency of the bureaucracy. In Australia, the biggest problem was with the unions, those working the mines, and then those at the ports, which made the flow very unreliable and put off many investors while periodically withholding goods from the market.

The other reasons some countries were a partial success, or a partial failure if you will, is that they did not take advantage of natural resources to launch the economy more broadly. They were content to receive their earnings on crude ores and crude oil rather than process them locally. What is most disconcerting here is that it was the advanced countries, not the developing countries, which missed the most opportunities. Places like Australia, Canada and the United States certainly had, or could acquire, the necessary capital and technologies. But they apparently lacked the will.

In industry there were also many partial successes. Thanks to Japanese investment, it was possible to create subsidiaries and joint ventures which built factories, recruited labor and produced manufactured products. This was usually a smattering of projects in various sectors, such as textiles, electronics, motorcycle and automobile assembly, machine tools or zippers. But in some cases whole industries were established or regenerated by the Japanese, such as textiles and electronics in East and Southeast Asia or color television in the United States. This was basically to the good. It stopped the influx of imported goods and promoted local production. It increased employment, generated wages, and raised productivity.

What made these successes only partial varies from the developing to the developed countries. In the more backward economies, it usually happened that Japanese investment was induced into relatively new sectors in which there were few domestic producers. They were actually "infant" industries and therefore gained support from the host government. This was perhaps justified, and did permit a more rapid rise of these sectors and the companies acting in them. But it cannot be entirely forgotten that the "infants" these countries were fostering were Japan's and not their own.

In more advanced nations, the situation was quite different. Usually, the full complement of industries already existed and what happened was that Japanese companies came to compete with local companies. If they were particularly dynamic and aggressive, the Japanese companies actually replaced some of their local counterparts but, at the same time, tended to indigenize and become local to some extent themselves. The most striking case of this is the television industry in the United States and a broader illustration is the motorcycle industry in America and Europe. True, the host countries did receive many benefits, the local production, employment, improved technologies, and so on. But the net addition, after subtracting any local companies that went under, was much less impressive.

Here, too, it looks as if the so-called advanced nations on occasion did less well than the developing ones. Their gain was seriously mitigated by what happened to their earlier producers. More surprising, once again, this occurred in countries which possessed, or could acquire, the capital and knowhow to reinforce their own industries and fight back. Something was evidently missing, either the will, or a realization of the seriousness of the situation, or misguided and defeatist economic policies. Still, those that gained even moderately were better off than countries like France and Italy which either kept the Japanese out or failed to attract them.

Aside from these relative winners, there were also a number of real winners, countries which benefited very considerably from overseas investment in general and Japanese investment in particular. They include its closest neighbors, Korea, Taiwan, Hong Kong and Singapore primarily. But a few other countries seem to be entering that small circle slowly, and less conclusively, like Malaysia, Thailand and Sri Lanka in certain ways.

These countries, and especially the "newly industrialized countries" or NICs, as they are called, are among the few which have made a success of development over the past few decades. They managed to attain very considerable rates of growth, ranging above 10% during the peak period in the 1960s and early 1970s, and still remaining well above the world average during the recession. Beyond mere growth, they have brought about a basic transformation in their economy through the rise of industry. While some only progressed as far as light industry, others now boast a heavy industry. This development also enabled them to raise per capita income substantially and create a much larger domestic market. For the foursome, the growth was also export-led.

This is a very intriguing phenomenon. There are few enough countries which accomplished any sort of growth for this rise to be spectacular. But, for students of investment, it certainly proves someone's case. Those who regard investment as akin to exploitation and feel that the more investment, the greater the risk already expressed their views on the highly perilous path these countries were taking. The conclusions could not be more blunt and dogmatic than what Halliday and McCormack stated in *Japanese Imperialism Today*.

"The effects of Japan's trading with Southeast Asia in the postwar period are obvious; areas like South Korea and Taiwan have been forced into positions of impossible

subordination, and lasting imbalance. It is impossible even
to fantasize that the new phase of heavy Japanese investment in the area can be anything but equally deleterious to
the masses of the countries concerned."[5]

This proved to be the most mistaken of many foolish
predictions made by these and other writers. It turned out
that the very countries which received the biggest doses of
Japanese investment in terms of yen per inhabitant were
those which did best. This is not because investment was
free of problems, or the Japanese investors had suddenly become charitable, but because they knew how to
handle investment and, more generally, how to construct
an economy.

If Japanese investment had indeed been the bulk of the
capital and knowhow that flowed into these countries, then
they would obviously have been dominated by the Japanese. In fact, it was not. Even while Japanese investment
was rising, the countries managed to boost their own
capital formation very rapidly. In Korea, for example,
direct foreign investment from all sources only amounted
to 1.2% of domestic capital formation throughout the
1960s and 1970s, with a much lower level at the end than
the beginning of the period. Far more capital was induced
through foreign loans, as much as 19% for the period. The
rest, about 80%, came from domestic sources. Thus, the
vast bulk of capital was owned and/or controlled by
Koreans and not foreign investors.[6]

Moreover, there was a long-term trend for local entrepreneurs to spring up in the very same sectors as the
foreign investors, something almost excluded outright by
the critics of neocolonialism and not really expected by the
multinationals either. Despite their head start, the relative
share of foreign companies in key sectors like textiles,
household appliances, electronics, etc. in Korea, Taiwan
and Hong Kong tended to decline because more domestic

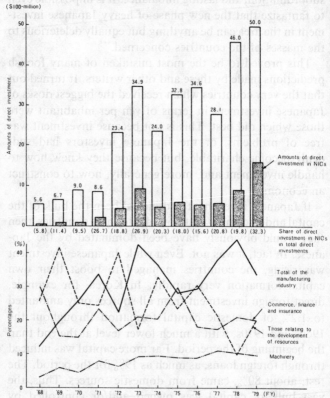

Japanese Investment In NICs

Source: *White Paper on International Trade*, 1981, MITI.

companies were created from year to year. In addition, other areas expanded in which there was little or no foreign investment, such as agriculture, transport, and services. Admittedly, some of the top companies were still Japanese and foreign ventures were usually larger and more efficient. But they no longer lorded it over the rest of the economy or even dominated their own sectors.[7]

Of course, one should not swing to the other extreme of underestimating the contribution of foreign investment. That would be equally mistaken. For, even if local entrepreneurs have become dominant in later years, they would never have gotten there if they had not had the possibility of copying and learning from outsiders. If the Japanese and Americans had not come to begin with, it is likely that there would never have been much of an electronics industry and, without foreign buyers, the textile and garment industry would never have flourished. Thus, one should not forget the crucial impact in the early, formative period. Nor should it be forgotten that investors tended to move upward in various ways, repeatedly acting as pathfinders. It was the foreign companies that kept upgrading equipment, introducing new products, and initiating more sophisticated technologies, thereby setting an example that is still useful.

In addition, foreign investment was not thinly spread over the whole economy but heavily concentrated where it could have the biggest effect. Much of it went into "strategic" industries or others that provided the impulse for growth, such as electrical and electronics, machinery, textiles and garments, chemicals, petrochemicals and fertilizers. Referring to Korea again, foreign-invested companies created a disproportionately large share of value added, 3.8% in general and an impressive 13.6% for manufacturing. Some of this investment was in labor-intensive industries, which enabled them to account for 10.5% of industrial employment. And there was a higher commitment to export-oriented sectors which resulted in their providing over 18% of total exports.[8]

Finally, it must be stressed that in these host countries there was a tendency not just to accept any investment but to screen the offers to select only those whose potential was most positive. More often than elsewhere, these were also countries whose investment authorities or, more likely than not, whose entrepreneurs went out and sought the kind of investment they thought was most useful. This greatly increased the chances of coming up with truly worthwhile projects. In this way, just as the "losers" seemed to attract the worst investors and projects (or turn them into a shambles even if they were originally all right), the "winners" had a knack for attracting or selecting better investors and projects (and then making as full use of them as possible).

So, by making a vital contribution and providing a sustained impetus, foreign investment—and, in the case of these countries, very heavily Japanese investment—was a key to the apparently miraculous growth.

If this growth was unexpected, and certainly went against the preconceived notions of some, what happened later was even more surprising and in some ways preposterous. Not only did Korea, Taiwan, Hong Kong and Singapore gradually create domestic industries to substitute for imports, they moved on to become major exporters. Unlike other countries, where the infant industries never really grew up, these became vigorous adolescents and sometimes amazingly mature youngsters. They managed to enter world markets and compete against products from developed countries, including their Japanese mentors. Then they began penetrating the Japanese market itself.

This scenario would have sounded incredibly far-fetched to those who warned of all the harm that could come from investment. Yet, by the late 1970s, the small band of NICs in the region was well advanced in the "chasing up" operation, taking over one sector after another almost as soon as they were opened up by the Japanese. In so doing, they kept treading on Japan's heels and forced it to push ahead more rapidly than planned. In short, the hosts were turning the table on the investors.

That helps explain why, despite an even greater density of Japanese investment than in places like the Philippines or Indonesia, a more xenophobic and anti-investment mood did not arise. If anything, there was a reasonably good relationship with Japan and its investors. This ranged from the highly flattering approach summed up in Singapore by the "learn from Japan" campaign and in Malaysia by the "look East" policy to reasonably correct but hardly cordial relations with Taiwan and Korea. This does not necessarily mean that any of them *liked* Japan or *cared* for the investors. In fact, they still remembered the war and found the Japanese a bit too aggressive. Yet, in the cause of better business, they could deal suitably with their partners and backers. And, turning the past hatred to good use, they redoubled their efforts to catch up with Japan.

Notes

1. See Woronoff, *Korea's Economy, Man-Made Miracle.*
2. See Woronoff, *Hong Kong: Capitalist Paradise.*
3. *Electronics Industry in Korea*, Electronics Industries Association of Korea, 1982.
4. MITI, *Overseas Business Activities of Japanese Enterprises*, 1983, and *Economic Impact of the Japanese Business Community in the United States*, New York, Columbia University, 1979.
5. Holliday and McCormack, *Japanese Imperialism Today*, p. 230.
6. *Machinery Korea*, February 1981, pp. 34–41.
7. See Bohn-Young Koo, *Role of Foreign Direct Investment in Recent Korean Economic Growth*, Korea Development Institute, April 1982.
8. *Machinery Korea*, op.cit.

9
The Mother Country

To Invest Or Not To Invest?

Although they tend to disagree on most things, there is a definite concordance between those who extol international investment and their opponents who decry neocolonialism. They look upon investment almost as a natural reaction of businessmen and intimate that there are so many reasons to invest that just about every company must be thinking of doing it sooner or later. The result would be massive moves of investors and more multinationals than ever.

Looking at the figures, or at least one set of figures, they would seem to be right. From year to year, the number of projects, the number of investing companies and the amount of investment have grown in Japan. Not only have they grown because new investments were added to the old, the flows themselves have become increasingly large. Thus, while there were only 729 new projects worth some $904 million in 1970, the figures for 1982 were 2,552 projects worth $7,703 million.

This is indeed impressive. On the other hand, it is just a drop in the bucket if one considers the total amount of domestic investment. From that, it can be safely concluded that not even 1% of all the companies have mustered the courage to make a try. And they are only risking a bit more than 1% of Japan's total investment capital for the year.

Moreover, even those companies that advance most resolutely into such investment would not dream of putting more than a carefully circumscribed portion of their capital into overseas ventures.

The reasons for this are numerous and fairly obvious. As was noted, one segment of investors consists of rather small companies, frequently in older and even declining sectors, which feel they must go abroad to obtain cheaper labor. And they are so poorly adapted to efforts of this sort that often the initiative, and certainly some crucial assistance, must come from the trading companies, banks and government agencies. That so many have taken the step is striking. But it is not surprising that the vast majority have not, even when that meant facing a dismal and perhaps fatal future in Japan.

Naturally, it is much easier for large companies to make the move. They have the capital, the experience, the manpower. But they also have many more alternatives. There is already less need of cheap labor since this can be replaced by further automation or robotization. Rather than save bits and snatches of their foreign sales, they can concentrate more intensively on the domestic market. If they gain only an extra percent or so of the Japanese market, that can easily compensate for the loss of clients in most developing countries. Moreover, if they are in a stagnant or declining sector, they can use their resources to switch to more promising fields.

With these alternatives to choose from, in addition to the possibility of overseas investment, they are likely to take other action in many cases. Since Japanese companies are actually rather conservative, and most are quite insular, the choice of overseas investment may well be the least appealing, or at any rate the most unfamiliar and riskiest, put before the board of directors. Only a minority of firms would have any prejudice in favor of it.

That is why host countries have gone to such extents to attract investment. They know it will not flow very freely unless they provide extra advantages. This they do in the form of subsidized land and good infrastructure, access to resources or cheaper labor, tax holidays and rebates. This may help overcome some of the resistance or at least make the alternative of investment more appealing than it was before. That is the carrot.

However, sometimes investment has to be extracted from investors. Here the stick is used. This can be done by putting up tariffs and quotas, making continued exports to the host country impossible, and encouraging foreign companies to salvage what they can of the market by getting inside the barriers. They can be further prodded by introducing local content regulations that make the investors move ever deeper into local production.

That often investors were indeed acting under duress was admitted by a Japan Economic Institute study which showed that "many companies" with a significant stake in the American market did not decide to build or acquire local manufacturing facilities "until they were faced with actual or potential import restrictions."[1]

The fact that the stick is used as well as the carrot and, in recent years, it has been used more than ever, should convince proponents and opponents of international investment that foreign investors are not as eager as claimed. The awesome difficulties of the world economy, relatively tight credit and increasing risks abroad have made them very cautious. True, more investment is still coming. But there is a definite polarization among the investors and the host countries.

Looking through the lists of Japanese projects, it immediately becomes clear that certain companies have a disproportionately large share. These are the good investors or, at any rate, those which are more inclined to invest. There are many others which seem to avoid investment as much as possible. While part of this division is due to the idiosyncrasies of each company, and its management, there are some general characteristics that typify the good investors.

One of them is largely historical. Before the war, the Japanese economy was dominated by a number of large companies, often joined together in closely knit groups called *zaibatsu*. Although these groups were forbidden and sometimes disbanded after Japan's defeat, they quickly reformed on the whole. Today, the economy is again dominated by major groups or *keiretsu*, often revolving around a bank or dynamic industrial firm. They are looser than they were in the past, and they do not quite control the market any more, but they do have a very strong position.

What changed their situation, among other things, is that just after the war, when the groups were still weak and disorganized, a number of dynamic young companies came to the fore. Among the better known are Sony, Matsushita (National, Panasonic), Sanyo Electric, Honda, Bridgestone, YKK, Idemitsu, Arabian Oil, and so on. They had to consolidate themselves to resist the encroachment of the older companies. To this end, they often found it more advisable to gain strength abroad and use that to support their position in Japan.

Another characteristic is whether the company has its major clientele at home or abroad. Most of the older ones, those related to the *keiretsu*, are strongly oriented toward the domestic market. Some of the newcomers like Matsushita have also developed a very solid and dense domestic marketing structure. For these companies, the bulk of their sales is at home and they must therefore concentrate more efforts than otherwise to holding onto, and hopefully expanding, this market.

Frequently, they have done so well that just a handful,

and sometimes less, of companies clearly dominate each sector. Other firms whose market share is restricted must either risk disappearing or make even greater exertions abroad. One solution is exports, another overseas investment. The purpose of this is both to boost sales and create sufficient economies of scale to remain competitive. Among the companies which have pursued this strategy most effectively are Sony, Sanyo and Honda.

A third characteristic is rooted in the management. Making overseas investment requires some sense of adventure and a willingness to take risks. This is not a very common feature among stodgy bureaucratic managers such as proliferate very widely in Japan. It is more the sort of thing that would appeal to the self-made man, the entrepreneur, who started from nothing and built up his company. It is also an alternative for the executives of companies whose ranking is somewhat lower and wish to catch up with the leaders.

Among companies noted for their overseas investment, some have such founders. Akio Morita of Sony is just as well known abroad as in Japan, and he was instrumental in making Sony an international company almost as much as a Japanese company. Konosuke Matsushita, even while cultivating the home market, launched a continuing chain of subsidiaries and joint ventures. Soichiro Honda also had the vision to create an international network as a counterpart to his domestic one. Tadao Yoshida, the founder of YKK, had no aversion to spreading his brand name far and wide. And Toshiwo Doko, as president of Ishikawajima-Harima Heavy Industries, tried to get around his rivals by seizing opportunities abroad.

Each of these characteristics predisposed a company to be more open to overseas investment. But the urge was even stronger when several of these characteristics combined, as frequently happened. Most of the entrepreneur-led companies were, quite naturally, among the younger, more dynamic entities. Since they arrived on the domestic market later than the others, they had to struggle with the older, more established companies for a slice of the pie. This was not easy to obtain, especially not in Japan, and thus they had to look toward other horizons.

Among the most prominent investors, we therefore find relative newcomers like Sony, Matsushita, Honda, Bridgestone and YKK. But there are also older companies like Nissan, which proved more energetic than Toyota, IHI, busily rivalling the top shipbuilder, and Kawasaki, doing a bit more than the other steelmakers. Among the trading companies, C. Itoh, Marubeni and earlier Ataka tried to raise their ranking through investment. Even further up in the hierarchy, it was Mitsui which first showed an interest in expanding its overseas base as opposed to Mitsubishi,

Sony's San Diego Plant
Credit: Sony

with a much stronger domestic position rooted in its related heavy industry companies.

There has also been an increasing polarization among the areas where investment is made. This, too, is perfectly natural. Each sector has different marketing, production, technological and other imperatives. What makes sense in one sector is hardly convincing in another. Given Japan's present situation, with high wage levels, it is natural that the more labor-intensive operations would feel a stronger pull than capital- or technology-intensive ones. Consumer goods, which must be produced on a large scale and sold widely, would also want to protect or conquer markets. Anything which can be manufactured or assembled readily would come under pressure from host countries to be localized.

Thus, one of the first industries to be attracted abroad was textiles, since it combined all three characteristics in many cases. However, while simpler spinning and weaving or labor-intensive garment making came easily e-nough, the synthetic fiber makers tended to drag their heels. Another major move was undertaken for household appliances and electrical articles which were sold directly to the consumers. Heavy electrical equipment, sold primarily to manufacturers or power companies, was quite another matter. Now successive waves of electronics investment are unfurling on foreign shores. This started with simple goods like radios, tape recorders and televisions. The passage to video tape recorders and computers is much more cautious and only occurs under special circumstances.

In the heavy and chemical industries, the situation is almost the reverse. This has various causes such as a need for less unskilled labor as opposed to technicians and engineers, high capital outlays, greater implications of economies of scale, and sometimes dependence on supplier and subcontractor networks. The steelmakers have made comparatively little overseas investment despite their tremendous sources of capital and their high technology. Aside from IHI, there has been even less investment in shipbuilding. While there has been a fair number of projects launched by automakers, most were just simple assembly operations. Heavy machinery and machine tool manufacturers have been timid to date. The only real exceptions arose for petrochemicals and light metals like aluminum, both for the same reason. It was essential to have access to cheap oil or natural gas, as a feedstock for the former and a source of energy for the latter.

Meanwhile, considerable polarization is taking place with regard to the host countries that are favored by Japanese investors. This can be described in various ways. There is a trend to pull out of the more dilapidated of the developing countries, quite simply because there is not much of a market and the prospects of success are dim. But the repulsion is even more marked for those countries which have an antagonistic leadership, aggressive opposition movement, or worrisome political instability. Even when the regimes are stable, there is no liking for those which change their policies frequently and unpredictably.

Perhaps the broadest move is to turn away from many of the developing countries. There is no longer much interest in most of Latin America, with the exception of Brazil and Mexico, and even there not quite the same heady optimism. Most of Africa is increasingly avoided and even some parts of Asia. There is a willingness to deal with the Middle East, but mainly because of its oil wealth. At the same time, natural resources are being sought more eagerly than ever in Australia, the United States and Canada. Manufacturing and marketing efforts are being shifted to America and

Europe and especially the rapidly expanding countries of East and Southeast Asia (but not their more sluggish neighbors).

These trends can just as well be summed up by another polarization, namely a shift from the "losers" to the "winners." This may seem obvious on the face of it. But the situation is far from that simple since, within each group, there are both advantages and disadvantages.

It is easy to understand that any investors would avoid the outright losers. These are countries where the infrastructure is so poor that nothing works, the government so venal that little can be done without a kick-back, and the economy so stagnant that it is hard to sell anything. There may also be risks of labor unrest, social disturbances, political upheavals and minor problems like nationalization. But it should not be forgotten that there are countries in an intermediate category where relative success (or failure) is possible because investors are overprotected. They enjoy strong support from the government, which sets up high tariffs walls so their goods can be sold and perhaps tosses in some attractive incentives and subsidies. There, profits can be made, sometimes very regularly and comfortably.

Among the winners, it really is not so easy to make a profit. A company must be extremely competent in its sector, it must have good technologies and hardworking staff, it must be competitive on quality and price. If it does not manage this, its profit margin can be depressingly slim and it may obtain little of the expected fruit. It also faces the risk of spawning its own competitors by letting them know what its products and technologies are like. On the other hand, even with a relatively low level of profitability, in an expanding market which keeps on generating more sales, the total profit can be much greater. There are also possibilities of selling large amounts of capital or intermediate goods (at least until they are cut off), introducing new technologies periodically and thus maintaining royalty payments, and using the overseas venture as part of an international network.

While it is obvious that most investors would write off the crumbling or dangerous host countries, it seems that on the whole they show not much more liking for those which guarantee their profits despite inefficiency and sloth. For, these are just good profits as compared to a relatively small and stagnant market. They entail unpleasantness and irritations that make serious businessmen uncomfortable. And they do not provide the more distant hope of turning the investment into a really satisfying venture.

For all their risks, the Japanese still come back to the countries which have demonstrated a reasonable ability to use investment intelligently and treat the investors correctly. This includes the United States and European countries like Germany and Great Britain. They also show a willingness to cooperate even with those countries which have periodically gotten the better of Japan, such as Hong Kong, Taiwan, and especially Korea. There is no doubt that today's investors are more prudent than yesterday's. But they still come. The same cannot be said as readily of the Philippines, Indonesia or Thailand, at least for non-natural resource projects, and most certainly not of the bulk of the Third World.

Happy Investors

Judging by most standard criteria, the Japanese investors would seem to have reasons for satisfaction. There is no doubt that more raw materials than ever are flowing toward Japan, taking an almost quantum leap that would not have been conceivable without the extra push of going out there and finding, then developing, the sources. Sales abroad are growing rapidly, something that would be equally unlikely without the excellent and increasingly dense marketing and distribution networks. In more countries than ever, Japanese factories are in operation.

This latter point is only a mixed blessing because, in most cases, it has resulted in somewhat less production at home and fewer shipments of finished products. But there is no doubt that the overseas factories are also making a positive cotribution. First of all, they are usually fitted with Japanese plant and equipment, marking a sale for someone, perhaps the investor or his associates. Then, for a fairly long time, the investor continues supplying raw materials and intermediate goods. And, if the factory does well, its owner will eventually benefit directly and indirectly.

In a broader sense, overseas investment has been Japan's primary entry into the glorified scene of "internationalization," a goal long cherished but only fitfully accomplished. Still relatively isolationist in other matters, the Japanese have not hesitated to set up shop in the most far-flung places. They have made investments not only in friendly countries but others which they do not particularly like or get along with on diplomatic or ideological issues. In turn, this has sometimes improved, and nearly always strengthened, relations with the host country.

The Japanese get so excited about investment as a key to mutual understanding that they do not hesitate to include it under the heading of international cooperation. Naturally, this is not very disinterested assistance, since the investor country also gains (sometimes more than the host, sometimes less). But it is the kind of cooperation the Japanese spokesmen seem to value most highly and are bound to encourage in the future.

In the narrower, more crass and commercial sense, investment has often been a source of satisfaction for the investing companies. Their overseas subsidiaries and joint ventures are growing and multiplying. Some are even prospering. They are sending back profits and dividends and repaying the initial capital and loans. Many are also paying royalties for patents, designs, trademarks, technology, and so on. Some have become part of an integrated international strategy by producing parts more cheaply or marketing in their region. Back at the head office, officially at least, very good things are said about their progress.

As with everything, some companies are happier with their investments than others. Some have followed a wiser policy or simply been luckier. On occasion, investments have actually been so successful as to become exemplary success stories that are written up in the press and cited as an illustration of "what can be accomplished if . . ." by economists, businessmen and government officials.

One area in which there has been a fair amount of success, although rather few spectacular triumphs, is textiles. Teijin, Toray, Kanebo and others have set up a broad array of ventures of various types in various locations. Among those that are doing well are Toray's Penfabric and Penfibre, which show exceptionally high sales figures for Malaysia. Teijin seems to be matching this in Thailand, where Marubeni and Toyobo also have good projects like Dusit and Erawan.

But it is increasingly clear that this sector is played out. The existing ventures may stay but few new ones will be added. According to President Tomoo Tokusue of Teijin, "We intend to put an end to new joint ventures in the textile field." Yuji Kosugi, a top textile trade businessman at C. Itoh quite agreed. "I am pessimistic about overseas fiber and textile ventures. . . . We have not the slightest intention of setting up new ones. Rather, we will try to increase exports from Japan."[2]

The household appliance and electronics industry has remained more enthusiastic. The number of investments either for parts and components, final assembly or local manufacture is much larger. Most of these operations would seem to be doing reasonably well, or at least serving their purpose, or they would not be allowed to continue. It is very easy to disband them when their usefulness is over, but this is rarely done. Still, there are already signs that much fewer new investments will be made in the future.

Among the companies that are prominent, certainly none has gone into as many different ventures as Matsushita. Whether this is because of its desire "to contribute to world development" or because it is helpful to harness cheaper labor, to procure cheaper components and to get around trade barriers is unknown. Perhaps it is a combination of these reasons. At any rate, group members have over eighty overseas ventures which definitely shows a strong commitment. Sanyo Electric, with fewer actual ventures, nevertheless holds the Japanese record for sales amount of overseas production since 1978. By 1981, sales from its 33 manufacturing operations in 22 countries reached $2 billion. This represented over a quarter of its total sales and it is intended to raise this to one-third.[3]

While it does not have the largest number of subsidiaries or the biggest overseas production, there is no doubt that the one Japanese company that is best known abroad is Sony. In fact, some Americans and Europeans do not realize that it is a Japanese company which is a striking sign of its naturalization. Among Sony's various operations, four are particularly notable. In little over a decade, it put up three plants in the United States. One is the color television plant in San Diego, California, another the world's largest magnetic tape facility in Dothan, Alabama, and the third may be its biggest, a factory in Columbia, South Carolina, to produce color televisions and perhaps VTRs. The fourth is in Wales. Together, they employ about 7,000 workers and cost Sony over $300 million.

What impresses many observers, aside from the ultra-modern machinery, is the apparent ability to combine the best of Japanese management techniques with American practices. There is much talk of managers eating with the workers in the same canteen, chatting with them on a first name basis, and being receptive to proposals and suggestions. More significant, there is an effort to retain workers, if necessary doing other tasks, rather than lay them off during slack periods. The result, according to some journalists, is a lot of very happy workers. As for Stanley Karnow, he called Sony's San Diego factory "a model of efficiency." The Japanese managers seem just as happy, since they talk of productivity as high or higher than back home and products whose quality is not only good enough for the American market but even to sell in Japan.[4]

Another sector with a tremendous amount of investment is automobiles. Just what this really means can hardly be determined since most of the ventures are rather small-scale assembly plants in which actual value added is minimal and operations are hardly run on a sound commercial basis. Profits depend, more than anything else, on the level of protection. There are, however, some exceptions. One is the Nissan truck factory that opened up in Smyrna, Tennessee. With an output of about 200,000 units a year, this will be a real operation and, if Nissan plays its cards well, it should be a money-maker.

More impressive in its way is Honda's automobile plant in Marysville, Ohio. It went up next to the existing motorcycle facility. Automobiles are considerably more complex products to make, requiring more parts and finer workmanship. And the market is much more competitive. Yet, Honda has been making cars there since 1983, accelerating completion of the factory to take advantage of the "voluntary restraint" imposed on Japanese exports. Producing at a rate of 150,000 units or more a year, it achieves economies of scale. It should also be a success due to Honda's own capabilities and because it was preceded by an intensive learning process with the earlier motorcycle production which Honda regards as a success industrially and financially.

What is most interesting is that, unlike Nissan and especially Toyota, Honda did not wait to be asked or invest just to get around tariffs and quotas. This investment was part of a longer-term policy which was adopted many years ago by the founder, Soichiro Honda, and endorsed by his successor Kiyoshi Kawashima. It consists basically of a three-way division: one third of production to be made in Japan for sale on the domestic market; another third to be manufactured in Japan for export abroad in built-up form; and the last third to be produced and sold overseas. With nearly thirty offices, subsidiaries or tie-ups abroad, the company is well on the way to that goal.[5]

Whether the Japanese automakers will really succeed, and become as well-known and highly praised as Sony, will depend more than anything on labor relations. Like many other Japanese manufacturers, Nissan and Honda are evading or resisting unionization. But this will be much harder in a strongly unionized profession like the autoworkers and the UAW is bound to fight. In fact, even Nissan's cornerstone laying ceremony was marred by demonstrations. If all their efforts at setting up a factory and running it the way they want are disturbed by similar

Honda's Automobile Plant In Ohio

Credit: Honda

mishaps, the chances of success will be much slimmer.

One food company has also done amazingly well. Kikkoman, whose name is nearly synonomous with soy sauce, is an oft-cited success story. When it entered the American market again after the war, it found that local companies monopolized sales and it could hardly get its product on the store shelves. Kikkoman International, established in San Francisco in 1957 and with a branch in New York as of 1961, tried to turn the situation around through an exceptional marketing and publicity effort. But progress was stymied by the high cost of shipping from Japan. To save on transport, get around tariffs, and especially take advantage of abundant local raw materials, in 1972, the company built an integrated plant in Walworth, Wisconsin. With this boost, and the lower prices it permitted, Kikkoman was soon the No. 1 brand.

According to Yuzaburo Mogi, a descendant of one of

the company's founding families and general manager for international operations, it was not easy to decide on this major step of building their own factory. "It was a big risk. A soy sauce plant is a capital-intensive investment— in that sense the soy sauce industry resembles the oil industry. Furthermore, America is geographically much bigger than Japan, which makes the cost of overland transport from plant to market high. Another point is that, while ordinarily machinery can be purchased inexpensively in the U.S., construction of a soy sauce plant required special machinery and this equipment was very costly." While he did not mention it, there was doubtlessly also concern about the potential labor force. Fortunately, Mogi discovered, "at our Walworth plant, the productivity of the workers whom we have gathered from the area just around the plant is excellent."[6]

Such successes seem to have been achieved in a more dispersed fashion by YKK, the world's leading zipper manufacturer. With its zippers proving so popular abroad, many of the sales agents came to Tadao Yoshida, the founder, with the request that he open a production facility in their country. This was done all the more readily since the company also produced its own machinery, parts and supplies. Not all of the ventures were successful. Still, on the whole, they prospered and, if not, could be quickly wound down. By now there are nearly forty subsidiaries or branches around the world and overseas production already represents over a quarter of YKK's total.

Bridgestone Tire is also pursuing its grand design of becoming an international manufacturer like Firestone, Michelin and Goodyear, the top contenders. This was first done piecemeal with ventures in several developing countries. Those in Singapore and Iran were anything but encouraging. Still, the campaign moved into high gear by taking over Uniroyal's factory in Australia. Now Bridgestone is launching into the decisive phase with production in the United States. It recently acquired an old facility of Firestone, complete with equipment and workers, and is trying to upgrade it. It may well succeed, especially if it can tie up with Japanese automakers like Honda and Nissan as well as domestic American makers.

By far the biggest investors among Japanese companies are the general trading companies or *sogo shosha*. Each has anywhere from several dozen to over a hundred ventures of one sort or another. Some are just overseas sales offices. Others are participation in the sales and production facilities of their clients. They also get involved in major resource development projects and sometimes even manufacturing. By 1980, they boasted some ¥879 billion in overseas investment and loans for some 1,452 projects as well as 969 offices abroad. In so doing, they clearly outranked all other firms and as a group provided 40% of the investment of Japan's fifty biggest companies.[7]

Among them were successes and failures and especially a vast middle range of subsidiaries which did reasonably well and provided little cause either for glee or desperation. These operations, depending on their degree of success, were either channelling back dividends and repaying initial capital or begging for more loans. It would be hard to tell just how much money they did bring into their parent companies. However, whatever that may be, it is only part of the picture. For, most subsidiaries and joint ventures were not established purely for themselves but as part of a broader strategy. Even factories or mines that were doing poorly in their own terms could provide all sorts of trading revenue. And those that did well fed the *sogo shosha* with raw materials and bulk foodstuffs which they moved and were their basic stock in trade or manufactured products that they distributed at home and abroad.

Hapless Investors

There are doubtlessly a fair number of Japanese overseas investments which could be regarded as a remarkable success. Many more would be included among reasonable or relative successes and even some of those doing poorly still possess the potential to improve with time and effort. Thus, the prevailing opinion is that investors on the whole are doing well. In the eyes of some, they are doing too well. But this does not mean that there are no failures.

Naturally, much less is known about the failures. The investors themselves are hardly inclined to reveal their weaknesses and setbacks. The press does not do a much better job. Whenever the Japanese advance into an overseas venture, this is played up in newspapers at home and abroad. It is given banner headlines and everyone knows that such-and-such company has great expectations of its latest investment. When, for one reason or another, the project has to be scaled down, or withdrawn, or just collapses, there is rarely any mention. The only sign of its passing may be a brief notice on a back page of the same newspapers or malicious rumors spread among those in the know.

Be that as it may, there has been more than just a trickle of failures. First of all, it is necessary to remember that Japanese investment statistics, as well as those of many host countries, carry a list of "authorized" projects. These are investments for which all formalities have been completed and the investor can go ahead. Even at that stage, they may be announced to the public. But it sometimes happens that the investor has second thoughts and holds back. Thus, the investments actually made may run 10% or 20% lower than the investments authorized.

In a corner of Japan's statistics, there is also a reference to withdrawals. This shows that, from time to time, investors have thought better and officially pulled out of a project. There were as many as 300 to 500 partial or complete withdrawals a year, representing between a tenth and a quarter of the number of new investments.[8] But this is not all. In many cases, projects are allowed to lie dormant or, since what can be retrieved is minimal, it is not deemed worth the fuss to actually put a formal end to them.

There are plenty of reasons for an overseas investment to fail, as many and perhaps more than for a domestic venture to fail since it is embarked upon in a strange country under unfamiliar circumstances. Some were flawed from the outset and should never have been made, others developed problems as they went along. Among the potential defects are unwise choice of investment site. The product, the technology or the production scale could be wrong. Even if they were right, the market may not have materialized. And, even if it did, there is no guarantee that other competitors would not come in from outside or rise up in the host country. This could lead to fierce competition in which only the fittest survive.

When we turn from the "hard" aspects to the "soft" ones, things become even murkier. The manager may not have been right for the project, he was good at home but not abroad. Or the local partner may have hurt more than he helped. Goodness knows how the local labor force shaped up. Then there are various bureaucratic barriers and pitfalls. Government policy can change radically, and frequently, each time throwing all the company's plans off. There can be social unrest, political disturbances, even war. Short of this, there is always the rise and fall of the economy. Projects that were doing fine when business was booming just peter out with the downturn.

Since it takes a certain amount of time to try out a new project, for it to be run in or admitted inappropriate, a good place to look for failures is in a sector that has been around for a long time, like textiles. Here, just about all of the investing companies, both the textile manufacturers themselves and their trading company partners, have one or more failures to their name. C. Itoh pulled out of five ventures in recent years, including one in Spain and another in Nigeria shared with Teijin. Teijin and Kanebo had trouble in the United States and Toray got into a worse mess in Kenya, Ethiopia and El Salvador. Asahi Chemical closed down its first venture in Ireland, Chori discarded its sportswear firm in El Salvador, and Marubeni dropped some of its subsidiaries. This list, it must be stressed, is not exhaustive.

But similar events have happened in other sectors, since business is never smooth sailing. Matsushita Reiko liquidated its Spanish freezer and air-conditioner plant. Marubeni, Sumitomo and Mitsubishi closed their steel fabrication and sales firms in Europe. A Sumitomo-owned grain trader went bankrupt. Even an otherwise successful sector like electronics got stormy on occasion. Toshiba and Sanyo broke with their erstwhile partners in Europe and Sony, Matsushita and others withdrew from joint ventures in Korea. After a decade of frustration, the three trading companies pulled out of their model farms in Indonesia. These are just a few cases among many.

It was mentioned that some projects were flawed from the beginning, or almost. This could apply to two of the larger natural resource ventures. Although closely related conceptually, Cenibra and Flonibra were located a considerable distance from one another which meant that the eucalyptus trees were far removed from the pulp plant that

was supposed to process them. Domestic transport costs
entirely upset the original cost estimate. As for Flonibra
supplying cheap wood chips, this plan was promptly
undermined by rising freight rates which made it nearly
three times more expensive to ship them to Japan from
Brazil than from Australia. While its later troubles over-
shadowed the earlier pains of the Iranian petrochemical
project, Mitsui was doomed to make a loss from a very
early date. Once it was decided that costly naphtha would
have to be used as the feedstock rather than cheap
associated gas, there was no real hope for profits. And
Ataka, the ill-fated trading company, collapsed largely
because it failed to check the credit worthiness of its partner
Newfoundland Refining.

Other problems have materialized over the years. One
widespread headache has been the unexpectedly high cost
of training workers, and then retaining them, so that the
company could work efficiently. All too often, no sooner
were employees trained than they left for other jobs. A
complete turnover of personnel in two or three years was
not unknown. There have also been strikes and work
actions. More generalized, and insidious, has been the
nasty tendency of wages to rise faster than expected,
making some labor-intensive operations pointless. While
this was usually a gentle movement, to which companies
could sometimes adapt, on occasion it was abrupt as in
Korea after Park's death. When wages shot up 30% and
more, some manufacturers even withdrew from the export
processing zones.

While relations with labor were sometimes painful,
those with partners could be even more troublesome. A
joint venture is an unwieldy creature even in the best of
circumstances. There are always differences among the
parties on a multitude of points that arise in current
operations as regards recruitment policy, production

scale, marketing strategy and so on. This is nothing compared to conflicts over whether to plough profits back into the company or to start repaying the investors. And even this pales against how to fix blame if business goes down. Thus, Toshiba broke away from Rank in Great Britain and Sanyo from Emerson in Italy, both reputable firms, and proceeded to establish their own subsidiaries for television production instead. Toyota was such a demanding suitor that it turned down Ford and could barely agree to GM.

The situation in developing countries was bound to be even worse. There, under one sort of legislation or another, investors were often forced to take on local partners. All too many of those which Japanese firms had to work with were relatively unprepared for business and tended to belong to the "comprador" class. They could arrange appointments, make connections, pull strings, but not much more. This did not prevent them from demanding obscenely high rates for their services and occasionally getting in the way. Worse, some subsequently tried to take over the company, running it primarily in their interest. This could mean making it a going concern. More often it was a case of diverting funds from the joint venture into their own projects or pockets.

Among the partners who ended up getting some Japanese investors in trouble is Ricardo Silverio, a close crony of Philippine President Ferdinand Marcos, who served as a middleman for leading firms like Toyota, Komatsu, Sharp, Daikin and Nippon Denso. While he was extremely capable at politicking, he turned out to be a rather mediocre businessman. Delta Motors, his main holding, got off to a good start and boosted sales of Toyota through assembly of knock-down kits. But the company never made much money, and it invested part of that in other unrelated projects, some of which did poorly. Toward the end of the

1970s, Delta could not keep up with its competitors and Toyota's sales fell from year to year while the market share slumped from 40% to 32%. This hurt Toyota, which was also pinched by slow repayment of huge advances to Delta. Buried under losses of its own, Delta turned to the Philippine National Bank and ran up a debt of as much as ¥1 billion ($130 million). With insolvency looming, Toyota stopped shipment of kits and the PNB urged a loan restructuring. In the end, Silverio's position was downgraded while the PNB appointed directors to the board and Toyota finally gained an equity position.[9]

This time the use of a "comprador" certainly hurt more than it helped. And it was not only Toyota which suffered by using a partner with no real flair for business. Sharp was doing even worse and had to reduce its scale of operations sharply. The other joint ventures were only doing somewhat better. Yet, they were luckier than those who entrusted their interests in Dewey Dee, head of another leading Filipino business family. In January 1981, he suddenly disappeared leaving behind corporate and especially personal debts of ¥635 million ($85 million). This triggered a banking crisis in the Philippines, since he was tied up with many leading banks. And it also caused losses for the Japanese partners of Dee's Continental Manufacturing Corporation and other companies, including such behemoths as Mitsubishi Rayon, Mitsubishi Coporation and Marubeni Corporation.[10]

For a while, Nissan was stuck in a no-win situation in Indonesia. When its trading company Marubeni sought a sales agent back in 1975, the firm chosen was Indokaya managed by a reasonably competent *pribumi* businessman with some government connections. Things went smoothly enough until he passed away, leaving control to his brothers who soon got in a wrangle with the Japanese. Despite Datsun's popularity in the rest of Asia, sales were running well behind other Japanese makes. Rather than boost sales, the management decided to go into local assembly and, apparently without consulting its partners, bought German equipment for this. In so doing, Indokaya ran up a $28 million debt, part of it on Marubeni funds. With its sales agent facing imminent default, Nissan's own existence in a potentially promising market was threatened. But there was no desire to help the Indonesian managers who had created the mess. Finally, despite anti-Japanese campaigns in the press, Nissan and Marubeni got rid of their local partners and, in return, agreed to revamp the operation and even open a major assembly plant.[11]

In other cases, the partners turned out to be more dynamic than the outside investors, or had only gone into the project on the assumption that it would one day be transferred to them. This sort of thing happened with Sony's television joint venture with Whashin in Korea. Once its partner acquired "sufficient technology" to operate the plant, it sold back most of its share. Pioneer transferred its whole share in a TV venture to Lotte. In the tie-up between Honda and Kia, once the motorcycle factory was developing smoothly and local content rose to 90%, the Korean partner seemed capable of running it. Honda thus gave up its 49% share but continued providing technical assistance.[12] Although the Japanese partners were always compensated, and often continued their links, they had unwittingly created competitors.

A more natural cause of failure was growing competition, which could become intense both between foreign multinationals and with local firms. While the Japanese subsidiaries usually held their own, and actually took market share away from earlier Western rivals, they sometimes did one another in. With each trying to boost market share, obviously something had to give. More surprising was that local firms also moved in. Among the casualties was Safron, a polyester fiber operation in Brazil run by Teijin and Marubeni, which had been highly successful for years but had to be sold due to competition arising from no less than twenty rivals. Teijin (with C. Itoh) also pulled out of Polynova in Mexico, a company which once had nearly 100% of the market for texturized yarns.[13]

A general recession, often coupled with even tougher competition, can hurt just as much. The recession is largely what drove the steel fabricators from Europe. It led a leading bearing maker Koyo Seiko to stop actual production in Australia and revert back to export. Showa Renko reduced its equity in a French aluminum joint venture when sales plummeted. Toray had to absorb enormous debts of its fiber and textile ventures in Indonesia. And Marubeni, Mitsubishi and Mitsui had to pump more money into Alaska Pulp as wood chip prices nosedived and the company was heading for insolvency.

Very special problems arise for investors who set up offshore operations to get into restricted American or European markets. For, in successful places like Korea or Taiwan, exports may rise to the point that quotas are imposed on them as well. Such countries are then more likely to grant larger shares to domestic firms than foreign ones or even joint ventures. Meanwhile, the domestic market may be partly or entirely closed to outsiders. This leaves them little choice but to shut down or transfer their holdings to local interests. This explains why Matsushita sold its share in Korean National Electric, Pioneer withdrew from its joint venture with Lotte, and many others pulled out more or less discreetly from once thriving operations, especially in the export processing zones.

While many of these afflictions seem normal in manufacturing, they have become an almost equally frequent companion to natural resource projects. Just a few years ago, investors thought that only long-term contracts and vast new projects could save them. Their exaggerated ambitions, combined with a worldwide recession, have resulted in a general slump in certain sectors. Sometimes they saw the downturn coming early enough to hold back on investments or slow them down. Often, they were stuck with excess capacity or output. Thus, one case among many, Oji Paper and Mitsui had to defer imports of printing paper from their Canadian affiliate, New Brunswick International Paper, which had just begun expanding production at their request.[14]

Much less visible is the loss of earnings which many of these projects will face because of oversupply and even a glut for certain products. The economic rationale of many projects is now badly in need of review. This applies to bauxite, alumina and aluminum with several major Japanese ventures coming on stream, including both the Asahan and Amazon projects. And this is occurring at the same time as many others in India, Australia and elsewhere. There is also trouble in the paper and pulp sector and probably later for petrochemicals. Even the steel complexes in Brazil are somewhat dubious, not in their basics, but because of the cost overruns which made them much more expensive than planned.

What is most worrisome is that Japan is not just having trouble with relatively small projects but also some of the biggest ever undertaken, including a number of highly touted "models of international cooperation." Indeed, each time the Japanese government and the host government intervened too strongly in promoting a venture, the chances of commercial success were reduced by that much. Pressure to go through with it, exerted both on the local partners and the Japanese investors, made them ignore some of their qualms or accept the greater risks in the expectation of government compensation or bailouts later on. In Japan's case, the safety net of insurance and promises of support made it *too* easy to enter commitments that would normally have been turned down.

This shows that many failures arise not so much from commercial miscalculations as political causes which are largely beyond the control of the investors. Even in relatively friendly and hospitable host countries, under a government that is supposedly promoting investment, there can be sudden changes in policy that create uncertainty and damage. Among them were an ill-advised decision in Indonesia to insist on exporters purchasing back some of its commodities in return for the right to sell capital goods, in the Philippines a provision in the new corporation code making companies buy useless government securities in order to have their business licenses renewed, or in Thailand moves to control prices, sometimes at ruinous levels.

Even more painful is to unexpectedly lose the support and protection of the government when it decides that it just isn't worth the cost to promote certain industries. A particularly poignant case is Nissan's participation in Motor Iberica, once a very profitable venture. It promptly started losing money when Spain lowered import tariffs on machinery in preparation for joining the European Community. In no time, the market was flooded with low-priced tractors from Italy and seven of its ten factories had to be closed. This is also a familiar phenomenon in developing countries. When Singapore decided to scrap its fledgling automobile industry, Toyota, Nissan and Bridgestone Tire all closed down. And over a dozen assembly plants may bite the dust due to Indonesia's "deletion" plan.

To show that advanced countries are sometimes no better, one of the most unfortunate measures was taken in California and a dozen other states which decided to raise more revenue through a "unitary tax" system. This meant that foreign companies, the vast majority of whose operations were abroad and which only had subsidiaries in the state, could be taxed as a function of global earnings. This would have serious consequences for firms like Sony and Kyocera. But the perpetrators were not even smart enough to figure out that it could also have an unfortunate impact on the state, as a former Sony executive explained. "It is clear that the unitary tax as applied to foreign-source income has the very definite effect of discouraging foreign investment in California. . . . Thus, while it is possible that California might enjoy a temporary increase in revenue by use of the concept of unitary taxation, it is bound to suffer in the long run."[15]

In other cases, the government may be viscerally opposed to foreign investment and have no compunction about nationalizing or expropriating companies with little or no compensation. In Ethiopia, this happened to Toray's textile mill, with any compensation paid in useless local currency. Yokohama Rubber more recently decided to pull out of Addis Tyre due to the government takeover and arbitrary reduction of its shareholding from 30% to 5% after the revolution. In Iran, the authorities completely took over the management of Bridgestone Tire, a once successful operation. They also halted repayment of sums due it by the joint venture partners. A copper mine run by C. Itoh, Nittetsu Mining and Toho Zinc fared similarly.

Aside from this, there are damages inflicted by social disturbances, civil wars and international hostilities. In El Salvador, two textile company executives were kidnapped by leftist guerillas, one of whom was later released for ransom while the other was found dead. This put a definite damper on the company's activities as well as those of Japanese investors throughout the region. When the Islamic Revolution erupted in Iran, followed by a lengthy war between Iraq and Iran, hundreds of technicians and managers had to be withdrawn from projects which then languished. The worst stricken was the petrochemical complex in Bandar Khomeini which was repeatedly bombed. Yet, what was at stake was not just a few projects but the fate of dozens of projects in Iran, which had accumulated $855 million in investment before the Shah's fall, accounting for about 40% of Japan's total investment in the Middle East and nearly 3% of its investment worldwide.

While outright nationalization is regrettable, at least it is a clear-cut situation. What is increasingly disturbing to many investors is the trend toward "creeping" expropriation of their holdings in less radical countries. This can occur when they are encouraged, whether they want or not, to sell increasing shares of their equity to local partners or the general public, pressed into boosting local content, faced with discriminatory taxation, or forced to leave sectors which were later reserved for locals. For example, when the Brazilian government decided to localize the telecommunications industry, NEC had little choice but to sell its 51% interest in NEC do Brasil.

That there can be failures among Japanese investments should now be abundantly clear. There is no need to press the point further nor to feel that the failures represent a much larger proportion of the total cases than they really do. No one knows for sure, but there is probably only about one failure in twenty or, at worst, one in ten. Unfortunately, even this rate is unduly high. For each failure causes more trouble and frustration in the local operation, more hassle and work at the head office, and more financial losses than can be balanced by several successes.

It should also be clear that the Japanese investors are not the only ones who can engage in questionable practices. They repeatedly run into competitors and rivals which threaten them. While this is expected, they can also be stabbed in the back by their own work force or partners. And they must constantly worry about what some governments, even those which are supposedly well disposed, may cook up next. It would seem that, seen in this light, exploitation is very definitely a two-way street and that as much opprobrium should be reserved for "ugly" hosts as for "ugly" Japanese.

Profit-Disoriented Investment

There is one other point on which both the supporters of international investment and the critics of neocolonialism would agree, albeit for entirely different reasons. They assume that investment must be a profit-making proposition. In fact, they would probably go much further. The former would speak of fair returns, juicy profits, and occasionally even a "killing" that could be made. The latter are highly vocal about the tremendous—and unjust—rewards of "plundering" natural resources, "exploiting" labor, and "subjecting" markets.

In theory, no one would make investments abroad unless he thought there was some possibility of earning a reasonable return or, more exactly, unless there was a good prospect of earning a greater return than at home. There is no sense in going to all the expense and bother of setting up a foreign venture if one could do just as well in Japan. True, for some of the industries fated to decline or disappear due to rising labor costs or growing competition, any profit would be better than none. Still, even then, the yield must at least be high enough to pay back the initial outlay, including any interest on borrowed funds, and then bring in some modest premium.

So, one simple yardstick for measuring the success of Japanese investors would be profits. This is not quite as good as actual return on investment, but certainly more accessible. Yet, although a vast amount of research has been done on investment in general, amazingly little of it has paid much attention to the financial side. Part of the reason may be that academics do not find the subject sufficiently scholarly while even business journalists take too narrow a view to follow trends. The other problem is quite simply that companies are not prone to announcing their profits, or at any rate stating them clearly and honestly, and thus accurate data are hard to come by. Still, what there is of it leads one to reject the idea that Japanese investors are earning a fortune and even makes one wonder whether they are doing very well at all.

The statistics collected annually by MITI show a far from encouraging situation. Prior to the oil crisis and the worldwide recession, the percentage of corporations a-broad reporting profits for the term edged close to 75% only to fall back to 65% or less during the recession. That was not bad... except that the profit margins were never terribly high. The peak average reached for profit, whether as a ratio of sales or of net worth, was just 5% in 1972. Until then it only wavered between 1% and 3% and after that it sank below 1% before returning to the 1–3% range. Profitability was, in fact, so low that only about a third of the companies declared dividends in good years and a quarter in bad. And the average dividend varied between 7% and 20%.

What is most distressing about this reading is that the trends were only really positive before the oil shock and it took nearly a decade to come out of the trough. Also, compared to the situation in Japan itself, profits were not very good and dividends were hardly better. These ventures are thus still in a period of relatively low return on investment and it is a bit premature to talk of success. Actually, with such low profits, it would take them decades to pay back the original capital and finally make some real

Profitability Of Overseas Subsidiaries

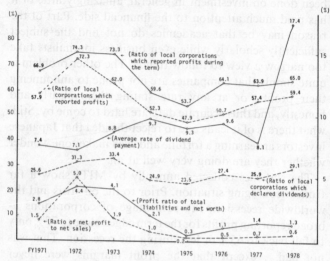

Source: *Overseas Activities of Japanese Business Enterprises*, 1980, MITI.

money. And that only applies to those which declare dividends.

Naturally, there is considerable variety among the investments. There are subsidiaries which are doing very well and quickly paid back their initial costs. Others are languishing and may never make it. There are also countries where profits and dividends are much higher than elsewhere. The MITI statistics do not go into such details, but there are sources which indicate reasonably good profits in places like Taiwan, Hong Kong, Singapore and Malaysia. Other countries have been a disaster as Japanese investors fell into an unexpected trap... inflation. From year to year, the value of their investments dwindled as inflation soared by 20% or 30% in countries with a mild case, like Indonesia, Thailand and Korea, and 50% to 100% where it is acute, like Brazil, Mexico and Argentina.

More embarrassing than deriving a rather meager return from their investments is that it appears the Japanese are doing worse than some other investors. Even when they are getting along nicely in some Asian countries, their profits do not look quite as good as those of prosperous local businessmen. Compared to other foreign investors, they also seem to be lagging behind. For 1980, the American Department of Commerce reported a 15% rate of return for all foreign subsidiaries; Nikko reported a profit rate of barely 1% or 2% for Japanese investments in the United States. The two measurements are not strictly comparable, but the gap is so great that the Japanese were obviously not doing too well.

There can be some valid reasons for this. The foremost is that many of the Japanese investments are still rather young since it is a latecomer to many countries. It takes a while to set up a company, to get things running smoothly, and to generate profits. But the situation does not seem to be improving with time. That may be due to the lingering recession. Still, there are a number of other explanations that probably deserve more weight.

The first, which should be dealt with immediately, is the possibility that the profit picture has been made to look worse than it really is artificially. There are plenty of ways of doing this. At the outset, when the value of the investment is assessed, it is possible to overvalue any portion that was provided in capital goods, especially used machinery. The parent company can charge more for any services rendered while the trading company or a sister company may pay less for products supplied. The bill for patents, royalties, processes and so on can be padded. But the most common method is through transfer pricing, especially when the level of local content is rather low. By charging more for its intermediate goods and raw materials, the investor can draw a lot of money out of the subsidiary. Of course, it is also possible just to falsify the tax returns.

There is no point in arguing that Japanese are more inclined to use such tactics, or more honest, depending on how one feels about their morals. It is likely that the degree to which any group of investors cheats is not terribly different. Moreover, over the years, the host countries have gotten increasingly adept in dealing with investors. They know all the tricks and have adopted stricter measures against them, ranging from fines and other penalties for incorrect tax declarations to evaluating the worth of intermediate goods and machinery themselves. Thus, cheating is surely not the whole reason and probably not even an essential explanation when compared with other investors.

What makes Japanese investors fare differently from most others is that their business practices are so different. This is manifested in various ways, some of which have a direct influence on profits.

One drawback is that so much of the investment is built on debt. There is not just one level, but several. The overseas subsidiary itself will not be capitalized to anything like the extent needed. Like its Japanese parent, it will be highly leveraged with bank loans and sometimes government loans. In those countries where it must seek partners, the Japanese side may also grant loans, or guarantee them, for the local partners. The subsidiary will have to pay interest on its loans, and eventually pay them back, which will naturally decrease its profits and make it wait longer to reimburse the parent company. If, for some reason, the overseas venture or even the partners get in trouble, then the parent company will be responsible for other costs that should not normally be its concern.

Another tic of some companies that keeps profits down is a yearning for prestige. Japanese companies aiming for the top of the market, or trying to keep up their image, will tend to indulge in unduly expensive offices and other premises, excessive publicity and public relations, and assorted representation costs. Much less willingly, they may have to provide better conditions for their personnel, not only somewhat higher wages but also more fringe benefits, welfare services like canteens and dormitories, and so on. Finally, if they insist on maintaining quality, which is an entirely justifiable concern, they will find that it can be costly. It implies greater training of workers, closer supervision of what is done, perhaps incentives to perform. It also means more rejects and waste if workers do not turn out high enough quality parts or products.

But the most serious cause is the urge for expansion and striving for larger sales as opposed to bigger profits. The Japanese system is driven by and large by these goals, which are very different from those of more commercially-minded businessmen in the West or even Third World. Thus, the Japanese will engage in fierce competition with local rivals, and especially with one another, in order to grab a bigger share of the market. This will involve, among other things, price-cutting and granting rebates. Part, but only part, of the loss may be compensated for by larger production scale among those which survive. But, as long as the competition remains hot, the profits will stay low.

In Japan, this sort of competition occurs in the beginning, until just a few producers dominate the market and the market shares are pretty much consolidated. Then, through collusion of one sort or another, they mutually boost prices and start reaping profits to compensate for the earlier price wars. This relief may not be possible elsewhere, either due to antitrust legislation or because they are being chased up by cheaper domestic producers. The outcome is that profits can be kept slim for much longer than they normally would in Japan where the parties know when to fight and when to cooperate.

Previously, the problem of low profits had not seriously upset the Japanese investors. They were still in a pioneering phase and assumed that eventually things would improve. Now that the situation has not gotten much better abroad and is sometimes tight at home, they are having second thoughts. This review is also caused by the fact that overseas investments are not really seen in the same light as investment at home. When they put up extra installations at home, the Japanese at least have the benefit of expanding their own base, hiring more workers or finding alternative posts for employees they are tied to, and so on. The only thing they really gain from an overseas investment is profit. And, if this is not forthcoming, the whole thing just doesn't make sense.

Of course, there is little point in talking of profits without saying a word about losses. This matter is even more obscure and there is hardly any information available. Worse, when a project collapses it is simply withdrawn from the investment statistics without its value being announced or deducted. The money that has already been paid out is forgotten at this macroeconomic level, if not the micro level. The parent company knows how much it has lost and is not likely to forget the experience.

Scanning the newspapers, however, it is possible to find some data which are enough to faze any investor. For example, Asahi Chemical is reported to have lost ¥12 billion in its first attempt in Ireland. Teijin may have lost ¥10 billion on its joint venture in Spain.[16] Toray's Indonesian subsidiaries ran up $100 million in debts. Bridgestone was out some ¥6.5 billion for its tire plant in Iran. Yet, this is nothing compared to the potential losses of the petrochemical complex. Mitsui and other companies paid in about ¥310 billion before balking. This is not offset by any profits or dividends since the project was aborted before it even went into operation.

Fortunately for some of the companies concerned, but not all, they are covered by investment or export insurance when the losses are due to political as opposed to commercial risks. Thus, it was rumored that Mitsui and its partners would recover as much as ¥239 billion while the various other ventures in Iran, including Bridgestone, could expect another ¥154 billion, making their burden considerably less. But this transfers much of the load to the national budget, since the insurance claims are too large to be covered by the fund, as much as ten times its annual income. This, in effect, means that the general public has to bail out the companies when too many investors get in trouble.

Obviously, such losses must be balanced against any gains. In so doing, one should consider that when a project is given up, this often only happens after a series of bad years has proven that it could not work or even be saved. This time, in addition to any current losses, it is necessary to write off the initial outlay unless plant and equipment or other assets can be sold to compensate. Therefore, if even one project in ten fails, it can be most discomforting.

Nevertheless, very slowly and not too surely, Japan's investment is entering a phase of maturity. The amount of profits paid to the parent companies has been rising steadily and already reached the level of $1,461 million in 1981. This may look like a substantial amount. But it is still only about 30% of the sum that was paid out in fresh investment the same year. More pertinently, it is only 4% of the cumulative amount of investment that was put up to yield it. It is also just a shadow, a mere 7%, of what American companies earned in the same period.

Hurting Japan

When the Japanese first began investing heavily, in the 1960s and early 1970s, they were very confident and enthusiastic. Without carefully looking into the situation, they optimistically assumed that things would turn out for the best. They felt that with their greater economic wealth, superior technologies, and smooth-running production machine, they could easily direct the many projects and also use them in their own interest as well as that of the nation.

By the late 1970s, there was a rude awakening when many investors discovered that things were not so easy. True, some projects had been a huge success. But they were not quite the overwhelming majority. Actually, the bulk were just moderate successes and the remainder were relative or outright failures. This has put a damper on the earlier hopeful mood and increased awareness of the problems that can arise.

The most evident are connected specifically with the host countries since it turned out that some were much better locations than others. Basically, this had to do with their general economic situation, the existence of natural resources, the ability of their work force, the growth of the market, and so on. Some countries simply did not have much potential. This could be excused. But a certain number also refused to play the game fairly. There were too many cases of investment regulations suddenly being revised, usually to the detriment of the investors. Loans were not always repaid and even nationalization occurred with worrisome frequency.

This led to growing concern about the problem of "country risk," something the Japanese had blithely overlooked before. As time went by, they began sorting out the various host countries, deciding in their own interest which were the most reliable partners and which could not be trusted. This distinction acquired a particular weight for various reasons. First of all, the Japanese lay great stress on correct relations and dislike doing business with untrustworthy or incompetent counterparts. They also tend, more than others, to take a long-term view and launch projects which will not pay off for substantial times. So, they cannot really afford major changes even in a distant future. Equally important, they have a very good memory when someone has cheated or mistreated them. Thus, the news was passed along the grapevine and it did not take long for bad experiences made by one company in a given country to become general knowledge, making everyone less than eager to deal with that country.

The rating of countries by risk was formulated more precisely on occasion, as when the highly reputed *Nihon Keizai Shimbun* began organizing country risk surveys. It checked a hundred leading companies doing business abroad about the situation they had encountered, whether for investment or exports. This included specific problems like non-payment, unilateral cancellation of projects or expropriation. It also covered the general economic status such as inflation, natural resources, market size and growth potential. But it could not overlook political factors like the ability to service external debt and stability of the government. The results were then tabulated with 10 points indicating a perfect score.[17]

Not even the United States hit that level, but it remained at the top of the list with a rating close to 9 points. Following below were other leading Western countries, especially those with a buoyant economy or raw materials, like Germany, Switzerland, Canada and Australia. Somewhat further down came the Asian NICs, Singapore, Hong Kong, Taiwan and then Korea. In this intermediate range were also the oil producers and other raw material suppliers as well as more Asian partners like Malaysia, Indonesia, Thailand and Philippines. Trailing further behind, somewhere beneath the 5 point level, were the East bloc countries and the more promising developing countries. The mass of the Third World remained under 4 points and a few countries in a particularly unstable condition took up the rear, Lebanon, Iran, Afghanistan, or whoever happened to be in trouble just then.

Country risk was far from an academic matter. Each time the survey was taken, it turned out that a fair number of companies, about a quarter, had actually suffered damages of one sort or another in the preceding year. It also became clear that companies were withdrawing their investments or had doubts about making new ones and those which continued were increasingly cautious. Countries with a very low rating would find it hard to court Japanese investors or even engage in normal commercial transactions with many companies.

By the early 1980s, country risk was not only an irritating issue for companies engaged in investing and exporting, it also preoccupied the government. With social disturbances, political reversals and even wars cropping up at a dizzying pace around the world, there was soon a plethora of unfortunate incidents involving Japanese companies. In fact, claims on the special investment insurance were already enough to bankrupt the system. Thus, MITI started pushing for more investment guarantee pacts, especially with closer partners. Meanwhile, it declared as many as fifty countries to be risks and recommended a very low ceiling for export insurance covering those areas. Deprived of this backing, more companies than ever hesitated or just refused to sell or invest there.

Although the more spectacular events such as the collapse of some major project or difficulties in a given host country were usually highlighted, a number of broader

problems gradually came to light as well. They had been
emerging very slowly, and not very visibly at first, until they
loomed up as even more serious matters than mere
bankruptices or expropriations. For they affected not just a
few projects or companies but the whole Japanese economy.

The first phenomenon the Japanese began to notice was
eventually dubbed the "doughnut." Over the years, certain
industries had been ceded without too much resistance to
the developing countries. These were the backward, labor-
intensive or "throwaway" sectors which Japan apparently
found insufficiently attractive. This happened, to some
extent at least, for textiles and garments, footwear and
toys, pottery and plastics, as well as many traditional
crafts. Most of these simple industries were migrating to
the nearby Asian countries where labor was much cheaper
and less demanding. This was not only, as sometimes
claimed, because Japan wished to shed them but also
because its own businessmen had to move abroad to find
cheaper labor.

However, the process did not stop there. No sooner had
the techniques of these rather simple industries been
mastered than some of the more dynamic entrepreneurs
abroad began seeking Japanese cooperation for more
advanced branches. Since some of them had widely known
technologies or required large inputs of labor, they too
started to migrate. This included radios, televisions, and
other basic electronics, digital watches and some chemicals. . . Then, before Japan knew it, places like Korea,
Taiwan and Brazil were also producing ships, automobiles,
and steel.

A similar process was occurring with regard to raw
materials. Japan had once imported only ores and then
processed them and turned them into finished products.
Gradually, either due to new legislation in the producer

countries or to perfectly good economic reasons, like cheaper transport, easier access to feedstock, or abundant energy, the Japanese began processing more of the raw materials on the spot. At the same time, the resource-rich countries began processing their own raw materials and selling them in processed form and ultimately in finished form. This was already occurring for aluminum, copper and zinc. It would eventually happen for most petrochemicals and steel.

As more and more goods were being produced in offshore factories or by foreign countries for Japan, less and less goods of the same type were being produced in Japan. The Japanese side of the operation gradually withered, with factories that once manufactured all their own products now importing the majority from abroad, and then one day becoming nothing more than a warehousing and distribution setup. Companies that once processed raw materials ended up importing processed articles. The vital industrial core was being eroded and emptied of its substance while the essential activity was taking place in the periphery.

If being the hole in a doughnut had its disadvantages, certainly being the butt of a "boomerang" was more uncomfortable. Yet, this was the second effect arising from investment. Not only had the Japanese been discarding their backward industries, they had been eagerly acquired on their own by some of the developing countries, especially those which won themselves the qualification of newly industrialized countries. Much to Japan's good fortune at first, and later its misfortune, they were the very ones it was located nearest to or worked most closely with, such as Korea, Taiwan, Hong Kong, Singapore and Brazil.

These countries not only learned the tricks from Japan, they were able on occasion to outdo the master in some ways. This process took place in two phases. First, the NICs and some others recovered control over their own industries. In each sector the investors had entered, the once predominant Japanese companies faced increasing competition and became just a few among many. It could even happen that particularly energetic or resourceful national companies would wrest away part of their market share. Anyway, once the local economies had reached a certain stage, they found it easier and easier to do without Japanese imports.

Meanwhile, these more rapidly developing countries were soon demanding access to the markets of the advanced nations, including Japan. They were producing goods of adequate quality at comparatively low prices and they could compete even against Japanese products. In the sectors they were most competitive in, they edged out some of the less efficient Japanese firms and then encroached on the share of more successful ones. Even when Japan ducked this boomerang by imposing quotas or hiding behind non-tariff barriers, it could not avoid the impact on third markets. There, the exports of real developing countries kept driving out those of Japan in all but some highly sophisticated sectors.

The "boomerang" and the "doughnut" were already serious enough if one could see an end to these trends. Yet, there was always something new coming up. The NICs did not stop at simple manufactured goods but tried to produce just about everything, with or without Japanese aid. The most unpleasant aspect of this, however, was the habit of certain countries of treading on Japan's heels. Whether coincidentally, since it was the handiest model, or purposely, because it was a rival, the Asian NICs almost systematically followed the same path as Japan. Thus, no matter which way Japan turned, it was bound to find one of its competitors trying to catch up.

Once upon a time, the Japanese had regarded the surrounding nations as such distant competitors that there was no need to worry. "By the time they figure out how to manfacture that, we'll have more efficient methods or we'll move onto something else," they used to say. The name of the game was to continue upgrading to keep ahead. This the Japanese did quite admirably, while managing to catch up with and then pass many Western countries. But they clearly underestimated the ability of other countries to pull off the same trick. They also forgot that it is much easier to follow in someone's footsteps than to become a path-breaker. So, Japan was gradually running out of new growth sectors while the old sectors it was losing its competitive edge in accumlated.

Another phenomenon might be labelled roughly "missed opportunities at home." Overseas investment was always an alternative to investment in Japan and the money that was put into foreign factories could have been used sometimes to expand or upgrade domestic facilities. Even in the older, labor-intensive sectors, another way out was to introduce larger doses of machinery and robots. The rest of the manufacturing investment more clearly took work away from the local economy. Only investment in marketing outlets or raw materials seemed entirely to its advantage, while investment in processing was again more dubious.

Similarly, the transfer of production to other countries, especially of labor-intensive but also of capital-intensive operations, took jobs away from Japan. Doubtlessly, new opportunities were opened in more sophisticated sectors that replaced the older ones. But they never amounted to quite as many as were lost, since the older the sector the more likely it was to be labor-intensive and the newer the sector the less likely it was to absorb much labor. In the days of rapid expansion, this was hardly noticed. However, by the late 1970s there was a growing problem of unemployment even if it was not openly admitted.[18]

It is extremely difficult to measure Japan's losses here. Some of the investment was unavoidable. Either the host countries extracted it or the domestic industries were really too weak to survive without unacceptably high levels of support. But certain sectors, or individual operations, could perhaps have been saved. Thus, local businessmen have been increasingly vocal in demanding government backing, especially those in the smaller companies and declining sectors. The trade unions and labor officials have also begun complaining about "exporting jobs."[19]

With this, a more fundamental change in the attitude toward investment is taking place. It is still much too early to see this reflected in actual policies since it is only of late that the government and ministry officials, businessmen and trade unionists even realized what was happening. But there is no doubt that there will be much more talk of the dangers of the "doughnut" and "boomerang" effects or "exporting jobs" in the future. And this cannot help having an impact on investment.

NOTES

1. *Japan Times*, May 8, 1981.
2. *Japan Times*, September 28 and July 7, 1981.
3. Nobuhiko Tsuchida, "Japanese Style Factory Management in the U. S.," *Oriental Economist*, May 1982, pp. 24–8.
4. *Japan Times*, June 12, 1980.
5. Kiyoshi Kawashima, "Investing Overseas," *Speaking of Japan*, March 1982, pp. 16–9.
6. Jiro Koitabashi, "A Symbol of Japanese Culture Now 'Made in America,'" *The Wheel Extended*, Autumn 1980, pp. 21–4.
7. Katsumi Shimada, "Japan's Trading Houses," *Economic Eye*, September 1981, pp. 27–32.
8. Ministry of Finance, *Japan's Direct Overseas Intestment*, 1983.

9. *Far Eastern Economic Review*, April 16, 1982, and *Insight*, June 1981.
10. *Far Eastern Economic Review*, January 30 and February 13, 1981.
11. *Far Eastern Economic Review*, January 16, 1981.
12. *Asian Wall Street Journal*, December 1, 1979.
13. *Japan Economic Journal*, October 14, 1980, and *Japan Times*, May 20, 1982.
14. *Japan Economic Journal*, July 13, 1982.
15. *Far Eastern Economic Review*, December 1981, p. 52.
16. *Japan Economic Journal*, October 20, 1981, August 4, 1981, and May 10, 1983.
17. *Japan Economic Journal*, September 1, 1981.
18. See Woronoff, *Japan's Wasted Workers*, pp. 229–43.
19. See Japan Institute of Labor, *Overseas Investment and Its Impact on Domestic Employment*, May 1981.

10
The New Order

Improving On The Past

Whether Japan likes it or not, it will have to live in the shadow cast by the erstwhile co-prosperity sphere. Although the war lies nearly forty years back, and all of its former colonies have regained their independence and some are progressing very nicely, the memories have not entirely faded. Any similarities in policy today, no matter how faint, can invoke the sometimes inept, sometimes outright cruel actions experienced by those who were subjected by Japan or fought against it during the Pacific War.

Nevertheless, Japan's present commercial empire is not like the old one, no matter how many invidious comparisons may be made or irate complaints raised against it. It is not, and could not be, the same kind of empire because the contemporary world is so totally different from that of the past. The sharp distinctions between strong and weak countries have not quite been lost, but at least the weaker ones now enjoy a situation of theoretical equality. They are all sovereign states. They belong to various organizations which defend their rights, and sometimes turn them into privileges. The host countries, even the weakest, are members of the United Nations and also Third World groups that happen to represent the vast majority of the international community.

When Japan wishes to invest there, it is now dealing with a government which it can perhaps influence, but certainly not coerce or impose its will on. In order to launch any project, there must be some sort of consent from the host country when the investment is first made and the host country maintains substantial control over the process throughout. If, for one reason or another, it feels that the arrangement was not sufficiently beneficial, it may even intervene against the investor to impose its will. Since the investor has more to lose than to gain by resisting, he is basically the weaker party even when Japan is stronger than the host country.

Moreover, much of the illusion that the new empire bears some resemblance to the old is attributable to the mistaken notion that Japan has again become a very powerful nation. That is not quite accurate. True, it has resumed its economic progression and become what is called an economic "superpower" which already produces about a tenth of the world's gross national product. It is a very dynamic trading nation. But it has no political clout to speak of, not being a member of the Security Conucil or even a leader in the group of advanced nations. Militarily, it can scarcely defend the home islands let alone send gunboats abroad. And, no matter what it might conceivably wish to do on behalf of its investors, it can do nothing effective for these reasons alone.

This means that, for the Japanese, investing is a process that must evolve on the basis of mutual benefit—or reciprocal self-interest—because the investors can do no more than make proposals which must be accepted by the local government and their partners. They enter the host country in the position of supplicants, not masters, and they have to obey the existing rules. In some cases they do receive incentives, but this does not mean that they can bend or break the rules with impunity. Moreover, since their investment has such high visibility, they have to be exceptionally cautious and any missteps they make will be noted faster than those of others.

Although the investors cannot lord it over local businessmen or the "natives," there are still some rough edges which create an impression of domination. Japanese companies happen to be larger than most and some of them are particularly extensive and tightly organized concerns. The businessmen who represent them, and even those from the smallest firms, are used to playing a very tough competitive game at home and they are under pressure to win abroad as well. Locals, even in the most advanced countries, may find them unduly aggressive and prove unable to resist their attacks. If they get hurt, they will not really care much why, and put the blame on the Japanese investors.

It is unfortunately true that Japanese investors also try to give less in return for what they receive, even when compared to the hardly generous Europeans and Americans. More staff is brought from the head office and fewer locals recruited in responsible positions. No more training is given than is needed to get the job done and technological secrets are rarely bared. Firms struggle to increase market share without the slightest concern about what happens to anyone else. This sort of thing can lead exasperated critics to make comments like the following from an Indonesian businessman. "If you really think about it, it took the Japanese 35 years, but they finally won the war."[1]

Yet, even here one should not exaggerate. Most Japanese companies do have some interest in long-term success and a nebulous recognition that this is only possible if they behave reasonably well. Although they are sometimes callous, they cannot really afford to be brutal. And, no matter how hard they push, the local companies and population can stop the game by convincing the government to intervene. Finally, although the Japanese businessmen are hardworking and ambitious, they are far from heros. If the situation gets ugly, they will more likely fade away or step back and hope to be forgotten.

Many of these rough edges have been smoothed by the passing years of experience as international businessmen, something they never possessed before. The ministries back home and the trade associations also impress on them the need to adopt a more exemplary conduct for the good of all. Where these largely verbal pleas fail to produce results, the Japanese may be called to order by the unpleasantness that arises when their action is too obstreperous and a nasty reaction sets in. Repeatedly, Japan has been taught its lesson. And it was perhaps learned most effectively since it took much the same form as *zazen*, the Zen Buddhist method of teaching where the slightest lack of concentration is punished by a sharp and sudden whack with a heavy stick.

There were periodic strikes and boycotts, tracts and riots, pointedly directed against the Japanese. The most memorable blow was delivered in 1974, when Kakuei Tanaka, the brash and freewheeling prime minister, undertook a "good will" tour of Southeast Asia. Scarcely had it begun than a revulsion against Japanese encroachment and "overpresence," doubtlessly borne by even deeper currents of anger at the local goverment, broke to the surface. This occurred with particular vehemence in Thailand and Indonesia. In Bangkok, the prime minister was treated to jeers and insults; in Djakarta, the crowd ran wild and two days of rioting ended with eight dead and dozens injured.

But there were also lessons of another sort, this time when Japanese investments were hurt, not so much due to the fault of the Japanese themselves but various misdemeanors of the host government or population. This was the other shoulder of *zazen*. Workers showed disloyalty by leaving the company for a paltry raise elsewhere or managers quit and joined the competetion, or set up their own office. Local politicians and businessmen intrigued against them. On occasion, assets were expropriated or a firm was nationalized. The worst shock came when Iran's revolutionary regime differed with Mitsui and the biggest private investment ever became worthless almost overnight.

What were the lessons the Japanese learned? Basically two. The first, mastered especially by the government and politicians, was that in the future they should use only the kindest language when dealing with other countries and that they should accompany investment with little gifts now and then to win the friendship of the natives. This was already noticeable when Prime Minister Takeo Fukuda made his swing through Southeast Asia in August 1977. In what came to be known as the Fukuda Doctrine, he promised to turn a new page.

"It is not enough for our relationship to be based solely on mutual material and economic benefit. Our material and economic relations should be animated by heartfelt commitments to assisting and complementing each other as fellow Asians. This is the message I have carried everywhere on this tour, speaking repeatedly of the need to communicate with each other with our hearts as well as our heads, the need in other words for what I call 'heart-to-heart' understanding among the peoples of Japan and Southeast Asia. You, fellow Asians, will understand what I mean. For it is in our Asian tradition, and it is in our Asian hearts, always to seek beyond mere physical satisfaction for the richness of spiritual fulfillment."[2]

However, it was perfectly obvious that the developing countries which received much of Japan's investment were not interested solely in "heart-to-heart" diplomacy. For that does not fill the stomachs of the millions of hungry people nor does it put a shirt on the back of those who

Prime Minister Fukuda Visits ASEAN

Credit: Foreign Press Center/Kyodo

cannot afford it. More to the point, it does not put any
money in the pockets of the ruling elites either. Thus, Japan
has boosted its development aid and intensified its economic cooperation, especially with countries that host
Japanese investment.

The businessmen also showed a somewhat better understanding of the need to seek friendly links and to make the
commercial side of their operations less crude and grasp-
ing. Jointly, they formed a Japan Overseas Enterprises
Association (JOEA) to "ensure sound development of
overseas enterprises and thereby promote coexistence and
co-prosperity with host countries." Individually, they contributed to civic causes, granted scholarships, engaged in
public relations and, in general, tried to behave like good
corporate citizens. Without becoming charitable in-

stitutions, the companies did think more of overall relations. This was done not only in the interest of the host countries but their own as well. For, Japanese overseas investments could hardly flourish if their presence created negative rather than positive reactions.

Thus, a series of "guidelines for investment activities" was adopted by the Japanese business community and endorsed by the Japan Federation of Economic Organizations (Keidanren), Japan Chamber of Commerce and Industry, Japan Committee for Economic Development (Keizai Doyukai), Japan Federation of Employers' Associations (Nikkeiren) and Japan Foreign Trade Council. They dealt with matters such as selection of Japanese personnel for assignment abroad, employment and promotion of locals, transfer of technology and training, development of local industry and cooperation with existing companies, encouragement of reinvestment, conservation of the environment, integration in local society and especially promotion of mutual trust. This last point, as the cornerstone of the new era, is worth quoting in full.

"In order to assist the economic and social development of the host country, our overseas investments must be consistent with the principle of contributing to the long-term interest and prosperity of both parties, the investor and the host country, on the basis of mutual trust between them. Due consideration should be given to matters such as, for instance, the clear statement of long-range business policies, establishment of sound relations between labor and management, extension of opportunities for greater capital participation to investors of the host country at an appropriate stage, and furnishing accurate information about the business operations of the local subsidiaries, as a means of promoting deeper understanding by the local population."[3]

The second lesson was completely different. The businessmen primarily, and the government officials or politicians to a lesser extent, learned the "lesson" that it was perhaps wisest not to have any close relations with countries which were unpleasant partners and to avoid investing where the host government or people could not really be trusted. Thus, during the 1970s, there was a striking decline in investment in certain countries, including some that treated Tanaka most rudely. This was not due to any love of the prime minister. It was just that the Japanese businessmen had been alarmed by the anger they knew was directed even more against them and, if they were already disliked for an "overpresence," this was hardly the time for fresh investments. Other countries which treated the Japanese investors more coarsely were avoided more thoroughly as well.

Amazingly enough, no sooner had Japanese investment begun drying up than people started screaming for more and this emanated not only from those in ruling or business circles but some segments of public opinion. In many countries, the host government or people had grown aware of the benefits that could be gained by them from receiving such investment. Even if they did not always like the counterpart, and sometimes felt cheated, they too realized that they must modify their behavior if they wished to do business with the Japanese.

So, the sporadic complaints and periodic crises could scarcely be regarded as telling the whole story. Much of the rest was barely noticeable since it consisted of investments that aroused little controversy, that progressed smoothly enough not to make waves, and where each party got something out of it. The result has been more reciprocal self-interest with each party accomplishing some of its aims, if not all. And it instilled a spirit of mutual benefit on occasion. Obviously, this is not the millenium. There are still frictions and conflicts, disagreements over which side gains more, and some bad projects that are a waste or worse. But what has been accomplished is enough to show that there is considerable positive potential.

Investor's Balance Sheet

Japan's new commercial empire has decisively answered a question that was hotly debated before the war when the co-prosperity sphere was being established by force. The military obviously thought they were doing business circles a favor by physically occupying territory from which raw materials could be extracted, absorbing populations that could work in Japanese factories, and spreading the borders of the empire to englobe new, relatively exclusive markets. Yet, even in the heat of the action, there were many businessmen who insisted that it was a terrible mistake, that the costs would be far greater than the gains.

Even while the empire survived, they were right. For, the cost of equipping the army and navy drew tremendous resources away from normal commercial uses, the soldiers enrolled under the flag deprived the factories of Japanese workers, and there was not much of a market in countries which were exploited rather than prospering. When the war came, the balance sheet became even more negative, as products were made simply to destroy assets or be destroyed. Gradually, anything resembling a normal economy, one run on rational grounds by people familiar with the needs, disappeared. Finally, having lost their gamble, the Japanese became some of the war's countless victims.

A balance sheet for the present empire would certainly be much more positive. With relatively little fuss, Japanese manufacturers and trading companies have been able to procure just about all the raw materials they need. Admittedly, prices rose periodically, especially when the suppliers got together as in OPEC. But, even then, it was much cheaper to pay OPEC's price than to obtain oil by force. Moreover, investment has provided a major key to the problem. By tapping new sources as old ones dwindled, by fostering new suppliers when older ones organized, it has been possible to keep the market reasonably fluid and avoid anything worse than the "oil shock," which the world has suffered from yet eventually overcome.

Some of Japan's industries, which were perhaps slated for extinction, have managed to keep very much alive thanks to investment. When the labor costs rose too much, many of the more labor-intensive parts and components could be produced overseas. If need be, Japanese manufacturers could actually shift the bulk of their operations abroad to cheap labor countries. Other industries which were blocked by tariff barriers or quotas could avoid the worst by migrating as well. Certainly, in none of these were they as happy as producing in Japan and exporting. But they did manage to keep their operations running, to sell products, and to make modest profits.

Certainly, there were negative points as well. Some of the projects were a failure due to faulty planning or excessive optimism. Assorted overseas subsidiaries went bankrupt and a much larger number have taken painfully long to generate any profits and start paying for themselves. Even the sounder ones have occasionally had troubles, perhaps with labor or local managers, perhaps finding markets, perhaps when competitors arose. In the worst cases, they were simply squeezed out or expropriated by countries that turned against foreign investment.

A much broader loss, one that is extremely difficult to decipher, is the trend for some industries to leave Japan and locate in other countries creating the "doughnut" phenomenon. To this can be added the even more unpleasant rise of competitors for products which Japan once regarded almost as its sole preserve, textiles, toys, electronics, etc. It has not been easy to keep ahead of the newly industrialized countries and it has certainly not been comforting to know that, without Japanese investment, they might never have gotten started and would surely not have made enough progress to tread on Japan's heels.

Nevertheless, there is no doubt that investment does solve certain problems and create certain opportunities. So, the investors are hardly likely to hold back very often. What they doubtlessly will do is somewhat different. They will become more selective and more discriminating.

After all, overseas investment is not the only way of solving some of the problems. It is still possible to buy raw materials on the spot market or obtain oil through the majors. Of course, the price is higher. But the risk is less formidable. As for the smaller developing countries that insist on local production rather than exports, it may be just as well to stop dealing with them rather than go to the expense of opening a major project there. When it comes to high labor costs in Japan, companies can also get around that by using more labor-saving machinery. It is not absolutely necessary to migrate. The same money could be used for greater automation and robotization.

So, one trend will be toward seeking other ways around the problems, ways which may require greater initial costs but will at least remove the element of risk that has plagued so many overseas ventures. Investment in more or better installations in Japan is very costly and the pay-off should be smaller. However, given the fact that some foreign projects just don't work and others only offer a rather modest return, the long-term profitability may be pretty much the same. This means that occasionally overseas investment will be rejected in favor of an alternative solution at home. Naturally, evidence of this action will be hard to find, companies don't announce the investments they fail to make. But there will be some.

The New Order

Another backlash arising from the past difficulties will be a trend toward selecting the specific projects for overseas investment with greater care. There is no doubt that the Japanese were too bullish on investment during the 1960s and early 1970s, when they were expanding more rapidly and had great expectations for the future. Money was available and with a rising yen costs abroad were falling swiftly. Now, with a duller economy and money more scarce and costly, they will have to think twice. They are liable to invest only when the prospects of success are much more favorable than before, and even then they are likely to start with somewhat smaller projects and only expand once their viability has been proven.

Meanwhile, the major trend should be for investors to select the host countries with more care. They have already acquired a lot of experience since the early days and they know the world much better. Larger companies do business, and sometimes have investments, in just about every corner of the earth. The smaller ones are often privy to their advice. There is no doubt that this has contributed to an emerging consensus on where it is safe to invest and where one should keep out. This is shown most clearly by the growing concern about country risk and the various ratings that sort out the good from the bad risks.

A look at the country risk list leads to some very interesting considerations. One is that the good risks are those which already offer the best investment climate, which have the most sensible investment codes, and which also have a relatively buoyant economy. Not surprisingly, some bad risks have already shown their lack of interest, or indeed antipathy toward investment, by not providing any particular assistance or a tightly regulated environment. Others offer exceptionally generous incentives, but only to make up for exceptionally daunting disadvantages. Their attitudes on investment can change rapidly, and radically, as circumstances develop. So, a long-term commitment to their economy by outsiders would be dangerous.

It is perhaps significant to add that the good risks are usually also countries which have already obtained very considerable amounts of investment. They have an economy which is reasonably well run on the whole, or at least in certain sectors, and which is growing or prospering. This means that they actually need investment less. The countries in most desperate need of investment are basically those which are listed as bad risks, and they will get less than ever. It is certainly a pity that they will not gain from the additional capital, or use of labor, or new technologies, but there does not seem to be any way of avoiding this.

But the most intriguing aspect remains the close correlation between the good risks and the successful economies, on the one hand, and the bad risks and what were called the "losers," on the other. Perhaps one main reason that some countries have sought so much investment is that they knew they were benefiting from it, and also knew how to benefit from it. The bad risks often complained that they gained nothing through investment and that it actually had a negative effect. In the most extreme cases they compared it to exploitation. This may well have been because they used investment so poorly.

Whatever the reasons, it is clear that Japanese investors will be pumping more investment than ever into like-minded nations while increasingly shunning those which reject the concept or claim to have lost through it. This is important. For, it utterly shatters the biggest myth about investment, namely that it is only another form of exploiting weak and backward countries. Basically, the Japanese do not want to have any more to do with such hosts than necessary, and that view is shared by most major capitalist states and even socialist ones. They only make exceptions when there are political reasons for helping out.

In preference to "exploiting" such countries, and turning them into "neocolonies," the Japanese investors much prefer taking any necessary risks with more advanced countries which are actually their toughest competitors or the more dynamic industrializing countries which nastily tread on their heels in the chasing up operation. No matter how unpleasant, they find their own self-interest coincides more often with the self-interest of these countries than the more recalcitrant, or confused, nations which doubt anything can be gained or cannot even figure out what really is in their self-interest.

Host's Balance Sheet

The host countries have also been drawing up their balance sheets most assiduously. It is usually easy enough to tell what the upshot is by reading the statements made by political leaders or economic planners from time to time, when they praise or criticize specific projects or partners. More intriguing undercurrents can be found in local newspapers, by chatting with academics, or studying the radical movements. But the situation is shown most palpably, and realistically, by the changes in the investment code and climate and the resulting rise or fall in investments.

Taking a broad view, most of these countries have gotten at least some of what they want. There is no doubt that the projects are employing more people and providing a living for a part of the population. Even more clearly, this investment helps to finance growth by opening new sources of raw materials or growing industrial crops which can be sold quite often to the investors themselves. Slowly but surely, industrialization is spreading and in many cases the pioneers, or at any rate the most advanced operations, happen to embody foreign capital.

Admittedly, the vast majority of host countries only gained from this marginally. Foreign investment merely blended with local investment or the government's own efforts to create a somewhat larger pool of capital and expertise to expand the economy. In some few places, however, the result was more spectacular. Investment really did provide the impetus that was necessary to change the whole economic structure or incite local entrepreneurs to innovate and really get things moving. In such cases there was a vital impulse that can hardly be evaluated in monetary terms and gives true meaning to concepts like the demonstration effect and spillover.

Also, in a certain number of cases, investment has appeared more as an evil than a good. It has disrupted the economy as locals failed to keep up with more advanced foreigners, new economic activities not only supplemented but crushed old ones, and more people were thrown out of work in earlier labor-intensive activities than were hired by subsequent projects. It has also happened that, due to poor planning or excessive optimism on the host's part, projects were launched that were bound to fail. When they did, this created more "white elephants" which gave a bad name to investment in general. Other projects failed because the investors could not get along with the local population, an affair where both sides deserve some blame. Thus, the money and effort were wasted, and the high hopes were dashed.

However, on the whole, investment has remained in a middle ground with a fair number of projects succeeding, even if just barely, and rather few becoming blatant failures. So, the biggest grief most host countries harbor is that they could have done better, or that foreign investors were doing better than they, or that other projects might have been wiser and more beneficial. In this mental balance sheet, the problems were attached more to specific projects than investment as such and the primary goal was to do a bit better next time rather than discard foreign investment as a suitable mechanism.

Of course, when the host countries are taken individually rather than as a group, the situation is significantly different. For the unsuccessful investments, and outright failures, have tended to clump together in some few countries rather than being spread evenly among them all. These countries have come to feel that the promise of investment was overdone or even deceptive and that it is better to close the country and work out a more autarchic policy. In so doing, they are liable to expropriate or nationalize what remains of the older projects and send the investors packing.

Since these economies are frequently among the less successful, and their governments are among the less stable, or at any rate less predictable, the Japanese and other investors will be annoyed at their losses and protest. In the future, they are hardly likely to undertake new projects there. So, the countries which reject investment as a tool and close up in practice will frequently also be part of the high risk group and be avoided by investors. This actually expresses a sort of mutual feeling whereby reciprocal self-interest discourages investment. If nothing else, it would seem to promise a world in which the countries that most fear exploitation by foreign investors will no longer be exploited because the investors do not want to come.

Meanwhile, the countries which have gained through investment will doubtlessly remain open for more. And those countries which have done best, the winners, will probably keep on looking more actively. The correlation here is clearly not between potential needs and possibilities but past experience. For, the more backward a country, the more it can gain from investment in theory. And some terribly bad risks, alas, offer very tempting prospects. In practice, however, increased investment is a function of past success. Thus, it is the degree of success which creates the two categories, a success that probably depends much more on the host country than the investors.

This will doubtlessly lead to a growing polarization of investment with Japan putting more than ever into countries which have treated its investors best. These countries will enhance the benefits offered by such investment or, at any rate, keep them on an acceptable level. Meanwhile, much less investments than ever will be going to the worst risks. In some cases, they will be quite happy to do without. In others, they may become more desperate than ever to get at least some investment and offer yet greater advantages . . . many of which will be snubbed. The relations between the Japanese economy and the places its investors favor most will grow and strengthen while its relations with the rest of the world become more distant.

However, even among the host countries that stay open to foreign investment in general, there are some which appreciate Japanese investments more than others. It is clearly inappropriate to lump all sources of investment, and all investors, together without considering that they show very great differences in types of projects, methods of operation, manner of relating to the local people and government, and so on. Much of what is happening now cannot be understood unless one accepts that Japanese investments and Japanese multinationals are not entirely like those from the United States, or Europe, or elsewhere.

So far most observers have pointed to the weaknesses of Japanese investment and local people have found it a handy scapegoat to blame anything on. There has been much talk to the effect that the Japanese are economic animals, that they are only interested in what they can gain, and that they have scant concern for the needs of the host country. They are criticized for bringing in massive projects that crush smaller local ones. And they have also been castigated for floating too many small projects that locals could just as well handle. To this has been added comments about their personal behavior and nasty remarks about the "ugly Japanese."

It is hard to grasp why those of the neocolonialist school, and some who are simply anti-Japanese, find it so diffiicult to give the devil his due. Even if the Japanese behave largely in what they think is their self-interest, there is no reason to ignore that some of the things they do are also in the interest of their hosts and that occasionally they are better partners for developing countries than some of the older industrialized nations.

When it comes to raw materials, Japan's voraciousness has frequently been a boon to the producer countries. The increase in demand has helped keep prices higher than they would otherwise be. More important, by appearing as an aggressive competitor to the Western countries, it has permitted the raw material producers to slip out of the grasp of their older partners and at least have one more alternative. Given its needs, Japan was sometimes willing to offer higher prices and better conditions. And, due to its concern with long-term supplies, Japanese companies were more willing to enter major projects that would take a long time to mature. In fact, they not only participated but often advanced some of the necessary funds while providing the essential knowhow and market.

Equally important, Japan showed more willingness to leave processing of raw materials to the producing countries. This may have been because some of it required huge amounts of energy, or because it wished to avoid pollution-prone operations at home, or because the economics were better. Whatever the reason, it gave the producer countries what they wanted, a chance to move upstream from mere mining. And, once again, this was often done with Japanese financial and technical support.

With regard to its labor-oriented investments, Japan also offered some benefits. Many of the factories it set up were at the lower range of sophistication and in sectors where it was easier for developing countries to advance, such as textiles, garments and footwear, simple electronics, and so on. Of course, inveterate critics complained that these were primitive operations in obsolete sectors. But they had the advantage of employing much larger numbers of workers and also provided what has come to be known as "appropriate technologies." Anyway, when the host country specified that it wanted nothing but the most advanced technologies and sophisticated plants, the Japanese had no trouble in obliging.

When faced with the alternative of losing exports due to protectionism or entering into local production, the Japanese companies had a greater tendency than other multinationals to accept the latter. They were also more willing than most foreign companies to concede that profits might be quite low for some time and even to accept losses just so they could maintain a foothold. Then, as each successive push for further localization came, they were still more willing to go ahead. This may be due to taking a long-term view or it may be that the cost-benefit calculations were not done meticulously enough. Whatever the reason, it proved far easier to lead Japanese companies around than American or European ones.

Since they were latecomers, the Japanese firms were sometimes not allowed to hold complete ownership and had to form joint ventures in order to get in. However, their unfamiliarity with the market and the fact that the smaller firms were quite happy to spread the risks, meant that they often sought local partners even when this was not oblig-

atory. Even the larger companies accepted this with less
fuss than most multinationals and they were also willing to
expand ownership by selling stock or accepting local
partners. In addition, subjected to substanial "administrative guidance" at home, they were less offended than
Westerners to find the local government meddling in so
many economic and commercial matters.

Finally, to soften the impact of purely economic interests, the Japanese government has made an effort to
improve its international cooperation, at least with congenial partners, by raising the amount of aid granted. It
also provided credits on a reasonable, if not always
concessional basis for projects that were of interest to both
countries. Meanwhile, unlike most other multinationals,
Japanese companies actually helped their local partners
(even those foisted on them) get loans from Japanese
banks, sometimes guaranteeing them.

There is no sense in creating an atmosphere around
Japan's efforts, or those of any country, where the investors
feel that they are "damned if they do, and damned if they
don't." Not everything the Japanese do is good; but it is not
all bad either. Japanese investors present some very definite
pluses for countries wise enough to realize this. Among
those which grudgingly concede that Japan offers something other partners do not are Korea and Taiwan. The
United States and parts of Europe are beginning to see the
light. And Singapore and Malaysia are much more lavish in
their praise. There is little reason to doubt that, within the
growing polarization between investors and hosts, such
countries will get an even greater share of Japan's overseas
investment.

The Bottom Line

Japan's old colonial empire, despite the fact that it was

acquired by military conquest and maintained by rigid control, only reached into neighboring Asia and soon began collapsing. The present commercial empire has spread much further, stretching around the globe, including not only friendly but also more neutral countries and even members of the opposing bloc. It began slowly in the 1950s but has not stopped expanding and the pace of growth tends to increase with time. Although there is not a single investment staked out abroad which could not be closed down by the local government at will, this rarely happens.

That is perhaps the strangest anomaly about the two empires. The first, built with bullets and blood, remained fragile throughout. It was never accepted by the local people because they had to sacrifice too much and got too little in return. The present one, despite its voluntary nature, remains fairly solid. That is because it offers the population enough for it to accept what to some appears as cooperation, to others more like domination, with relative equanimity. Indeed, there are many cases in which Japan is encouraged to extend its commitments.

This arises from the fact that the new commercial empire is built on nearly invisible ties of mutual benefit or, as previously explained, reciprocal self-interest. Most of the conflicts have not been over the principles but the details. They consist of haggling over who gets what, a rather undignified procedure, but one that is more likely to result in some reasonable compromise. Thus, as long as each side, host and investor, has its own interests for engaging in investment, it can be assumed that this will continue almost indefinitely. After all, the causes that led to the present stage have hardly changed, and the effects also stay the same . . . with some minor exceptions.

There is no question that Japan will continue being in need of more raw materials, given its insatiable industry and plentiful population. Japanese labor cost are bound to rise, and it will need cheaper labor for some functions at least. It will still want more markets to ship its products to and have to arrange for distribution there. And it will gradually go over to more local production for one reason or another. While the search for raw materials, labor and markets will proceed at its own pace, the conversion to local manufacturing will be hastened by measures taken by the host countries.

Meanwhile, the developing (and developed) countries will continue needing Japan. Who else can buy as much raw materials and is as eager to obtain a smooth and substantial flow? Who else can provide so many manufactured goods at such cheap prices? Who else offers the latest technologies to transform the economy of both backward and relatively advanced nations? And who else is willing to make such massive investments at present?

So, Japan will keep on investing and the empire will grow. Actually, Japan can be expected to rise higher in the ranks of investing countries. It is still only third for cumulative investment, ahead of Germany. There is no reason it should not pass Great Britain as well. And, since it has a more outward-looking economy than the United States, it may just conceivably become No. 1. At any rate, the fact that the per capita amount of its outstanding investment was only 26%, 38%, and 62% respectively of that of the United States, Great Britain and Germany as late as 1981 shows that there is plenty of potential for growth.

The basic difference—the minor exceptions referred to—will be that the growth should become more skewed in the future. There is little doubt that investment in certain countries which have proven to be bad risks will dwindle. On the other hand, countries which have offered a good climate and in which projects flourished, can expect to receive proportionately more. It is a pity that the former will not get the investment, since they really need it. But that is the way things are bound to develop if they do not change their approach.

Thus, the growth will not only be skewed but will fail to attain its full potential until more countries adopt a positive attitude toward investment. Certainly, if some countries can gain moderately, and others can forge ahead, there must be some advantage to investment no matter how difficult it can be to handle properly. It should be sought by all concerned.

A first step would be for the host countries, and particularly those which fear investment, to figure out just what can be gained so that they can direct the investment toward the appropriate sectors. It would help if they also made the effort to figure out how their economies should grow in general so that investment could be inserted more intelligently in the broader scheme. Then, the host government and local partners should more carefully study the specific projects to see what the prospects of success really are. For their part, the Japanese investors might select their own projects more carefully, paying attention not only to their immediate interests but also long-term ones such as creating better relations with the host country. With a bit more wisdom on each side, the projects could evolve more smoothly and increase the gains of both sides.

This care and caution is essential in dealing with investment. For, as we have seen, it is just a tool. It is not inherently or inalterably good or bad. Investment is what you make of it. And those who use it wisely are bound to gain. In fact, unlike what happened in the old empire, it can contribute to mutual benefit and co-prosperity.

NOTES

1. *Far Eastern Economic Review*, November 21, 1980.
2. Takeo Fukuda, Speech of August 18, 1977, Manila, Philippines.
3. *Guidelines for Investment Activities in Developing Countries*, Japan Overseas Enterprises Association.

Acronyms

Albras	Aluminio Brasileiro
Alunorte	Alumina do Norte do Brasil
ASEAN	Association of Southeast Asian Nations
Cenibra	Cellulose Nipo-Brasileira
CST	Companhia Siderurgica de Tubarao
DAC	Development Assistance Committee
D & I	Develop and Import
EC	European Community
EFTA	European Free Trade Association
Exim Bank	Export-Import Bank
Flonibra	Empreendimentos Florestais
ICDC	Iran Chemical Development Company
IHI	Ishikawajima-Harima Heavy Industries
IJPC	Iran-Japan Petrochemical Company
Inalum	Indonesia Asahan Aluminum
Ishibras	Ishikawajima do Brasil
JAL	Japan Air Lines
JBP	Japan-Brazil Paper and Pulp Resources Development Project
JETRO	Japan External Trade Organization
JICA	Japanese International Cooperation Agency
Jilco	Japan Indonesia LNG Company
JNOC	Japan National Oil Company
JODC	Japan Overseas Development Corporation

JOEA	Japan Overseas Enterprises Association
JPDC	Japan Petroleum Development Corporation
JSPC	Japan-Singapore Petrochemical Company
Keidanren	Japan Federation of Economic Organizations
Keizai Doyukai	Japan Committee for Economic Development
MITI	Ministry of International Trade and Industry
MNC	Multinational Corporation
MOF	Ministry of Finance
Nalco	Nippon Amazon Aluminum Company
NIC	Newly Industrialized Country
Nikkeiren	Japan Federation of Employers' Associations
ODA	Official Development Assistance
OECD	Organization for Economic Cooperation and Development
OECF	Overseas Economic Cooperation Fund
OPEC	Organization of Petroleum Exporting Countries
PCS	Petrochemical Corporation of Singapore
PRN	Power Reactor and Nuclear Fuel Development Corporation
Siderbras	Siderurgia Brasileira S. A.
SPDC	Saudi Petrochemical Development Company
UNCTAD	United Nations Conference on Trade and Development
Usiminas	Usinas Siderurgicas de Minas Gerais
YKK	Yoshida Kogyo K. K.

Bibliography

Bryant, William E., *Japanese Private Economic Diplomacy, An Analysis of Business-Government Linkages*, New York, Praeger, 1975.

Evans, Peter, *Dependent Development, The Alliance of Multinational, State, and Local Capital in Brazil*, Princeton, Princeton University Press, 1979.

Halliday, Jon, and McCormack, Gavan *Japanese Imperialism Today, 'Co-Prosperity in Greater East Asia'*, Harmondsworth, Penguin Books, 1973.

Hasegawa, Sukehiro, *Japanese Foreign Aid, Policy and Practice*, New York, Praeger, 1975.

Heller, H. Robert, and Heller, Emily E., *Japanese Investment in the United States, With a Case Study of the Hawaiian Experience*, New York, Praeger, 1974.

Hellmann, Donald C., *Japan and East Asia, The New International Order*, New York, Praeger, 1972.

Japan Institute of Labour, *Overseas Investment and Its Impact on Domestic Employment*, Tokyo, 1982.

JETRO, *China: A Business Guide*, Tokyo, 1979.

———, *Overseas Investment*, Tokyo, various.

———, *Study of Japanese Companies Located in the United States*, Tokyo, 1981.

———, *Survey of Japanese Firms Operating in ASEAN Countries*, Tokyo, 1981.

———, *White Paper on Overseas Markets, Investment Edition*, Tokyo, 1982.

Jones, F. C., *Japan's New Order in East Asia, Its Rise and Fall*, London, Oxford University Press, 1954.

Katano, Hikoji, *Japanese Enterprises in ASEAN Countries,* Kobe, Kobe University Press, 1981.

Kojima, Kiyoshi, *Japan and a New World Economic Order,* Tokyo, Tuttle, 1977.

————, *Japanese Direct Foreign Investment, A Model of Multinational Business Operations,* Tokyo, Tuttle, 1978.

Lebra, Joyce C. (ed.), *Japan's Greater East Asia Co-Prosperity Sphere in World War II,* London, Oxford University Press, 1975.

Marubeni Corporation, *The Japanese Edge,* Tokyo, 1981.

Ministry of Finance, *Japan's Direct Overseas Investment,* Tokyo, various.

MITI, *Economic Cooperation of Japan,* Tokyo, various.

————, *Overseas Business Activities of Japanese Enterprises,* Tokyo, various.

Oriental Economist, *Japanese Overseas Investment, A Complete Listing by Firms and Countries,* Tokyo, Toyo Keizai Shinposha, 1981.

Ozawa, Terutomo, *Multinationalism, Japanese Style,* Princeton, Princeton University Press, 1979.

Rix, Alan, *Japan's Economic Aid,* London, Croom Helm, 1980.

Sekiguchi, Sueo, *Japanese Direct Foreign Investment,* Totowa, New Jersey, Allenheld, Osmun, 1979.

Tsuda, Mamoru, *A Preliminary Study of Japanese-Filipino Joint Ventures,* Quezon City, Foundation for Nationalist Studies, 1978.

Tsurumi, Yoshi, *The Japanese Are Coming, A Multinational Interaction of Firms and Politics,* Cambridge, Ballinger, 1976.

White, Michael, and Trevor, Malcolm, *Under Japanese Management,* London, Heinemann, 1983.

Whiting, Allen S., *Siberian Development and East Asia,* Stanford, Stanford University Press, 1981.

Woronoff, Jon, *Hong Kong: Capitalist Paradise,* Hong Kong, Heinemann Asia, 1980.

————, *Japan: The Coming Economic Crisis,* Tokyo, Lotus Press, 1979.

————, *Korea's Economy, Man-Made Miracle,* Seoul, Si-sa-yong-o-sa Publishers, 1983.

————, *World Trade War,* Tokyo, Lotus Press, 1983.

Yoshihara, Kunio, *Japanese Investment in Southeast Asia,* Honolulu, University Press of Hawaii, 1978

————, *Sogo Shosha,* Oxford, Oxford University Press, 1982.

Yoshino, M. Y., "Emerging Japanese Multinational Enterprises," in *Modern Japanese Organization and Decision-Making,* Berkeley, University of California Press, 1975.

Young, Alexander K., *The Sogo Shosha: Japan's Multinational Trading Companies,* Boulder, Westview Press, 1979.

INDEX

412

Books by Lotus Press Ltd.

NON-FICTION

THE JAPANESE	J. Seward
MORE ABOUT THE JAPANESE	J. Seward
AMERICA AND JAPAN	
—The Twain Meet—	J. Seward
THE EMPEROR'S ISLANDS	
—The Story of Japan—	G. Matsumura
HARA-KIRI Hard Cover	J. Seward
NINJUTSU	
—The Art of Invisibility—	D. Draeger
READING YOUR WAY	
AROUND JAPAN	B. DeMente
JAPAN: The Coming Economic Crisis	J. Woronoff
JAPAN: The Coming Social Crisis	J. Woronoff
JAPAN'S WASTED WORKERS	J. Woronoff
PIONEER AMERICAN	
MERCHANTS IN JAPAN	H. F. Van Zandt
IMAGES OF JAPAN	A. Tsuchiya
—A Photographic Souvenir—	& B. DeMente
INSIDE JAPAN, INC.	J. Woronoff
WORLD TRADE WAR	J. Woronoff
SHOPPING YOUR WAY	
AROUND JAPAN	B. DeMente
IAI	
—The Art of Drawing The Sword—	D. Craig

FICTION

THE CAVE OF THE CHINESE	
SKELETONS Hard Cover	J. Seward
THE DARNED NUISANCES	J. Seward
	& C. Beardsley
THE DIPLOMAT	J. Seward
SAMURAI SIX	J. Stanley

Books by Jon Woronoff

WEST AFRICAN WAGER

ORGANIZING AFRICAN UNITY

HONG KONG: CAPITALIST PARADISE

KOREA'S ECONOMY, MAN-MADE MIRACLE

JAPAN: THE COMING SOCIAL CRISIS

JAPAN: THE COMING ECONOMIC CRISIS

JAPAN'S WASTED WORKERS

INSIDE JAPAN, INC.

WORLD TRADE WAR

JAPAN'S COMMERCIAL EMPIRE